GUARDIANS
ON TRIAL

GUARDIANS

ON TRIAL

*The Case Against Canada's Political
Leadership*

EDITED BY
ANTHONY HALL

BREAKOUT EDUCATIONAL NETWORK
IN ASSOCIATION WITH
DUNDURN PRESS
TORONTO ·OXFORD

Publisher: Inta D. Erwin
Copy-editor: Amanda Stewart, First Folio Resource Group
Designer: Bruna Brunelli, Brunelli Designs
Printer: Webcom

National Library of Canada Cataloguing in Publication Data

Guardians on trial/edited by Anthony Hall.

One of the 16 vols. and 14 hours of video which make up the
    underground royal commission report
Includes bibliographical references and index.
ISBN 1-55002-419-1

    1. Canada — Politics and government. 2. Canada — Economic policy.
3. Waste in government spending — Canada. I. Hall, Anthony.
II. Title: underground royal commission report.

JL86.P64G82 2003   351.71   C2003-902299-1

1   2   3   4   5   07   06   05   04   03

Printed and bound in Canada.
Printed on recycled paper. ✆
www.dundurn.com

Exclusive Canadian broadcast rights for the *underground royal commission* report

intelligent television

Check your cable or satellite listings for telecast times

Visit the *urc* Web site link at:
www.ichanneltv.com

About the *underground royal commission* Report

Since September 11, 2001, there has been an uneasy dialogue among Canadians as we ponder our position in the world, especially vis à vis the United States. Critically and painfully, we are re-examining ourselves and our government. We are even questioning our nation's ability to retain its sovereignty.

The questions we are asking ourselves are not new. Over the last 30 years, and especially in the dreadful period of the early 1990s, leading up to the Quebec referendum of 1995, inquiries and Royal commissions, one after another, studied the state of the country. What *is* new is that eight years ago, a group of citizens looked at this parade of inquiries and commissions and said, "These don't deal with the real issues." They wondered how it was possible for a nation that was so promising and prosperous in the early 60s to end up so confused, divided, and troubled. And they decided that what was needed was a different kind of investigation — driven from the grassroots 'bottom,' and not from the top. Almost as a provocation, this group of people, most of whom were affiliated with the award winning documentary-maker, Stornoway Productions, decided to do it themselves — and so was born the *underground royal commission*!

What began as a television documentary soon evolved into much more. Seven young, novice researchers, hired right out of university, along with a television crew and producer, conducted interviews with people in government, business, the military and in all walks of life, across the country. What they discovered went beyond anything they had expected. The more they learned, the larger the implications grew. The project continued to evolve and has expanded to include a total of 23 researchers over the last several years. The results are the 14 hours of video and 16 books that make up the first interim report of the *underground royal commission*.

So what *are* the issues? The report of the *underground royal commission* clearly shows us that regardless of region, level of government, or political party, we are operating under a wasteful system ubiquitously lacking in accountability. An ever-weakening connection between the electors and the elected means that we are slowly and irrevocably losing our right to know our government. The researchers' experiences demonstrate that it is almost impossible for a member of the public, or in most cases, even for a member of Parliament, to actually trace how our tax dollars are spent. Most disturbing is the fact that our young people have been stuck with a crippling IOU that has effectively hamstrung their future. No wonder, then, that Canada is not poised for reaching its potential in the 21st century.

The *underground royal commission* report, prepared in large part by and for the youth of Canada, provides the hard evidence of the problems you and I may long have suspected. Some of that evidence makes it clear that, as ordinary Canadians, we are every bit as culpable as our politicians — for our failure to demand accountability, for our easy acceptance of government subsidies and services established without proper funding in place, and for the disservice we have done to our young people through the debt we have so blithely passed on to them. But the real purpose of the *underground royal commission* is to ensure that we better understand how government processes work and what role we play in them. Public policy issues must be understandable and accessible to the public if they are ever to be truly addressed and resolved. The *underground royal commission* intends to continue pointing the way for bringing about constructive change in Canada.

— Stornoway Productions

Books in the *underground royal commission* Report

"Just Trust Us"

The Chatter Box
The Chance of War
Talking Heads Talking Arms: (3 volumes)
No Life Jackets
Whistling Past the Graveyard
Playing the Ostrich

Days of Reckoning
Taking or Making Wealth
Guardians on Trial
Goodbye Canada?
Down the Road Never Travelled
Secrets in High Places
On the Money Trail

Does Your Vote Count?
A Call to Account
Reflections on Canadian Character

14 hours of videos also available with the *underground royal commission* report.
Visit Stornoway Productions at www.stornoway.com for a list of titles.

TABLE OF CONTENTS

DEFICITS, UNFUNDED LIABILITY, ENTITLEMENTS
— *The Monsters We Create*

THE GUARDIANS
— Government Management or Mismanagement from Participants Who Should Know

THE LOBBYISTS
— Interest Groups and the Shaping of Public Policy

QUEBEC AND THE FEDERAL GOVERNMENT
— *Maîtres Chez Nous*

CLOSING THOUGHTS
— *Parting Words of Wisdom*

INTRODUCTION

Perhaps because of too frequent use or just sheer longevity, the term "public trust" has become hollow, even banal, as a phrase intended to enshrine a standard of civic conduct. Similarly, the use of "guardian" to describe an office holder charged with custodial duties on behalf of the public has undergone an erosion of meaning. *Guardians on Trial: The Case Against Canada's Political Leadership* makes a case for a return to the values that both terms were meant to convey.

In this collection of essays, economic mismanagement and government policies that are responsible for creating a legacy of debt for future generations are discussed. A range of people who agree on the need to change direction and stop the spiral of deficit and debt that has been the hallmark of Canadian government for more than 30 years recount their experiences and offer keen insights.

The edited conversations which comprise this volume trace their origins to a documentary television series, *Days of Reckoning*, which was produced by the Breakout Educational Network and Stornoway Productions. In that series seven young Canadians travelled across the country to uncover the truth behind 30 years of out-of-control public spending and the devastating disregard for its long-term consequences. In essence a compelling brief for the prosecution was assembled. On trial were the elected politicians and the voters who had allowed spend-thrift policies to mortgage the futures of succeeding generations of young Canadians. Viewers of that series would be hard-pressed not to return a guilty verdict. Hundreds of hours of "expert evidence" were compiled for the television project, but time constraints permitted only brief extracts to be included in the completed project.

This volume allows the reader to gain a more complete appreciation of the views expressed by an informed cross-section of Canadians. A guiding principle that is implicit in the television documentary and that carries over to *Guardians on Trial* may be stated directly: government policy is not the exclusive domain of experts. It is within the competence of the ordinary citizen to understand and evaluate the purpose and effectiveness of such activity. If a jury of laypersons is expected to assess the testimony of experts in our legal system, why should we expect any less in our political system? This is especially true in the sphere of economic policy where, for example, it takes little to convince even a casual observer that money spent servicing a huge debt is money denied to other ends. Yet in our history we find an overwhelming number of examples of government policies that defy common sense and historical experience.

The edited conversations of *Guardians on Trial* are a "user-friendly" exposition of insights from a unique assembly of knowledgeable speakers. As a colleague has reminded me, readers should be encouraged to listen to, rather than simply look at, the text. Since the conversational tone of edited interviews transmits to some degree the speaker's personality and often the force of his or her convictions, the reader may see a few instances of opinions that do not conform with what is usually called "political correctness." The various contributions started out as open-ended dialogues in which leading figures from business, political, public service and academic circles addressed their opinions to a panel of young Canadians. It will become evident to the reader that the panel feels a deep sense of moral indignation about government practices that blur the lines of accountability and obscure the real effects of misguided programs.

Seven years have passed since the first interviews found in this anthology were recorded. We now have an opportunity to see whether the conditions and practices described by the various contributors have changed or have undergone reform. As I write, in the spring of 2002, the present auditor general, Sheila Fraser, is reporting that the federal government, by numerous sleights of hand, has managed to hide at least $32 billion from Parliament's scrutiny. After reading the words of Maxwell Henderson and Kenneth Dye, the reader should not be surprised by this development. On the other hand, the recent controversy concerning conflicts of interest created by the relationship between federal Liberal Party leadership candidates — who are also ministers — and the registered lobbyists who support their candidacies is not foreshadowed by the words of the lobbyists interviewed in this volume.

Readers of *Guardians on Trial* may further examine the consequences of misguided federal government economic and administrative policies in a companion volume, *Taking or Making Wealth?*. This collection of edited conversations provides an examination of the same policies discussed in *Guardians on Trial*, as they were applied in particular regions across Canada.

Anthony Hall
Barrie, Ontario
April 15, 2002

THE VIEW FROM OTTAWA

In the Belly of the Beast

JOHN CROSBIE

A former finance minister describes the political realities that confront a politician determined to eliminate deficit spending by the federal government.

When I came into office in 1979 I don't know if the public was alarmed about the deficit and the debt, but the Conservatives were. People who are conservative by nature, conservative with a small "c," were concerned by that time with the fact that there'd been regular government deficits for about 10 years. So there was a feeling of alarm about the growth in the debt and the deficit situation. On the other hand, the PCs wanted to get into power. So on their way to getting into power, one of the policies proclaimed was a mortgage interest deduction. On the American side, down in the States you can deduct the mortgage interest you're paying from your income. You get income tax relief from it. We don't have that in Canada.

Normally you don't get into power by saying, "Vote for us and we're going to really tighten up under you and make sure you don't get anything further. In fact we're going to reduce what you've already got." That's not normally the way to get elected. So it wasn't the PCs who tried it. We had the concern about the deficit and the debt. But on the other hand we also had commitments for new programs. I was being appointed the minister of finance and I was caught in this dilemma. You know, you're caught in the dilemma between what you promised and what you really should be doing, which in my view was reducing spending and starting to get the deficit reduced. So that's what we attempted to do.

The results of the election that followed my budget showed, of course, that it wasn't popular with the public. The public doesn't want to pay anything more. It was 18¢ a gallon, I think you remember, it was an excise tax on gasoline. This was in the middle of the energy crisis and everybody went ape at this savage gouge of the public oil and gasoline price in Canada. They were far too low because the Liberals had kept them down there artificially. They didn't allow the world market price to operate in Canada — a very bad policy in a number of ways. But anyway people liked that, they thought that gasoline in Canada was less than it was in the United States. It made every Canadian feel proud and stand tall in the saddle that Americans were coming across the border to buy our gasoline because it was cheaper.

So the 18¢ a gallon excise tax, which was good from the point of view of conservation (and the government needed the revenue), was unpopular with the public. This did not help in the election that followed, and although I think we were defeated for other reasons than that, that was just an additional reason.

Politics is a series of compromises. Very few people can get their own way in every issue in politics. You've got to give here to get something else somewhere else. That's the system. In fact, I would argue that politicians who don't observe principles of compromise and accommodation are very, very dangerous. I'll give you one example: Clyde Wells. I consider Clyde Wells to be a menace to the successful function of the democratic system because he's too stubborn. He won't accommodate anybody else's views. He's too rigid, too inflexible, not prepared to compromise. I'm thinking now of Meech Lake. Clyde Wells was the reason that we're in the present difficulties with Quebec, as far as I'm concerned. Anyway, that's getting off the topic here a bit.

You've got to be prepared. In a liberal democracy you've got to be prepared to accommodate other people's views, so you can't always have your own way 100 percent of the time. Now, finance ministers get caught between the promises their parties have made to get into power and what might be the sensible financial decision that's in the best interests of the country, financially, to do. There's always that dilemma with the finance ministers and normally everybody's hand is against them.

Now, in the last few years finance ministers have had the edge on the rest of the Cabinet because everybody realizes that our financial situation is not good in the Government of Canada. So he's in quite a strong position, he or she, but it's always been a he so far, federally. So they have the edge. For example, in this present government Paul Martin is in a much stronger position than the spenders are. The spenders are running around the country looking embarrassed. Imagine Lloyd Axworthy suggesting that you shouldn't spend as much money or you should reform the system so that those receiving social assistance don't get as much or that unemployment insurance should be tightened up. Lloyd is fooling himself. He doesn't believe any of this stuff. He's forced into it by their fiscal position and by the fact that the minister of finance is in a dominant position and that the government is in the hands of foreign moneylenders.

Here in Canada we put ourselves in the position where anytime foreign lenders want to stop lending to Canada, we're going to have to reduce government spending by about 25 or 30 percent or go bankrupt. That's the position that we've gotten ourselves in. I laugh when I hear people being indignant about these little twerps in the financial markets and so on. They'll ask them for their opinions and what's going to happen to the dollar. Well, if Canada doesn't do such and such and tighten up its finances, dire things will happen to the Canadian dollar, they'll say. Or somebody evaluates our credit rating and lowers the standard and whoever it is that lowers our credit rating, people get very indignant toward them. Imagine, Americans telling us what to do.

We've put ourselves in the position where we've got to do what these little twerps say or we'll suffer tremendously. You see, we've put ourselves in that position. They didn't cause it. We caused it because we don't want to pay for our current consumption. The people of Canada are living about a third better than they should be as far as paying for it is concerned. They're living off the crowd that's coming after us, you people. You're going to get it right in the neck — not to mention other parts of your anatomy. So I've forgotten now myself what the question was. But this is the dilemma of not just Canada but other countries, for example, New Zealand. I was in New Zealand several times but New Zealand's a small country, straight out in the bush, let's call it, a long distance away. And they're on their own out there. They had a socialist government come in and they had to reverse all of this. Now they go around telling the rest of the world how to do it. This is quite remarkable. A socialist, Mr. Douglas, was a finance minister in New Zealand, but now he's an expert on how you can reverse this and what you've got to do to do it.

The younger generation, you're going to pay and pay and pay for the spending that's gone on in the last 20 years because our debt is now $500 billion or $600 billion, I think, including provincial debt. I have the figure here somewhere — $789 billion — and that's got to be paid off and you're going to pay it off. And you're going to pay the interest on it. This year you're going to pay $42 billion in interest. Next year you'll pay $49 billion in interest. I think it's 37 percent of all the revenue of the Government of Canada's going to go on interest payments. You're not going to get anything for all that money, except 37 percent will go on interest, which is being paid on past borrowings.

Even with Mr. Martin's budget the process doesn't stop. Even if he follows the budget exactly, and that remains to be seen whether he will, we'll still at the end of that time be borrowing $27 billion or something of that nature in the year after next. So all of this you're going to pay for. Your other option is you could persuade the Canadian people and instruct the government that they're to stop incurring deficits and to start paying them off. You have your chance now as we're doing this interview.

Ontario doesn't have a ray of sunshine. It's got Bob Rae, who's just called an election. He's one of the worst spendthrifts there is. He's the same guy that moved the motion of non-confidence in my budget and sabotaged my budget in 1979. He's been in charge of matters in Ontario for the last five years and Ontario's in a pitiful financial condition — pitiful. And they haven't learned their lesson. They're borrowing away. His finance minister says they're going to continue doing this. So here's a chance for the people of Canada to show whether they're worried or concerned about the deficit or not by putting this spendthrift out and putting someone else in that may reverse this. Even the Liberals have changed their spots. The only ones that haven't changed their spots are the socialists.

Election promises are different from what really happens because the politicians are convinced that the public will not accept any tough measures or any tightening up. If you ask them ahead of time, they'll reject you. That's my own analysis as well. If you say to the public, "Look, vote for me, I'm going to get in, we've got a serious financial problem. I'm going to have to do X, Y and Z and cut back and we're going to have to stop this lavish unemployment insurance and make changes in the social security system," the public will vote against you. They simply will not support you if you go to them on that basis. The public knows that these things need to be done, but they don't want to approve what you're going to do in advance. They would sooner see you get in power with soft soap and promising X and promising Y. After you get in power you do this so that they can say, "Those dirty politicians, bunch of liars, you can't trust them." They'd sooner look down on the politicians than give them the go-ahead.

The Liberal Party, last election, didn't go around and say, "Look, vote for us and we are going to change the UI system." They never mentioned the UI system. They didn't go around and say, "Vote for us and we're going to bring in a budget that tightens everything up. We're going to reduce the deficit and stop this process," because they knew or they felt that the public would be very angry with this and they'd vote for somebody else. So that's the dilemma. The real issues today in Canada do not get discussed at election time. One thing that politicians are convinced of is that they can't discuss any serious issue during an election.

Poor old Kim Campbell was foolish enough to almost say that during the campaign. That got her into tremendous trouble. She mentioned the complicated issues of the social security program but you can't very well discuss them during an election. It's quite true that you can't discuss them sensibly during an election, but she was jumped on and pummelled because of this statement, even though that's what every politician believes. The last thing you want to do in an election campaign is discuss the real, serious issues affecting the country.

In the Ontario election now, you see the same phenomenon will probably be true. So it's very, very difficult to deal with these problems because then when you get in power and you have not said you're going to take tough measures, naturally the public can say to you, "You never said you were going to do that." And you're on very weak ground morally. The difference in Alberta with Mr. Klein is that he did say during his election, "We're going to tighten up and we're going to do certain things" and then he got in power and did it. But nobody can come into his office and say, "You fooled up." So he's in a stronger position vis-à-vis his electorate than the politicians in Canada usually are.

We didn't do that in 1979 because one of the difficulties was that we had this promise about mortgage interest deductibility. It was a direct, specific promise that Mr. Clark felt had to be carried out. Now, I changed that to a mortgage interest tax credit, which was far less expensive to the treasury. But it was the same concept only you would get a tax credit. You wouldn't be able to deduct your interest but you would be able to get a tax credit for the interest you paid. That saved us some money. In our budget, despite having to introduce this tax credit, had the budget been carried out, we would have reduced the deficit the following year by $900 million.

We were starting the process of reducing the deficit. So despite the fact that we had some embarrassing promises like that, the budget did cut back considerably on spending. We achieved a $900-million reduction despite having to put in this mortgage tax credit, mortgage interest tax credit. As it happened, the Canadian public didn't give a damn about the mortgage interest tax credit. The middle-class suburbanites were supposedly very influential back in 1979. They didn't seem to care about this. It wasn't an issue in the election. The opposition didn't support the program in any event, but the feeling was that you could not just disregard a promise made like that during an election campaign. Today of course you would disregard the promise. We have a financial crisis today so you haven't got any option. Back then we thought there were options.

The Canadian public are unwilling every year, not just 1979, to take some short-term pain. The Canadian public is the author of their own misfortunes. They are getting exactly what they bloody well deserve. They don't deserve any better because they don't expect any better — because they don't respond to politicians who are frank and honest with them. I remember the night I got ready for the 1984 election. Mr. Mulroney had become leader of the Conservative Party and he started everybody on preparing policy and so on. I was the finance critic so I had to prepare projections of the financial positions — if we did certain things, what they would cost, etc.

We were going to have a meeting to discuss all this stuff. On the way into the meeting I had a bunch of papers under my arm and my chief of staff had done a memo as to what our promises were going to cost. These were promises we were going to make during the campaign. They came to a considerable figure, I've forgotten the figure — but it was a couple of billion dollars. But everybody was conscious at that time of the financial position, even in 1984. I got stopped by a press crowd in a scrum; while I was answering their questions, one of the journalists, a woman I believe, got down underneath my leg somehow and read the document on the top of this bundle of papers. The top document was the one that had all the figures and Tory promises. She made a few notes there reading under my arm. Now, I'm an innocent type of person. Can you imagine? Dastardly. But anything goes with the press these days and of course the headline was "Tory Promises Will Cost Several Billion." So they're quoting me right because this was my memo.

Naturally everybody in the PC Party thought I was a damn fool. Christ, I should be taken out and buried somewhere because you don't want to give the public the facts. These were just facts that I was going to give the party. I wasn't proposing to give them to the public. And now this woman reporter, using this unorthodox means, had gotten a look at it. So the point is that political parties don't feel they can expose all this stuff to the public because the public does not want to approve tough measures in advance.

I don't know if the public is any different now than it was 50 years ago. The difference now, of course, is that the public's attention is caught. Television is the big influence on the public today. So it's all visuals that have the most influence, but I don't think that the nature of the public has changed that much. Back in the 1940s and 1950s the atmosphere, as far as financial matters were concerned, was quite conservative with a small "c." The general atmosphere was that it was very important to get the debt down and not to owe money. So that was the prevailing thought and the governments just acted on that basis. The Liberal governments of those days did so and I imagine Mr. Diefenbaker's government did as well.

Then that started to change. Today there's actually a large body of opinion in Canada that thinks the debt doesn't matter at all. That you can go on indefinitely borrowing money and this has no serious bad effects. In fact there's a book; I haven't read the book yet, just published by this left-wing woman writer from *The Globe and Mail* whose whole argument is this: that this is nut stuff, paying off the debt and being concerned and worried. It's what I call kinky Keynesianism. It's based on Keynes. You're supposed to have deficits during the recession and then you have surpluses in the good times. The only trouble is we adopted Keynes and we forgot about the surpluses in the good times. So we've nothing but deficits whether it's good or bad economic times. Which is why I name it kinky Keynesianism.

To me it's just elementary common sense. I was in Mulroney's government for nine years. You had no options, except in minor areas, because every year when you started out it was 30 percent or 32 or 35 percent of all your revenues committed to interest. Now we're up to 37 percent. There's an interesting thing I came across in Newfoundland because of this book I'm trying to write. It was in 1931, 1932, I think it was, that 35 percent of the revenue of the Newfoundland government went to pay interest on the debt. Their whole budget in those days was $10 million or $11 million. It was a little country of 289,000 people. Because of the Depression, the year after that it went up from 37 percent to I think it was 41 percent. Within two or three years 65 percent of the Newfoundland government's revenues went to pay the interest on their debt, which at that time was about $98 million, the total debt of the country. Newfoundland couldn't survive. It would have gone into bankruptcy had Britain not come in and established its commission. Britian started to meet the deficits and helped the island through until World War II to remedy this.

It's only a difference in scale. If that could happen in Newfoundland, it could happen in Canada. Now, this year the funny thing is, 37 percent of Canada's revenue is going to go on interest on the debt. So to me, I don't see how anyone can argue that we should sit back and let this go to 41 percent or 45 percent. I mean, what will happen is we'll have an immediate crisis because you've got to stop a third of your spending immediately.

Despite the fact that finance ministers are in increasingly powerful positions vis-à-vis their colleagues over the last 10 or 15 years, they're still part of a government that wants to be re-elected. No government wants to institute a massive regime of cutbacks and so on, and it'll only do it when it has absolutely no choice about it. We're just about at that position now because that's the only reason Mr. Martin would bring in this kind of budget. One of the reasons I think the public is accepting it is that finally, the last three or four years, the public is starting to accept that the deficit and the debt are a problem. The public is now getting more convinced of that.

The second thing that helps the Liberals is — this is my theory — that people say Liberals are all heart. They're all heart, those wonderful Liberals. They instituted all these programs and they love the common people and they wouldn't bring in a regime like this and cut back if it wasn't absolutely necessary. But Tories, they're hard-hearted bastards. They have no hearts. They're black-hearted accountants. The Tories are going to cut back anyway, whether it's necessary or not. But the Liberals will only do it if it's necessary. That's what I think the public thinks. I could be all wrong. I've never been shown to be wrong yet about too much, but it's a possibility, I admit.

So those are some of the complications. At the moment the Liberal government has a golden opportunity, which they appear to be seizing, but we have to wait and see if they carry out the budget because there are a lot of quite tough things in this budget. One of the excuses for the Tories, Mr. Mulroney's government, was that we had savage opposition to every attempt to cut back. Savage. We had a bunch of savages in the opposition, in the Liberal ranks. Remember the rat pack? It was Lily Tomlin who said that the trouble with the rat race is that even when you win you're still a rat. In this case they had lost and they were still rats. But we had the rat pack going berserk about everything, any kind of a cut.

The best example I can give you is about a year before our government was terminated we changed the unemployment insurance so that voluntary quitters would not receive UI. Now, why should you receive UI if you voluntarily leave your job? It's inconsistent with the whole concept of unemployment insurance. Well, the opposition said this was a terrible attack on women because apparently nearly everybody who voluntarily quit their job was a woman who was sexually harassed. This raged on in the House of Commons for three or four weeks, that this was anti-feminist, you know, anti-woman, savage Tories exposing them to risk all across the country where they're being sexually harassed because this is the only reason anybody ever voluntarily quit their job. This was absolute nonsense but it was a serious political problem for four or five weeks.

Today, however, they don't have this kind of opposition. They've got the Reform Party who can't criticize at all because they're saying, "Cut even more. You're not cutting enough." They've got the Bloc Québécois, who are only interested in Quebec, and then you've got a couple of

NDPers, and nobody's paying any attention to them, and you've got our two buckos, and nobody's paying any attention to them either.[1] So they haven't got an opposition. The Liberals have got a much better chance now to accomplish necessary changes because of that.

Generally speaking, in the Conservative Party the members are quite supportive of reining in spending. They are fiscally cautious, but a lot will depend upon where a member is from in the country. Generally speaking, members of Parliament in our party or any party from Atlantic Canada will want government spending because Atlantic Canada is living on transfers from the rest of Canada. The dependency in Atlantic Canada is frightening. This is one of the things in the U.S.–Canada free trade debate that really shocked me. You'll remember from your history how the Maritime provinces always complained that Confederation had cost them and interrupted north-south trade and they were sacrificed for tariffs in central Canada.

The original tariff policy, the national industrial policy, was Sir John A. Macdonald's. So here was free trade. They were getting their chance down in Atlantic Canada after all these 90, 100 years of complaining for free trade with the United States, and they were paralyzed with fear that they were going to lose. They believed that medicare was going to go and the social security system was going to be badly affected, etc. We had a helluva job selling the free trade agreement in the Maritimes and Newfoundland because the region now is completely dependent on transfers of income from governments to their own governments, and from governments to people. Therefore the members of Parliament from Atlantic Canada, despite concerns about these spending issues, will support more spending because they feel they can't get elected otherwise.

As far as I know, until the last four or five years the public never showed any alarm about the amount in the budget that was going on interest or on the deficit question generally. For some reason the public or individual citizens feel remote from government. The rules that apply to them don't apply to government. They want things done for them and they don't want to accept reasons and arguments why they can't be done. They may know that in their own lives they can't just keep on borrowing, borrowing and borrowing, but they think the government is different. That somehow government creates the currency so the government can just print more. They don't like the Bank of Canada tightening up on interest rates. They're always blaming the Bank of Canada for the increase in interest rates. We don't have the power in this country any longer to control our own interest rates anyway. It's foreigners that determine what interest rates are going to be in Canada. But the public separates themselves. They don't believe that what applies to them in their own life in these areas is true of government as well.

It's not a question of morals; it's a kind of sublimation or denial. If you want the government to do something, you want to believe the government can do it. You don't want to accept the argument that it's beyond the government's powers to do this any longer. Now that's changing and has in the last four or five years. There has been a significant change in that attitude, and the proof is in the fact that our Liberal government now in office is doing the things they're trying to do. You know that's a major change.

Politicians are indeed responsible for that dependency. They will reflect whatever the view of the electorate is that they're representing. This is natural. You can't be elected in a democracy if you're going to go directly against what your public wants you to do. Look at the demands for recall. Look at what happened to the Conservative Party in the West. The Reform Party developed simply because the right-wing people in British Columbia, and Alberta in particular, felt the Conservative Party was ignoring them. They weren't doing what the people wanted them to do, which are some of the things that we're discussing. They wanted government to reduce spending and do certain other things and we weren't responding. They were against the bilingualism policy, and here the Tories get into power and they're just as bad on the bilingualism issue as Mr. Trudeau was. This is the way they thought. Eventually they felt that the PC Party no longer represented their views or wouldn't carry them out, so they left and created the Reform Party, which has crippled us. Only the future will tell whether this can be overcome again or not. So if the politicians don't reflect the wishes and views of their constituents, how can they hope to continue in any place where they're going to affect policy?

I agree with you 100 percent that ideally leadership involves persuading people to come in the direction you think is the right direction, even if starting out they don't think so. That's the essence of leadership. But it seldom works. I used to say that about my budget in 1979, 1980. That was supported by *The Globe and Mail*; you know, all the papers, generally, and editorial speakers were all very supportive of that budget.

But I used to say after we were defeated that you quote the Bible: and you shall tell the truth and the truth shall set you free. I said that's certainly true, here we are free as the breeze. We're set free because in this budget we gave them the truth. Well, most politicians think that if you give the public the truth, you're going to be set free. Just as we were set free.

I must say that when the Conservatives are in opposition they're just as irresponsible as the Liberals are when they're in opposition. Unfortunately that would be true of the NDP as well because when you're in opposition, you are arguing that you should be spending money on this or that. The government says, "Take away the lighthouse keepers," and the opposition opposes — this is one of the tricky issues on the East Coast and has been going on now for eight or nine years. Now, you don't need light keepers any longer. We have all this modern electronic machinery, so the government wants to save a few dollars. Well, opposition members of course oppose this because the public opposes it. They like the romance of lighthouse keepers.

So when you're in opposition you tend to be irresponsible and it's when you're in government that you'll have no way of avoiding the fact that you are responsible. I had to plead guilty to some of that myself when I was in opposition. In fact, take UI. We had this Forget report.[2] If we had carried out its recommendations it would have meant the loss of hundreds of millions of dollars in Newfoundland, which is heavily dependent on UI. I think over $1 billion a year now goes into Newfoundland and UI. Well, the way I looked at it was this: I can't go to the people of St. John's West and say, "Elect me," and then turn around three weeks later and kick them in the face and change UI so that thousands of them are no longer eligible for it, or do away with fishermen's UI or whatever these changes might be. So that's a factor. If you went to them and said, "Look, vote for me and I am going to change UI," that would be different. But you don't do that. So these are all factors. You're representing people, so you have to be careful.

Parliament in Canada is extremely ineffectual. Ordinary members of Parliament, that is, government members who are not in the Cabinet or opposition members, are pretty well powerless and have very little influence. They may occasionally have some influence in their own party caucus, but outside of that they have very little influence because of the party system. If you're going to buck the party, well, there were three Liberal MPs that voted against gun control a month or two ago and they were punished by the party whip. They're not going to get certain things that members like to have in the future. They're taken off committees and so on. You need to have party discipline because you can't have a government based on the parliamentary system until you control a majority of the members in the House, so you've got to have that. But on the other hand, it takes away most of the influence of the members. So that's our system as compared to the congressional, where members have a tremendous amount of influence and control and the parties have little leverage over them. That's got its advantages and its disadvantages as well, but our Parliament is very frustrating for the members because they are by and large ineffectual.

As an MP I wouldn't go home to my district and say, "Look, I'm ineffectual, vote for me. I'm ineffectual but still I'm the best ineffectual candidate that you could send up." I mean, you have questions of pride and so on. They can still do a job for their constituents. They can still be a good representative of their area and so on, but as members of a party influencing policy, what a government actually does, rather than straightening out this man's unemployment insurance problem or this woman's rent problem, they basically don't have much influence. And they're a very frustrated group.

Unfortunately the level of debate in the House of Commons is, well, there's a great quote by the Victorian writer who said that the level of intelligence in politics is so low that you had to stoop in order to reach it. That's not exactly the quotation, but the level of intelligence in parliamentary debate is so low that it's about disappeared. Since the press and the media pay no attention to parliamentary debate, and since the fate of governments doesn't hinge on it, and since your own colleagues aren't even in there listening to you, there's very seldom a debate in the House of Commons that anyone pays any attention to.

Occasionally there is one. For example, there was one on the Gulf War when John Turner, who was then no longer leader of the Liberals, had a different view than Chrétien's and the party's. He gave a very good speech and there was a lot of interest in that particular debate, so there is the odd debate that can be effective. But for the most part there's nobody watching or listening. The House of Commons today is a TV adjunct — the only thing that counts is Question Period. And Question Period is a play. It's like preparing for a play on Broadway. The opposition spends all morning thinking up questions: how can we embarrass the government? And the government is thinking up all morning, how are we going to respond if X question is asked, and how can I put down the other guy? So this show goes on every afternoon in Question Period and that's all that Parliament amounts to any longer.

There aren't easy ways to overcome this problem. There have been suggestions of the recall and the referendum and nonsense of that kind from the Reform Party, which would simply put the kibosh on members altogether. If I get elected today and in six months' time the turkeys down in my district can have a referendum to have me recalled because I did something they didn't like, this will worsen the situation. We're just talking now about the fact that MPs are basically ineffectual. Well, if that's the position they're put in, they'll be completely ineffectual. They'll have to be nothing but just echoes of the people's prejudices and views at any moment in their own district. That's terrible and not the solution to making Parliament more effective. It doesn't lie there.

There have been some serious suggestions that you have very few votes of confidence. That you allow the government's legislation to be defeated more often and not taken as a vote of non-confidence because in an election some changes like that that might help. We're sliding toward the American system. The bill of rights here in Canada was a major change in the parliamentary system of government. The prime minister is becoming more like a president. It's really quite humorous to see how it operates. The prime minister has got staff in the PMO, the Prime Minister's Office, and the PCO, the Privy Council Office, and their job is to look after the prime minister. They make sure that he can't be blamed for something, that if anything bad happens, it's one of those turkeys' fault (some Cabinet minister).

They organize Cabinet shuffles on a regular basis because they now regard the leader as sacrosanct. He's not the first among equals, yet in your political science classes they used to say the prime minister was the first among equals. This is not the case anymore. The prime minister is a supreme being and the Cabinet ministers are peasants down below lucky to survive. At any moment they might be shuffled or put out and somebody else put in. So the prime minister today, in our system, has got tremendous power. In election campaigns the focus is on the three leaders of the three parties. Where will the rest of the candidates be? They'll be down in the local areas, you know, doing the local battles, etc. But all of the media attention will be devoted to the leaders. This is another major change in the parliamentary system, that the Cabinet ministers are no longer anywhere near on an equal basis with the prime minister. Now, I don't know whether this is good or bad.

Prime ministers naturally would like to be re-elected but Mulroney was very conscious of the need to restrict spending. The whole nine years we were in there were nothing but expenditure reviews and cutbacks and so on, but none were too successful. We did restrict the deficit spending so that the proportion of the GNP that was going for those purposes was reduced and we had an operating surplus, when you forget the interest and the debt part of it. For the rest of the government's program operations there was an operating deficit. It was $16 billion a year when we took over and that became an operating surplus. So there were some improvements, but not major enough because he had major political problems, which I've gone into before, whenever we attempted to cut.

I believe that Mr. Chrétien recognizes there is a problem because you'd have to be a complete and utter dolt today not to see this is a major problem for Canada. I think he's convinced of it. But he will have to try to evaluate the question: am I going to get chucked out of office in two or three years' time if I keep going in this way? He'll have to try to make those kind of judgments because he will convince himself it's in Canada's interest to keep him here rather than to have Jean Charest here or the leader of the Reform Party, Preston Manning, and so on.

If the public wants spending to be controlled, and they clearly demonstrate it and punish those who don't accept these principles or who are not advocating them, then the system will respond and this will be the policy. That's why in the last five or six years the governments have taken the steps they've taken. Because a number of provinces have cut back, as you know — Alberta, even Newfoundland. Clyde Wells, despite the fact that I think he was all wrong on Meech Lake, is very careful financially. So at least five or six of the provinces have cut back and this is all a reflection of the fact that the public is not prepared to endorse the former levels of spending. The public does understand it and so as long as the public demonstrates this is the way they want to go, that's what will happen.

The interesting thing is senior citizens. They're one of the most difficult groups to deal with and you would think that they wouldn't be because by and large they're the most interested in politics. They're the most enjoyable people to campaign — knock on the door, you know a person over 40 is usually interested. Younger people couldn't care less, they just want to get you out of their face, get you off somewhere else. But the senior citizens as a group are tremendously selfish. You can't touch a thing that senior citizens now believe to be their entitlement. And they've gone through the system and they get more and more selfish as they get older. It's quite an interesting phenomenon to observe.

You'll recall that in our first budget I think it was, Michael Wilson announced we were going to do away with automatic cost-of-living increases in old age security. Well, boy, the older citizens went bonkers. They finally nailed Mr. Mulroney, you remember that French-Canadian woman said, I forget the exact phrase she used now, but she got him outside of the House of Commons and told him, "You've had it." And this decision was reversed. There's the old dilemma because the senior citizens have gone through the whole system and by and large they're more intelligent, they understand. Well, when it comes to their own share of the pie, they don't want it touched at all. So when I start to see senior citizens saying, "Cut back on our entitlements," I'll know that the country's in a bad financial state. Then I'll know that the system is going to respond. So you watch and see what the organizations that represent senior citizens do.

I think you have to decide whether the governments should be concerned by regional disparities or not. We have had programs in Canada to try to overcome regional disparity for, say, 30 years at least. And they haven't been too successful. ACOA (the Atlantic Canada Opportunities Agency) has been the most successful of them, but every provincial government pretty well has programs to encourage industry, to try to attract industry to its own bailiwick. Most of them are not successful.

In Newfoundland hundreds of millions of dollars were wasted by Mr. Smallwood on crazy cockamamie develop-or-perish strategies for Newfoundland. So none of this has been too successful. Regional development spending has been cut back, so it's a question of whether the governments believe that they may as well go on the rest of the way and do away with all regional development spending or not. This will be very unusual if they do because even in the European Community they have huge programs of regional assistance. So it's difficult to know. Unfortunately the people today have a tendency to believe that it doesn't matter where you live; you should have the same services as everywhere else. If you live on the coast of Labrador, they firmly believe they should have the same access to everything as though they lived in Toronto. So this is a popular conception that's a bit difficult to overcome.

I'm involved in politics and there are various interest groups and pressure groups, but in the last 20 years I would say that it's gotten out of control altogether. The governments were the authors of their own misfortune because they went and financed these interest groups, which in my view they shouldn't do at all. For example, they financed the advisory group on the status of women. The governments used to meet with them every year and I've never met such a bunch of savages in my life. These people who are allegedly representing the women of Canada. They would come to a meeting with the prime minister and ministers, when I was minister of justice, and they'd ask a question. You'd get up to answer and hear "boo, boo" before you got your mouth open. They'd howl you down, shout at you and wave their fists at you. I mean, this is not dialogue. No one should have to put up with this. So after two years of this we said we're not meeting with you anymore. Of course we were savagely attacked because we wouldn't meet with them anymore. So the government has created a lot of this problem by financing a lot of these groups.

Now, what else has happened is the media. The media are usually anti-government anyway. I mean, talk about the Ottawa national media. They're certainly anti-PC and were anti-Mulroney. But generally speaking they're anti-government, in any event. In the last 10 years the government announces a policy at 2:00 in the afternoon. Say I announce a policy on behalf of the government before it's on the news at 6:00. What my new policy might get is 15, 20 seconds' coverage and no details. Then the reporters start going to all the special-interest groups. "What did you think of this policy?" they ask. "This is a terrible policy," the groups respond, "it's not enough." It's never enough money.

I was given a cheque to take down to Newfoundland for the Association for the Short of Stature. I didn't know what the hell this association was. What is this Association for the Short of Stature? So we had their representatives come into the office so I could present the cheque, $8,000. In came two dwarfs, or midgets is what we used to call them. The same size as you saw on television, you know, the wrestlers. So I said to the two men, "Now, gentlemen, what's the situation here in Newfoundland that we're recognizing your association?" "Well," they said, "in Newfoundland we have a very high percentage of short-statured people." I said, "Is that right? What's the percentage?" "Oh," they said, "two per 100,000." So that meant there were 10 on the whole island. Oh well. So there's all kinds of grants of that nature going out. It's really astounding.

The only real representatives of the youth that politicians come across would be the university student organizations or bodies that represent the university students. By and large their viewpoint is quite a narrow one. They're politicians as well. They got elected to head up university student groups and they're not going to get re-elected to head up university student groups if they don't act on the basis that students should get more. They say they're not being properly looked after and fees should be lower and so on. So normally the views they express are quite narrow and quite selfish, from the point of view that they want more for students. That's to be expected. I can't blame them for that.

Otherwise youth is difficult. Student groups are the main place you come across them, other than in the political parties. The youth is listened to a lot in the political parties because every political party thinks it's the youth group that their future lies with. So there's no problem in political parties with young people putting forward their views and getting recognized and having their own associations; and they're very active in organization. If you're a candidate for leadership and you have a good group of young people working for you, it's a big advantage. There's no difficulty in youth getting recognized, whether their views are any better than anyone else's. Normally they're based on self-interest, the same as everybody else's.

The fact that the younger generation has to pay off the debt is a failure of the system. Not just in Canada. We don't want to blame just Canadians. It's the same problem in the United States. It's the same problem in France and the same problem in Italy and so on. Where it's not a problem as much is more in the Southeast Asian countries, I suppose. There's no reason why people shouldn't be blamed because the system has failed. Whether it's the chicken or the egg — who knows? If somebody with a different attitude than Mr. Trudeau had been there in 1968, what might have been the situation? You simply don't know.

We were widely regarded as fools to bring in a budget, with a minority government, that was restrictive in any way. I think the mistake we made was we were not polling and we weren't acting like a minority government. We made a fatal mistake; Joe Clark did. In the first couple of days he said we were going to act as though we had a majority. That was an arrogant mistake. We thought we had the Liberals somewhat on the run, they wouldn't dare cause an election for two or three years. So we said, "We're going to act as though we have a majority." Well, that's a fatal attitude when you're a minority. So we failed to be listening and we went boldly onward. We were going to act as though we had a majority, so that's the basis I brought the budget in on. The Liberals wouldn't dare defeat it.

Well, they did dare defeat it and they threw us out for a number of reasons and put Mr. Trudeau and the Liberals back in. They didn't pay the least bit of attention to any need for financial control in Canada. We had ever-increasing deficits for four years. Marc Lalonde today is still saying that what they did was perfectly correct, right. He's not admitting any mistake. He's not like me. I'm prepared to admit the odd mistake. Marc doesn't admit any. The public seemed to approve it. A lot of that had to do with the energy policies and not wanting to recognize that the world crude oil prices had gone up and all this kind of thing. So I suppose we're all to blame.

If you of the younger generation want to get out of paying this debt, where are you going to go? You'll have to find a place where you'd be better off. I don't know where that place might be. Could be out in Southeast Asia somewhere but any of the Western countries pretty well have the same problem. Sweden is an example of excess. They went to hell with it in the social system. They have a fantastic taxation system, discouraging everybody from showing any initiative or enterprise. So you're not going to go to Sweden. If you go to Norway, you'll see the same problem there. You go to Denmark, it's no different in Denmark.

You go anywhere in Western Europe and you're going to find the same problem. So you'll have to leave Western civilization. You'll have to disappear to Korea or somewhere, and there may be other problems in Korea. I mean, you don't speak Korean, for example, and you may find difficulty in learning it. So I think you're stuck with staying here and dealing with the situation. It's only going to take five or six years of proper government, maybe seven or eight, to reverse this. They've reversed it in New Zealand. They're not all home free yet, but we can reverse this pretty quickly. In 10 years certainly. So there's no reason why you shouldn't stay here. It's still a great place to live. We still have all kinds of opportunities.

You're not paying for another generation's mistakes. You're paying for their enjoying life more than they should have enjoyed life because they didn't pay for a lot of the benefits that they had while they were here. Why should you pay? Because you've got no choice, you know. It's not that this is just or fair. It's that you can do nothing about it. Now, what you should do is try to get the system straightened up and not pass on the same situation to your own children, but you're going to have very serious problems as well. Not caused by frivolity or whatever, you'll have serious problems with the pension system — Canada pensions, which are not self-financing. These kinds of things are going to have to be tackled, so you have some real, bad problems. But I have no doubt that if you work 12, 14 hours a day, save your money, pay heavy taxes, that you can overcome it.

In terms of taking on the political system, it will respond to what the people of Canada think about it. One of our problems is the very excessive regionalism. The feature of our system I always found most discouraging is that the government does something in Quebec and every other region says, "You're always favouring Quebec." If they do something in Newfoundland, they'll complain in New Brunswick. This doesn't happen in the States. I've never heard anybody in California say the federal government shouldn't be doing as much as they are for those people in Alabama or New England or vice versa. But here in Canada there is a constant cacophony of complaints that one region is preferred over another. This makes political life in Canada even more difficult.

Politicians will respond to the general beliefs and atmosphere of their electorate. That's why the government in Alberta responds differ- ently than the government in Newfoundland or the government in Quebec. It's a funny thing. It's the two largest provinces, Ontario and Quebec, that are ignoring debt concerns. The Quebec government is completely irresponsible in its deficit and debt policy. Parizeau — he's not cutting back at all or trying to restrain because he wants to per- suade the people of Quebec that it's to their advantage to become sov- ereign. In Ontario you've had the New Democrats, led by Rae, who don't believe that these are important issues either. So the two main provinces of Canada are going blithely on their way. The federal gov- ernment is going in a different direction and most of the other provinces are as well.

Ontario now complains about how badly treated poor old Ontario is. They've suffered a bad loss of confidence in the last four or five years. They're no longer the cornucopia that the rest of us could dip into for transfer of money from time to time. So I think it's Quebec and Ontario where people who are concerned about these matters, as you people seem to be, and very properly so, have got to try to get a change in attitude and approach. I think you're a group of intelligent young people who are onto the right issues. This is the essence of the present problems of today — you're interested and involved in what counts today.

I liked politics and public life but, you know, after 28 years it was time to change. Also, I think I could have been elected again in my own district, my own seat, even with this disaster that happened to us, but I wouldn't have wanted to be in the opposition. The opposition is good for politicians on their way up, when they're younger, because it teaches them a bit of humility. It teaches them a life that's hard; things are not as simple as they might appear to be. It decreases their natural arrogance, which most of us politicians have because we think we're the greatest, right? If I didn't think I was the greatest, why would I be in politics?

When I ran for the PC leadership it wasn't because I thought I was some germ cell. I ran because I thought, I'm the best. Now, I was very disappointed with the people in our party who didn't run because Kim Campbell was showing fantastically in the polls. They didn't run because they didn't think they could beat her or get support. When I ran for the national PC leadership we'd done a poll. I had about two or three percent. That was as high as I was. That didn't stop me from running because I knew once they got to know me, jeez, that would change 75 percent.

Unfortunately it didn't. The percentages didn't get that high, or stay there. So politicians have to have a lot of self-confidence and so on or else they shouldn't be in public life. But opposition is good for them because it diminishes your arrogance and makes people more reasonable and humble. At my stage in life I wouldn't want to go back into opposition again because, after all, you're in politics because you want to do something. You can only do something if you're in the government. You can't accomplish anything in the opposition except your part of making it function and keeping the government on its toes, etc. So it's in government that you can actually do things.

I don't know how much I did. I did quite a bit, I think, for my native province and so on. I wouldn't have wanted to go back to opposition. Now I'm 64 and I don't feel used up yet. I've got things I still want to do. I'd probably run again except my wife, who's been my wife for 43 years, might no longer be my wife. So I don't want to risk that. She didn't want me in public life any longer, so I think it's unlikely I'll run again. But there are lots of other things you can do. I'm going to attempt the book. I don't know whether it'll be accepted or not. I can still speak. I'm practising law, black-letter law, really, trying to attract business for the law firm for which you're counsel. I do a bit of consulting work, get a chance to travel, speak occasionally. I'm a chancellor of Memorial University, which gives me the opportunity to work in the university and find out what's happening there.

I'm going to lead a campaign for funds for Memorial. It badly needs private funding. I'll be looking to you all, by the way, as you accumulate more wealth; I'll be around seeing what we can get for Memorial.

My life is very interesting. It's amazing. Today 64 is nothing. I used to think that everyone should be chloroformed at 65 — this would solve our old age security problem. As you turn 65 they take you over to the hospital and apply the chloroform and off you go. Now I've changed that to 75.

NOTES

1. "Buckos" refers to the two Progressive Conservatives who kept their seats after the Kim Campbell defeat in 1993, in which the PCs lost 167 seats.
2. The Forget report was produced by the Commission of Inquiry on Unemployment Insurance, with Claude Forget acting as chair.

GORDON ROBERTSON

*As clerk of the Privy Council under prime ministers
Pearson and Trudeau, Mr. Robertson had a key insider's
view of the growth of government spending programs at a
crucial stage in Canadian history.*

The period before the war, of course, was the period of the Great
Depression. Anybody who didn't live through the Depression can't
understand how totally different it was from anything that we've had
since. It was in magnitude an infinitely worse economic disaster than
anything we've seen since. Just to give you an idea, the levels of unemployment in Saskatchewan, where I was brought up, were around 30, 40,
50 percent. It was similar in other parts of the country, although not as
bad elsewhere as it was in Saskatchewan and Manitoba and Alberta. But
it was an economic disaster. It was not only an economic disaster, it was
a human disaster. We're awfully used now to the idea of social security
and support programs. The only form of social security at that time was
an old age pension introduced in 1927 for people aged 70 years and
over. It was $20 a month. That was the only underwriting of the posi-
tion of people at all. There was nothing of any other kind whatsoever.

When the magnitude of the economic disaster became apparent
and people were in desperate straits, it was the municipalities, not the
provinces, not the federal government, but the municipalities, that had

to develop programs of what was called "relief," and relief was handled in a very humiliating way. It was absolutely means-tested and means-tested in the most frugal, penny-pinching way because governments, too, were desperately hard-up. Frugality was the order of the day because it had to be the order of the day.

I mention this purely and simply to give you an impression of what the last decade before the war was like because it was a full decade. The crash on Wall Street was in 1929, the Depression began in 1930, and it didn't really end until we were into the war in 1939. Of course, when we got into the war it was totally different as far as the war effort was concerned. Whatever was necessary was what was done.

There are very few great things about war, but one of the great things about this war was the total unanimity of the effort. There was some effort on the part of Mr. Duplessis, who was premier of Quebec, at the beginning to create a difference between Quebec and the rest of the country but that failed when he lost an election in 1940. The French-Canadian ministers, led by Mr. Lapointe, in the federal government made it clear that unless Duplessis was defeated in that election, they would resign. Well, that finished it. Quebec rallied around and there was no problem from then on. So you had complete unanimity. There was no question that whatever was necessary financially had to be done. There was a commitment against conscription for overseas service, but apart from that it was whatever was necessary.

The handling of finance by Canada during the war was superbly well done. In fact, post-war, I remember an article in *Fortune* magazine that surveyed the various countries and their economic handling of the war effort which said that the financial handling of the war in Canada had been the best. I think that's not a reflection of Canadian chauvinism, it's the truth. It was a total effort.

All of that is background to the fact that when it became clear in 1944 that the war was going to end and the Allied side was going to win, planning began for post-war. The really great determination, and this was with unanimity like the wartime unanimity, was that there must never again be the kind of economic and human situation we had had during the 10 years of the 1930s. It's absolutely vital to understand that thinking or you can't understand what was done after the war.

The planning had a number of aspects to it. In the first place it ensured that there was not going to be an economic recession with a high level of unemployment once the war was over. You were going to have a few hundred thousand men coming back, demobilized from the services. You were going to have a lot of women, too, who were in the Forces, and there had to be planning for that. What were they going to do?

One of the things that was planned was a major increase of financial assistance in secondary and post-secondary education so these people could go to school and university. Then there was going to have to be someplace to house people, so amendments were introduced. With the new national housing act, for the first time there were guaranteed mortgages so people with low incomes could hope to get mortgages at low cost to build houses. This produced not simply housing but an active construction industry that would employ people to build houses. They wanted, number one, to see that the economic aspects of the Depression did not recur. They also wanted to see that some degree of social security was put under people so human suffering would not occur if there were any kind of economic recession or economic difficulty.

Unemployment insurance, old age security, health insurance, all of these things were planned and then were gradually implemented over the 1950s and into the 1960s. The attitude toward post-war spending was conditioned by, number one, the need to avoid an economic recession after the war. There had been one after the Great War; there was serious unemployment in the 1920s, but after the Second World War they did avoid any significant economic recession, they did avoid unemployment, and the attitude toward spending was that to the extent that it was necessary to achieve those purposes, it was going to be done.

Now, on the support programs, these came in at different times and in different degrees. On the whole, it was a matter of determination to get a social security net, but it was conditioned by the frugality of the pre-war period. It wasn't a sky-is-the-limit kind of thing the way it was during the war, for wartime expenditure. I can illustrate that by just one anecdote. I can indicate the attitude toward spending by simply recounting what happened in the late 1950s. The Old Age Security Program was made much more extensive in the late 1940s. But by the late 1950s there was a certain amount of inflation, not a lot, but a certain amount that was thought to be too low.

There was a Liberal government in power. Mr. St. Laurent was prime minister and Walter Harris was minister of finance and it was decided to increase the old age security payment. Walter Harris was a good, prudent, frugal man, and he decided the amount by which it should be increased was precisely the amount by which inflation had reduced the value of old age security. The real amount of the old age security payment had been eroded to a degree by the small amount of inflation there had been in the early 1950s. So it was decided, under the pressure of Mr. Harris, that old age security payments would be increased by precisely the amount that the loss had been in real terms by inflation, and that turned out to be $6 a month. Six dollars a month! Well, that was just leaped on by Mr. Diefenbaker, who was leader of the Conservative Party, and he denounced the Liberal government as heartless.

Now, this was significant for two reasons. In the first place it was reflective of frugality that was still the conditioned approach to money and spending at that time. It was also significant in that it was the Conservative Party that attacked the Liberal Party, which was traditionally the more spendthrift party, if you want to put it that way. They were more concerned about social welfare and it was the Conservative Party that attacked them for being frugal. So the attitude was not one of wholesale handouts.

I don't know whether it's right to say there was a radical change of thinking after the war. The implementation of these things was spread over from about 1946 to, I think, when medicare finally came, in 1968, if my memory is right. So they're spread over 20 years. As far as I was concerned, the first sense I had that perhaps it was going too far was when the Canada Pension Plan was proposed as something on top of old age security. The Canada Pension Plan was contributory; old age security was not contributory — the Canada Pension Plan was universally related to income and so it's quite different.

I began to worry if we would have the resources. A lot depended on whether they got the actuarial calculations right as to how the contributions would relate to the benefits. I don't know how carefully and how thoroughly the actuarial calculations were done, but some unforeseeable things have come in, you know. The longevity of people, on the average, has increased. There are more old people hanging around to get paid. So I think the calculations of that day were not right, given the facts of today.

I'm not sure that it's right to think that there was any wanton disregard. Certainly there was almost no criticism from any political party, and you'd expect the Conservatives to have been critical. It was usually the Liberals, from 1963 on, who were doing these things. There was no attack on the government from that point of view, so certainly frugality went out. I would agree with that. But whether anything that you could regard as lack of concern came in is another matter. The circumstances altered, calculations altered, and I think nobody really foresaw the kind of situation we've got now.

I think post-war planning was extraordinarily successful. There was no recession. There was no significant amount of unemployment. There was some, of course, but not a great deal of it. Industry got shifted over from a wartime base to peacetime. A large number of people got the kind of education they had missed during the war and the economy became remarkably prosperous. Indeed, I think Canadians got a sense of pride at that time that I think has only been equalled perhaps by the first decade of this century, when Sir Wilfrid Laurier said that the 20th century belonged to Canada. Canada was the third industrial power in the world at that time. This was pretty heady stuff.

Now, part of the reason we were the third industrial power was that a lot of the major industrial powers were flat on their backs, Japan, Germany, France and so on. But we were the third industrial power in the world and convoys came from various countries to get assistance from Canada, to establish trade relations. All of this was just a demonstration of the success that had been achieved in the development of our economy and it was translated into peacetime, from wartime into peacetime. It was a very successful operation right through to the 1950s. It was a very long period of remarkable success. I wouldn't know for sure how long it had gone on without a significant bump, but maybe 15 years. I mean, it was a very long time in terms of economic operation.

The pride in Canada's economy coming out of the war could indeed be described as euphoria. That's not too far off. It was a very good time to be a Canadian. One had the sense that Canada had done a first-class job in the war. All the Armed Forces had done a splendid job. There was also a sense that, industrially, we had changed from an agrarian peacetime economy to an industrial wartime economy. C. D. Howe was one the architects of this and, as you know, he brought in from all kinds of industry in Canada people working for $1 a year in Ottawa, or wherever it was required. He did this to make this conversion from peacetime to wartime, to build up the industries that were required for war, and this was done with great success. So there was post-war pride in the operation of our Armed Forces and pride in the operation of the economy and industry. Then there was a good deal of pride in the post-war success in swinging back to peace. It was a very heady period.

In terms of these dollar-a-year men, there was a completely different sentiment in regard to working for the Government of Canada back then. As I mentioned at one point, there are a few good things about war, but one of the good things about war is that you get a degree of unanimity that you just never get in peace-time circumstances. And there was a complete commitment to the winning of the war. The result is that you lost any sense, really, of what the differences were in the roles that people were playing, as long as they were constructive to the war effort. One didn't hear any attack on the government except in relation to the adequacy or inadequacy of what it was doing. There were attacks if the opposition thought that certain things were unwise, but there was no attitude that criticism is desirable just as criticism. That was out. On the whole, support was the matter of the day.

As far as the public service was concerned, but Canada was considered to have the best public service in the world. And this was said not just felt; it was said in newspapers of the day that we had a superb public service. Not all the way, not everybody by any means, but the total operation was first class and this was recognized. The dollar-a-year people were picked for their efficiency, their knowledge and what they could contribute. As far action was concerned, it was a great time to be in the public service because everybody was working for the same object. Everybody was doing it to the best of their capacity. It was a great time to be around.

I'm not an economist by training. My background is political science and law. So I was in no position to have any confidence about my own feeling on going too far with the Canada Pension Plan. But one of my very good friends is Bob Bryce. He was deputy minister of finance at the time. I remember very clearly being in a Cabinet committee meeting where Bob was discussing with the ministers the extent of the total load taken on in various programs and commitments of this kind. I recall him saying to the Cabinet committee, a committee of, say, eight or 10 ministers dealing with the financial aspects of government, saying almost word for word, "Ministers, you can do all of these things but you can't do them all at the same time."

They were spreading it over 20 years, but what Bob meant was that the load was getting a little bit more than what the economy would be able to stand without difficulty. But one of the problems in that sort of a statement is you can't point to anything specific and say, "See, that proves it." There's no clear proof. There was no demonstration at that time that the burden of debt was getting too heavy. You've got to remember here, too, that during the war the country incurred an enormous burden of debt. It was just a staggering amount of debt that was taken on, and that debt was paid off almost entirely in about 15 years after the war, by budgetary surpluses that were incurred in order to specifically pay off the debt.

So there was no history to point to, really, to say that at some point the burden has passed a point where it cannot be handled. Bob Bryce was worried. But how do you prove it? I don't think Bryce's statement made an awful lot of an impression, quite frankly. I think the ministers didn't really believe it. I think that at the end of the year there was no evidence. The sky hadn't fallen. The Canadian credit hadn't suffered, so there was no feeling that, yes, after all Bob Bryce was right. The feeling was that you'd expect the deputy minister of finance to say that.

I don't recall ever stating my opinion on this matter. It wouldn't have been worth very much, but Bryce's opinion was worth something because he was an economist by training. He had facts and figures and all that sort of thing. My advice was worth something on legal, constitutional things of that sort, but not on a matter of this kind. Others saw it as well. Certainly people in the Bank of Canada were concerned and I know they expressed concern at various times. I suppose people in the Treasury Board; it was their job to be watching programs. I don't want to give the impression that there wasn't an attempt to put a check on programs; there was. When I entered the public service the Treasury Board, which is a committee of ministers, was a part of the Department of Finance. In order to make the scrutiny of expenditures more effective the Treasury Board was set up as a separate department of government. It was separate from the Department of Finance, so you had two financial departments: Finance on the taxation side, Treasury Board on the expenditure side. Also, you had National Revenue operating the administration of the thing. So in a sense you had three departments in the financial scrutiny business. In addition, one had the Office of the Auditor General, and the auditor general's office was built up greatly because the auditors general at different times said the spending was getting out of control, so they got increased resources. Things were done to try to do some checking on spending. It wasn't a case of saying, "Oh well, what the hell, it doesn't matter." That wasn't the approach. But certainly the fact of prosperity and success led to a diminution in scrutiny about frugality and saving.

The public's attitude toward debt in one sense is reflected by the fact that a major and successful effort was made to pay off the wartime debt. It was run down; I haven't got the figures but you can find them with no trouble at all. It was run down almost totally in about 15 years after the war. So the view was that of course debts have to be paid, but the question is what amount of debt becomes unmanageable in the economy. And this is not purely and simply economics; it's also politics. In order to pay off debt, you have to have a conviction on the part of the populace that it's better to have a budgetary surplus, which means more tax than you have to have for immediate purposes, in order to pay off the debt. Well, this is not a politically attractive proposition at first glance. Unless there is some clear demonstration that this is required, you can't expect a politician to leap to that conclusion. That's not the kind of conclusion you leap to.

In the last few years, when the debt was an awful lot worse than it was in the 1970s and in the early 1980s, how much outcry did you hear from the public, press or politicians, before 1993? Almost none. It astonishes me that in the last six years there wasn't more concern about this, but there wasn't. One of the things that concerned me, and it concerns me still, is that my generation has lived high on the hog and your generation's going to have to pay it off. But there hasn't been much sense of that. People don't really accept it or believe it. It's only very recently, in the last 18 months, that people have had a sense that it's real.

Back in the late 1940s we had a bigger debt, but it was incurred for war purposes. It was incurred for war purposes because you couldn't fight the war without borrowing. There's no way you could tax enough to do it all on that basis, so there was no concern at all about borrowing to the hilt in order to fight the war. It was quite different from now. If there had been peace-time borrowing, yes, there'd have been concern.

I think today there is an increase in tax evasion — in the sort of attitude that the normal standards of morality don't apply when it comes to one's taxes. Mind you, this is not something absolutely new. I think that when I was a kid in the 1930s people regarded it as perfectly fair game to try to smuggle in a radio or something like that and avoid customs, so it's not as if this is something brand-new. But I think there is more of it than there used to be. I suppose part of the reason there is more of it is because of the weight of taxation being much greater. There's more to evade. There is more profit in evading, if you can do the evasion, but I don't think we should exaggerate. I think Canada is still, in comparison with a lot of other countries, a very law-abiding country, even including observance of tax legislation. But I think there's more evasion than there used to be.

The whole area of social security falls strictly into provincial jurisdiction. All social security programs are provincial jurisdictions and the only reason the federal government can get into them at all is because it can spend money on anything at all. That's the spending power. It was able to say, for example, "We will mount a program for the assistance of post-secondary education and pay 50 percent. We'll match dollar for dollar whatever the province spends." It could say the same kind of thing about health. It could say the same kind of thing about hospitalization. So it got into areas of provincial jurisdiction not because there was federal jurisdiction, because there wasn't, but because it could spend. It could offer money. And the province of Quebec objected on principle to this invasion of provincial jurisdiction by the federal government simply through use of the spending power.

One can't really generalize about provincial pressure because the provinces took different positions, depending on the financial position of a province and depending on the political complexion of a government. The province of Quebec, not for financial reasons but for reasons of concern about the protection of their distinct culture and language, was more reluctant than any other province to see the federal government getting into programs of the kind I've talked about, such as social security, income support, health and that sort of business.

In most cases the attraction of dollars overcame the objection of principle because they too had pressures to provide health services, to provide post-secondary education, to do all those things. Sometimes special arrangements had to be made, sometimes not. But Quebec came in on virtually all these things. Sometimes it was with kicking and screaming and sometimes it was with a special program that would be a little bit different. The Atlantic provinces are in general the poorest of the provinces, so by and large they were the most ready to come in on programs. Their only worry was, could they find the other 50¢ to match the federal spending to make up a dollar?

Saskatchewan, when it had an NDP government, which it did for a number of years, was out at the front on a lot of the spending even though it's not a very rich province. But it was Saskatchewan that invented medicare as we've now got it. They introduced it in 1962 but we didn't get it on a national basis until 1968. They led the way on medicare. Ontario was the most reluctant on medicare. The government of Mr. Robarts came in last — with a good deal of pressure. So the attitudes of provinces were different, but they were all highly relevant to these very major programs that we've got.

I agree it was something of a poker game but there was no consistent theme about it. What I mean is that there wasn't any particular government that wanted things to get up and up and up. There were a number of different considerations in different circumstances. The Atlantic provinces wanted more money, yes, but they didn't want to have to put more money in to match. So you had different considerations from all sides. But all of these things had to be discussed among 11 governments, and there had to be a certain amount of agreement or a program wouldn't work.

Good luck trying to trace where your tax dollars go. You won't get any help from me because I don't know. I told you that I'm not an economist by training. Following our tax dollars would have been easier for us to do in the 1940s, partly because government was so much smaller and so much simpler. I mentioned the fact that on social security there was only one program. There was the old age pension plan of $20 a month and nothing else. The government was very, very small. It wouldn't have been desperately hard. It would have been a bit of a problem to follow a dollar, but it would have been an awful lot easier than it is now. I don't know what the magnitude of the multiplier of growth is, but certainly the complexity is far greater than it was.

I was surprised when government started growing exponentially because I grew up in the Depression, and my wife and I have often said that you never quite get over having been brought up in the Depression. We don't think of $1 or $10, or whatever the dollars are, the way our kids do. It's different. So I was surprised and I was rather concerned, not really about the social security, unemployment insurance, health insurance, medicare, not about those things, but just about the proliferation of government programs and about the very great growth in government apart from these social security things. I can think of, for instance, the many, many programs that were related to the multiculturalism thing, with all sorts of subventions for all sorts of lobby groups of different kinds. These kinds of things did concern me a bit, but to a degree people like Bryce and I were regarded as sort of prehistoric remnants of a day when frugality was the rule.

As far as the social security net is concerned, and post-secondary education, which isn't part of social security strictly speaking, I don't think there has been much public concern. There hasn't been much concern by the man or woman paying taxes, so I don't think there's been much concern about those expenditures. There's even still a great deal of reluctance about endangering these programs. Yet there isn't any sense that we've got to cut expenditures back, and in order to cut expenditures back we must reduce medicare, we must reduce old age security. I don't detect that. There is a feeling that, yes, we've got to do something about this debt because these boys in red suspenders that trade in dollars seem to think that we have to, but it's painful and we don't like it. That's my feeling about what the attitude still is. It's a great reluctance to see these things diminished.

I have this sense that Canadians in general have lived through so many years in which the kind of programs that I've been talking about were built up and established and in which there was no economic or financial difficulty in supporting them. People find it very, very hard to accept the proposition that what they perceive to be a rich country like Canada — far richer than it was in the 1930s or the 1920s or even in the 1950s — can't support the kind of programs that are so obviously beneficial to a lot of people when they get hit by any of life's hardships. I think that Canadians not only have had, but also are having, great difficulty today in coming to terms with this idea, that this country perhaps can't afford all those things.

Well, why can't it afford it? We've never had any demonstration clearly, until now perhaps, that too much debt is a problem. We've always been able to support our debt, so I think we have a kind of confused attitude in which Canadians are being asked to accept the proposition that these desirable programs are too great a burden, that somehow they have to be reduced. And they don't want to do it. I can understand why they don't want to do it.

To a certain degree we're going to have a return to frugality forced upon us. We won't like it. We don't want it but I think the financial circumstances are going to force it. We see it right now. It's starting and I think it's not going to stop. The last budget is simply the first step and the steps have to be carried further, so I think the pain will increase. There'll be resistance but I think we will have a return to something closer to what we can afford. Simply because we've got to. I don't think it's because of any new morality or because of any new wisdom, but simply because of a recognition of facts. As Canadians contemplate this situation in which they have to decide that things that are obviously good and helpful have to be reduced or done away with, I think they'll be very mixed-up kids as they contemplate it.

ALAN ROSS

A senior public servant talks about government money mismanagement.

I was in government for 31 years. I came out of the private sector where I was a chartered accountant and joined as a treasury auditor and worked my way through different positions, finally to long-range planning in communications. Then I was five years with the Treasury Board and financial policy development. I spent seven years as an assistant deputy minister of agriculture at Agriculture Canada. I finished up my career at the Department of Supply and Services as a senior assistant deputy minister for eight years.

I started in 1962, just after something called the Glassco Commission, which was to bring a bunch of new management controls into government. I was very excited about doing that, bringing in financial management to government. You can see that after 30 years we succeeded, so I retired in April of 1993.

This was a time when government had grown to such a size that there was a highly centralized control that just wasn't working anymore. There was a strong movement to bring in more modern management practices. That was the beginning of the philosophy of "Let the manager manage and get out of his face," that sort of thing. Those were the basic messages behind Glassco, which was to bring these modern management techniques in and to get rid of this highly centralized control.

Absolutely there were some major impacts. There were some major structural changes and much of it was very positive, in the sense that the stultifying effects of highly centralized control basically were overcome. I guess the major flaw that I see after all these years is that they never replaced it with an adequate accountability mechanism, if you will. They never really found a way to make everybody efficiently manage the cost of their programs. It's very hard to get people focused on the total cost of government. So there have been a lot of new systems, new processes, new organizational structures, but we really aren't much further ahead.

My background was as a chartered accountant, so obviously the numbers are important to me. When you start talking about the cost of the program you have to calculate what the major cost determinants are and what some of the cost strategies are. We might have to manage the costs of government, whether it is in Agriculture — the costs of research or the inspection programs — or whether it was at the Department of Supply and Services — the cost of payroll systems or processing cheques or whatever. Those cost strategies have always got a political overtone.

For example, if you decide you want to increase cost recovery, obviously that has a political overtone. If you want to rationalize offices and you want to close some down, that has political overtones. But there's never been a way to make those cost strategies visible, to make people really interested in disciplining them over a longer period of time. I think they're still wrestling with that.

The auditor general in 1976 said that the government had lost control or was about to lose control. That wasn't long after the reforms for Glassco, which came in 1968, 1969, it wasn't a long period of time. It was the fact that they took away one set of controls and they didn't replace it with another adequate set of controls. At that time "control" in that milieu was a very dirty word. You didn't use the word control in polite company. There was a misconception by a lot of the senior managers at that time, and it remains, that control is kind of a bookkeeping term, that control is managing from the centre again. Well, it doesn't mean any such thing. What control means is, how are you making visible whether people are managing or not? It's that simple. You don't have to do the managing for them but you want to make sure they are managing. If they are not managing, then they are either replaced or given the tools they need to manage, and I don't think that the government has done that well yet.

I think that is true for a number of reasons. Those years were the years of free resources. The tax base could never get used up. There was revenue coming and it was a growth time. As a matter of fact, it was almost as if money was a free good, so it's kind of hard to get people interested in accounting for money if it's a free good. As well, the currency of that day, as far as the major bureaucrats were concerned, was ideas and new programs.

That's what you got your good marks for. Any idea was a good idea and any program was a good program — as far as politically it was an exciting new program. You were giving people things, you were building bridges, you were building monuments and you could do anything you wanted. You were opening offices, therefore creating employment and better services.

Politics today is not fun because now you're saying no. You're closing offices and that's a lot tougher. But the mentality and philosophy of the managers at that time was growth: "I'm going to have more people reporting to me. This is just a wonderful time." The whole idea, therefore, of accounting for your resources, demonstrating your cost-management strategies, just seemed to be redundant. The people who were in power generally considered those kinds of discussions to be what they called the bookkeeper mentality, and real managers didn't bother themselves with that kind of nonsense. They were interested more in the big picture, the strategic thinking and those kinds of things, and I think we're paying the price for that today.

At that time there were a number of people who were concerned, most obviously the auditor general. In 1976 he blew the whistle and did it in such a way that it was politically embarrassing and that generated a lot of discussion. We had a royal commission on accountability. I think that was partly a cosmetic response by the government. While intellectually it was an interesting exercise, what it did was basically emasculate the auditor general and that was more important. They created the Office of the Comptroller General and the comptroller general was going to be the most senior bureaucrat, at the deputy minister level, to look after these things. In fact he had no mandate to do any of that. The comptroller principally was hired to put in systems and procedures and processes, which you can do forever and ever and ever, but if it doesn't come down to who's doing the job and who's not doing the job, that's not comptrollership. They've now disbanded the comptroller's office and they are trying to resurrect that function with the Treasury Board — the Treasury Board being the committee of ministers responsible for the management of the public service. Therefore the secretariats supporting that are trying to create the skills to be able to do so, but I think the jury's still out as to whether or not the rest of government will let them do that. There have been other people concerned and interested and many, many exercises and a lot of words spoken about it. In some cases some good work has been done, but, collectively, in government it has never been the major priority.

In 1976 there were two schools of thought on government's reaction to the auditor general. There were a lot of people who said, "Right on, this is correct and we've got to start to do this." But there was a larger school, I believe, in particular the senior managers at the time, that felt this was just another thing to be managed, another constraint, another political embarrassment. "We have problems with rotting tuna on the East Coast and we have to manage that. Do we have a problem with the auditor general making rotten noises? We have to manage that."

That's another aspect of the whole environment that I am a little concerned about because the bureaucracy and the major politicians, that is, the Prime Minister's Office and the Privy Council Office, became more concerned with managing the cosmetics. The major sin in a government is to have the government embarrassed, to have a minister embarrassed. So a lot of time has been spent and there have been a lot of communications experts involved in putting the correct slant on a problem or managing embarrassing situations.

For example, the auditor general's report is now extremely well managed as far as the government is concerned. They know the public can only absorb so many major headlines a week, and they make sure that the auditor general has his headlines for two days, and then some other major announcement will be made. I can guarantee that two days later it will make the auditor general's report a bit of a two-day wonder, as they say. So this whole question of managing the media, managing the public, managing the cosmetics, has become too high a priority by the senior managers in the government.

Certainly at the time the auditor general's report and the various mechanisms, the creation of the Office of the Comptroller General, made the point that there should be a senior financial officer in government. So they gave him one. Now, that did two things. One, it shut him up because he got what he wanted. But they never gave that senior financial officer the powers that Mr. Macdonell (the auditor general) had intended — that was to ensure there was visibility and that people were held to account, that people used the financial information to see whether or not people were managing costs. Instead they got very much into building systems, building processes, doing all those nice things that are part of the management process. But I believe that was part of managing the cosmetics.

As I said, visibility is the most important ingredient in accountability. By that I mean that the currency, as far as politics is concerned, is visibility. The only time anything really happens that's important and gets a politician's attention is if there is visibility. So if it's the opening of a new research station, a ribbon-cutting ceremony or something on the positive side, growth, creation of the jobs, all of those nice things are good things and good politics. Therefore granting money, contributions, subsidies, those are all good things because they create jobs and improve service. Going the other way around though, closing offices, cutting back, usually means a loss of service, loss of jobs and bad politics. Therefore there's been a lot of time and attention given to the correct cosmetic.

If we want to increase the public awareness of the cost of government, then obviously we should be making the cost strategies of each program visible. The cost strategies for one year, three years, five years, which might mean we're going to rationalize a bunch of research stations in agriculture. No politician is going to want to say that in five years he's foreclosing some research stations, that's just not good. They will fight those things. They will resist that kind of visibility. Until you get that kind of visibility you're not going to get accountability because you're not going to get the public debate, the public understanding and the public demand for a fiscally responsible government.

For the average person, figuring out these governmental systems would be very, very difficult. Particularly, understanding the cost part of government is very difficult. Firstly, we haven't made it easy in our form of the Estimates or public accounts. Secondly, it's so convoluted, but again, there's never been a real big demand. If the Royal Bank is in trouble, for example, because it's made a lot of bad loans in Mexico or wherever, it's all over the *Financial Post*. If you wanted to pick up and see what the financial analysis has been on the operations of any major corporation, you can do that.

Well, has anybody asked to see the financial operations of the Department of Health and Welfare or National Defence? If nobody asks the question, nobody cares. If nobody cares, who cares? That's the biggest problem we have — nobody cares. Nobody is making real efforts to try and create that need. The auditors general have in the past, but I don't think academia has done its job. I don't think that the financial bodies, the Institute of Chartered Accountants, which is, if you will, a group of informed citizenry who should be asking those kinds of questions, I don't think they've made an issue of it. Neither has the Chamber of Commerce. I don't think anybody's really gone after those kinds of issues and made them political issues until now. Now people are saying, "I'm not playing anymore." Now it's becoming politically embarrassing, so the government is taking it seriously.

Why? Not because good management is intrinsically good but because it's politically embarrassing. They have got to do something about it. Whether it's the bond rating or whether it's the fact that people are saying, "I'm not paying any more taxes," they have to do something about it. If you yourself are to go and say, "I want to know what the cost of the Indian program is. I want to know what the cost of the Old Age Security Program is, or the young offenders program," you would have a very difficult time understanding what those costs were. You'd have even a more difficult time finding out what anybody was going to do about it. Are they going to manage those costs in any way over one year, three years and five years? If you asked about the major cost determinants, I wonder if some of the senior managers would even know. Because "it's not important." If they did know and you asked them, "What are you doing, are you going to re-engineer, are you going to rationalize, are you going to get out of the business, are you going to automate?" you'd have a very difficult time finding those answers. If they don't have answers to those questions, i.e., they don't have cost-management strategies, you have to ask yourself the question, are they really managing those programs?

I think government and the bureaucracy have become extremely conscious of managing the public and managing information to the public, so in that sense I guess it is deliberate. Visibility is not a good thing. It is not perceived as a good thing. They usually hide it behind things. They do not want to undermine the accountability of ministers. What does that mean? Well, it means that each minister is supposed to be accountable to Parliament, so let's make it visible to Parliament. That's a whole question of parliamentary reform but even if it's visible to Parliament, it should be visible to the public. Nobody was working hard at using the information available to see whether or not somebody's managing the overall cost of government until, as I say, recently; with the program review and the policy review they are attempting to do that.

Even with the program and policy reviews, do we get to see the whole picture? Do we know what all those deliberations are? Or do we just get to see a little bit when they pull up one corner of the curtain and tell us in a budget speech, "Well, this year we're going to do this, this and this." What are you going to do three years down the road? What are you going to do five years down the road? We don't get to see that.

When the auditor general comes with a report like that, it becomes food for the opposition. The opposition's job is to then exploit that, to expose the government for poor management techniques. So there was a great cry in the House and then it was all forwarded to the Public Accounts Committee. The Public Accounts Committee is the only committee, I believe, that is still chaired by a member of the Opposition. At that time there were some really tough members of the Opposition in the Public Accounts Committee, such as Don Mazankowski and Lincoln Alexander and people like that, who were smart people and incredibly sharp. The auditor general's staff briefed them so they knew whence they were coming. Now, they were critiquing the lack of government controls and the poor financial-management process. Unfortunately, at that time I happened to have been the director of financial policy development, of those new mechanisms, if you will, and I had to go up to the treasury, to the Public Accounts Committee and defend them. Well, there was no defence because the auditor general was right. We knew he was right. It takes time to correct it, so again we would try to tell him, "Well, this is what we plan to do to correct that." But the biggest technique you had is you knew that a parliamentarian had very limited time. They had lots of demands, whether it's the constituency, the various committees they work on, and the time for the House, so you just worked hard to consume the time they had in front of the Public Accounts Committee. You made sure you survived those one or two hours or whatever it was, and you knew that if you got through that one day, the problem had gone away. It sounds callous but in fact that's part of managing the whole process.

This is one instance where the House, through the Public Accounts Committee, was asking us embarrassing questions and pushing us for answers that we didn't have. The only thing we could do was say, "Well, we're going to try to address that." That's not very satisfactory. So basically what you had to do was string out your time. Today, if people go before an estimates committee, before any committee of the House, you know that you can manage those exposures. That's part of the problem with visibility. We're not going to get visibility by parliamentarians unless we somehow modify that. If you talk to the Honourable Paul Dick, he will tell you that he remembers when there used be a Committee of the Whole. That is, the whole House reserved the right to scrutinize a department's estimates. Through parliamentary reform the House lost that particular facility. As a result they lost some of their control. What I'm saying is, until you reform parliamentary committees to allow the kind of visibility and exposure that can't be managed by the bureaucracy, then you're not going to get that visibility.

There's no question that the ethics and integrity of government have changed. It's a mirror of our society. When you hear that the Department of Finance used the most advantageous estimates in their interest rates of their foreign exchange, of their unemployment figures, when they were preparing a budget, you have to conclude that they lied. If they knew that they were using the very best estimates, that's a morality issue. I don't believe, in times gone by, that the deputy ministers of finance like Bob Bryce or people like that would allow that to happen. Today people manage the cosmetics, which means, if you will, a different morality, a different essence of integrity. Unfortunately I believe it sort of mirrors what's going on in society as a whole.

Everybody likes to point their fingers at politicians, but it is absolutely more complex than that. We had a generation of Canadians who drove politicians, who had great expectations, who insisted that government become more involved in the issues of Canadians, whether it be grants to business, whether it be subsidies, whether it be immigration. It doesn't matter what it is, there was an acceptance by the public, generally, that government's going to look after us, whether we're students or whether we're businessmen. We created, therefore, this monster that we can't pay for. It's not the politician. The major reason for a bureaucracy is to serve the ministry. You may disagree with the ministers but you're not there to disobey them; you're there to make it happen. So we have a whole bureaucracy that grew up to support a growing government, you know, a growth industry. That is why we are where we are today. The people who are in senior management were the young officers who were recruited to be part of that growth industry.

A lot of people in government saw it coming and tried to do things. I think politicians tried to do things. I remember when Mr. de Cotret was president of the Treasury Board and they brought in a major review in an attempt to try and bring the budget under control. If you listened to the budget speeches of many ministers, you heard people saying, "We have to get this deficit under control." Intellectually they knew that. They intended to do that in their heart and their souls but it just didn't come. It's hard, politically, to reduce anything.

I remember in Agriculture trying to rationalize some of the research stations, which meant closing some research stations. Ministers don't want to do that. The Western caucus wouldn't let certain offices be closed. The Quebec caucus wouldn't let certain offices be closed. I remember when we were trying to look for efficiencies and one of the things we thought we were really onto very quickly was a direct deposit. Instead of mailing a cheque to all of the citizens, whether for family allowances or for old age pensions, we could have a direct deposit. We paid a penny for direct deposit and we paid 10¢ per cheque, plus the envelope, plus the printing of the cheque and all the paper. So it doesn't take much to see a business case for going electronic. While the business case was there, politicians for nine years fought that — for nine years. The first politician who spoke out against it was the minister of health. He said, "We think the political benefit of having the government communicate with citizens every month with a little piece of paper and a cheque is worth it." And that means that it's politically more expedient to spend a whole lot of money. We had to convince them that their advertising dollars could be spent better. The other major issue was that it was a hidden subsidy to the post office. The post office was supposed to be a good business venture and was supposed to be getting off the public purse, but if every month you're sending out a whole bunch of cheques and paying them the full postage, that was a hidden subsidy. So we had to wait until a minister said, "We're going to make those suckers in the post office be efficient and we're going to make them pay as they go, so we're not going to give them that hidden subsidy." It took us nine years to bring an efficiency reform like direct deposit.

There are many, many, many examples of that, of rationalizing regional services, of rationalizing bureaucracies. Sometimes the automation would be short-term pain for long-term gain; that is, there's a major up-front investment. Well, that means there is going to be a negative impact on the budget this year and the election's next year, I don't care if there are efficiencies in the future, I don't get any benefit for that, the hell with you. So it's very tough when your planning horizon is so short that it's the next election. It's very hard to develop a longer-term view of cost management.

We don't do a good job of holding ministers accountable for their spending. I don't think you'll see any minister who has ever got up and said, "While I am the minister of fisheries, I am going to reduce the cost of this program and then be held to account to do it." He'll say, "I'm going to do this for cod or I'm going to do this for the fishermen." He's never going to get up and say, "I'm going to drive the cost of this program and never be held to account for it." We just don't do that at all.

Collectively, for the government as a whole, you can ask whether they met their deficit target or not. That's about the only performance indicator that anybody ever seems to care about. It seems to be a big plus if you say you can reduce the deficit. In the private sector, if you reduced your deficit, you'd be bankrupt because the bottom line is that your debt continues to increase. It's only been recently that people have begun to focus on the fact that *reducing* the deficit is not a good thing; *eliminating* the deficit is a good thing. Let's get a few surpluses and let's begin to manage that public debt because the public debt really represents our collective bankruptcy. That's what it's all about.

We have to change the inflationary psychology we have. In other words, more and more government is not the answer to all the problems. Smaller government is better government. That's the first thing, and I think we're well on the way to that. The second thing we have to do is expect and demand and have proven to us that government is fiscally responsible. We have to develop all kinds of mechanisms so we can see the collective costs of government and the individual portions of government and know that that the cost of government is being managed properly. That's what this debate is all about. How do we make that happen?

Finally, we have to demand a little more integrity about managing the relations with, and giving information to, the public. We have to get away from this managing by cosmetics. Again, I think that that's an exceedingly complex and difficult problem to deal with but those are the things we have to do. There is a certain amount of naiveté among Canadians. I think we all think, I don't have to do that, somebody else will look after that. But if you're a citizen and if you're exercising a vote, then the person who says, "You get the government you deserve," is probably right on. That's why collectively we have to become more demanding. The fact that people are getting more involved in finding out the issues and participating in tax revolts is hopefully a precursor of more involvement between governments, politicians and their constituencies. Until that happens, until you no longer say, "I'll let George do it," we're not going to get the kind of government that we should have.

Let's not be too hard on the Canadian people and the Canadian government. This is universal. This has happened in every democracy. The Americans have had the same problems, and the British, and the French. But it's interesting that in Switzerland, it's my understanding, that constitutionally it is *ultra vires* for one parliament to leave the next parliament in debt. I don't know what the sanctions are, but certainly that mentality is there. That is, they pay as they go. I think that that's where we came undone, where we began to think that tomorrow's dollars will be cheaper than today's dollars, so let's buy it today and pay it tomorrow.

When we entered into a growth mode we thought we'd have more population tomorrow; we'll be able to spread the cost over more people, so therefore we can afford these big programs. But we deluded ourselves, as a generation. Not just the politicians — collectively as Canadians, or collectively as world citizens, at that time we deluded ourselves into believing this growth mentality, this inflationary psychology. We're beginning to recognize that there was a price to pay for it. The fallacy was the cost of foreign exchange and the interest rates. And they've caught up with us.

In terms of guidance for younger Canadians, I would say, "Be a responsible citizen. Understand your government. Understand what it is you're paying for and demand the best." If you demand the best and if

61

it's important to you, you'll get the best because politicians are very sensitive creatures and they will respond to what you want. If you care, as citizens today are demonstrating, your governments will respond. If you don't care, governments will respond as well.

I don't think these past generations owe younger Canadians an apology. I think they faced their own challenges. They faced challenges, whether it was the Second World War, post-war, whether it was nuclear arms. I think in many, many ways they broke new ground as far as social programs — the ones that are good programs — are concerned. We just have to find the right balance. We have to leave some challenges to the next generation.

In my time in government I ran across the term "bean counter" many times because I was an accountant. Whenever we raised these issues at a senior management committee down at the Treasury Board, there would be a laugh in saying, "Well, this is typical bean-counter mentality." The people who were kind of on the rise were the economists or the political scientists and the policy people. There was kind of a love affair with policy, that they were the only people who could have a vision. In the early 1970s the people making policy decisions and not thinking about the spending down the road were young officers. They came in to develop new programs, to have vision, and they attracted some really great minds, I mean, some really wonderful and creative people. But they had no sense of the importance of the cost of a program because, as I said earlier, money was a free good.

Anybody who had this kind of mentality was a little bit to be felt sorry for because obviously they didn't have the same visionary skills, the same creative skills. They were restricted by this anal attitude, if you will. I can remember, for example, when Jim Macdonell, the auditor general, was creating difficulty for the government. One of the most senior bureaucrats, one of the most senior deputy ministers, after an interview with Mr. Macdonell, simply was exasperated and said in the taxicab back to the office, "You know, Macdonell is a man of the times but he's an intellectual pygmy." And believe me, Mr. Macdonell was not an intellectual pygmy. He was a powerful, powerful mind. I think this comment demonstrated the overall attitude of the senior managers of that time: that anybody who would be concerned with such things as costs and the appropriate management obviously were small-minded people. That was their attitude.

Anyone who disagreed with spending money, it was felt, shouldn't be constrained by those thoughts. Think big. Think large. Let's not constrain ourselves with such things as money. Look after that later, or somebody else will.

DONALD SAVOIE

A leading academic and former DREE mandarin provides a critique of regional spending programs and an insider's view of the federal public service.

To understand the philosophy behind regional development we have to go back to the 1960s when Pierre Trudeau was talking about a "Just Society," and that's where he took flight. Diefenbaker had first tried something but that was on a smaller scale, that was a rural-based kind of economic development. Trudeau felt that there were two main problems in this country. One was language and the other one was poor regions. He set out to solve both.

He appointed his most trusted advisor to lead the charge and they initially sought to focus exclusively on Atlantic Canada and eastern Quebec because that's where the real problems were. But over the years it got pushed and pulled into every nook and cranny of this country. Initially the focus was clearly on Atlantic Canada and eastern Quebec, and they introduced a number of programs. Some were fairly well thought out; some were not.

I think politics came into play because, if you recall, in the late 1960s and early 1970s we had an FLQ crisis in this country. We had a separatist problem, as we've had since. A lot of people in Quebec made the case that regional development was going to be tied to growth pulls because back then that was the key. You looked at the main urban centres and said, "Let's build on these strengths." Hence you built on Halifax, Moncton and so on. And people in the province of Quebec said, "If you're going to focus on that, our growth pull is the same in Montreal. Regional programming should apply there."

In 1970 this was agreed to. However, the moment something was started in the City of Montreal, you can bet your bottom dollar that Cornwall would say, "If it's good enough for the City of Montreal, it's good enough here." Over the years it was pushed and pulled into Cornwall, into Alberta, into British Columbia, including Vancouver. Whistler Mountain was a project that was financed at that time under DREE (Department of Regional Economic Expansion). The program was pulled and pulled all over the place, which wasn't the original intent.

In fact, Jean Marchand claimed in 1968 that if ever the federal government spent less than 80 percent of its regional development budget outside of the areas where it was first launched, that is, eastern Quebec, Gaspé, up north and Atlantic Canada, it would fail. That's where the main focus was, but we've lost that. We lost that in the early 1970s and we've never been able to go back to it.

I think that once the federal Cabinet agreed to supply some of these programs to the City of Montreal, then it opened a floodgate. MPs from Alberta could go back home and claim that they were able to pull such programming to the local chamber of commerce: "I've been able to get our city, our urban area, our towns designated." Once the City of Montreal was tagged, then you really opened it up because anybody with any claim could knock on their door. This happened — bear in mind that one thing that motivates a lot of politicians, perhaps most politicians, is visibility — if they can go back home and say, "I've done this," it's a hell of a coup. And so it became a part of politics.

Claiming to help build struggling East Coast economies doesn't win votes in Red Deer. If you're from there, having climbed up the greasy pole to become the local MLA or MP, the last thing you want to do is go home and say, "I've helped Corner Brook." You want to go home and say, "Look what I've done for my area." That's what motivates them. If you go back to a riding in southern Ontario and say, "What I've done over the last month is to really help the cod crisis in Corner Brook or

St. Anthony," that doesn't sell. People elect their MPs to represent their riding, their cities, and they are expected to go to Ottawa and fight on their behalf. That's what the game is about.

Regional development projects expanded all over the place. I think the height of it was in 1983 when Ed Lumley was appointed the minister. I think at the time DREE had been abolished and it was now DRIE (Department of Regional Industrial Expansion). He got up the new regional programming that applied in every city, every town, every community, Toronto included. I think that was the height of it; and from there we've never been able to go back.

In 1983 the Liberal government lost. Brian Mulroney came into office and he got an awful lot of pressure from people on the East Coast saying, "If that's the best then scrap it. If regional programming means that a firm can apply to make potato chips in Hamilton and get more assistance by going there than to Nova Scotia, scrap it."

The prime minister attended a special Cabinet meeting which was held in St. John's in 1986. On the way he stopped to see premiers Hatfield and Buchanan and they really tore into him, urging, "Cut this nonsense. This doesn't make sense anymore. Cut it — best to cut all of it and have absolutely nothing than to have this kind of nonsense."

Bear in mind that in the mid-1980s the Ontario economy was starting to take on speed and the East Coast was in really bad shape because it never recovered from the massive recession of 1981 and 1982. So they really came down hard on him. He came back to Ottawa and John Crosbie also got after him to do something here. They decided to scrap the existing programs. "We'll have a Department of Industry that will look at all of Canada, but we'll also have an Atlantic Canada agency."

This was launched and given over $1 billion. Within three weeks Mazankowski, who was the minister as well as the senior chap from the West, saw the need for a similar agency in Western Canada. Within three weeks there was a new Western agency with a budget of $1.1 billion, whereas on the East Coast it was $1.8 billion, just a notch above.

At this point the province of Quebec asserted that if it's good enough for the East Coast, we need one here as well. So they got a federal organization for regional development in the province of Quebec and funding of $1 billion, plus perhaps a bit more. It became a bastardization of regional policy, if you like, so every region had similar programs. What we've seen is that one community in one province is in competition with the next one. It makes no sense but it's the essence of politics.

As I stated earlier, it was Ed Lumley who got up and said, "I have good news. Finally we have a program, a regional program, that every member of this House can stand up and say, 'I agree with this.'" Why? Because it applied in every riding. This was a bit of good news. But it broke down. It broke down because premiers from have-not regions said, "This is nonsense. This doesn't make sense at all." It doesn't make sense when you have the economy of southern Ontario booming and you have somebody — and this was an actual case — applying for a grant to make potato chips in Hamilton and in Nova Scotia (he applied in both places) and, lo and behold, the offer was more generous in Hamilton.

So the premier of Nova Scotia protested that this had gone crazy and you had to fix this thing. The premier of New Brunswick agreed, as did Brian Peckford. And so the prime minister said, "Let's fix it." Well, he fixed it. He abolished that program. But he replaced it with a patch-work of programs: each region having its own programs. It wasn't fixed. It was a different format.

If you give a billion bucks to Atlantic premiers, they're pretty happy for a while; it's a good fix. I mean, a billion bucks could fix a few things. They weren't as worried about the billion bucks going into Western Canada because they had their own fix, if you like.

In one of my books I suggested a theory which could also apply to regional policy. If you have 10 people that go to a restaurant and sit down, they have to make a decision. The decision is whether they're going to share a cheque or each pay for their own meal. The theory is that if they agree to share a cheque, the total bill will be higher than if each agreed to pay for his or her own meal. The reason for this is that if you're sitting down and you order a hamburger and the person next to you is ordering scallops, especially if they're from the East Coast, there will be hell to pay because the person who's paying for a hamburger is also paying for those scallops. He will be tempted to buy a sirloin steak. And so the common cheque, if you like, is going to be much higher than if you buy your own meal. I said the same theory applies in this country. It's not in the interests of Newfoundland or the province of New Brunswick to cut spending so long as they see Saskatchewan back at the trough. So a common-cheque theory applies in my view.

One never had to worry about the province of Ontario up until now. I think now one has to worry. It was in the interests in some way, a perverse way, of Ontario to see equalization payments flow into the province of New Brunswick; Ontario was assured that because of protection policy, it could sell its fridge, its stove, its TV into the province; it had a captured market. So it was in the interests of Ontario to have people on the East Coast with a few bucks to buy a fridge. This has now changed and it's going to have massive fallout. We are starting to see that from Bob Rae — I mean, you can even see him changing the whole nature of the debate. Up until a few years ago it was in the interests of everybody to see the federal government spend. Equalization payments, in my view, were as helpful to the province of Ontario, to manufacturers in Ontario, as they were to people living in the Maritimes. They really had a captive market. They didn't have to worry about manufacturers in Boston, knowing that if there were people on the East Coast capable of buying fridges, their fridges would sell. They were being manufactured in Ontario. A lot of people drew a lot of benefits from such arrangements. Although the have-not provinces benefited from regional development and equalization payments, I happen to think that in the process those regions lost a great deal of initiative, entrepreneurship and self-starting. I think it hurt because it was a fix. It was an annual fix and in the process it hurt those provinces.

One must also look at the role of the prime minister of this country. You have to look at what motivates him or her. In the case of Trudeau, clearly it was national unity. It was the Constitution. Budgets were not something that he would wake up in the morning and say, "I've got to do something about that." Brian Mulroney was not terribly worried about spending. He said one thing but did quite another thing. He was above all a politician, a very good one; let's have no illusion about that. He could out-politic a lot of people. When he went to the East Coast people thought he was from there. He went to school in Chatham — he went to St. Francis Xavier University, he's part of us. In Quebec he was from there, he could play that card. He went into Cape Breton and said, "You think that you had it good with Allan J. MacEachen, well, I'm going to outdo him." He believed that. I think he was above all a politician.

Allan J. was a bit of a phenomenon and in the short term it was very good. In the long term it was not as good. In the short term he brought a number of things into Cape Breton. He was able to go to the Cabinet table, grab the juicy morsel, if you like, and run. He brought a number of things, like heavy water plants, into Cape Breton. There's no question that this was a coup, no question about that.

In the longer term it hurt because the plants closed down and an adjustment process had to take place. But he could go back home after. You must remember that he both won and lost elections. Once a politician loses and comes back, he doesn't want to lose again. Bill Clinton in the United States is a good example: they become good politicians. Allan J. knew that the best way to hold onto that seat was to act and to be seen doing good things for Cape Breton. He never lost a trick, he was a master of it. And things that flew around the Cabinet table — he could smell it coming and so grabbed them and ran.

In the process the Government of Canada invested millions and millions into that economy. Whether it was in Devco, mines or steel, an incredible amount of money was invested. So in the short term he was viewed as a saviour, and in Cape Breton if you see manna coming down, you know it's Allan J. In the short term it makes sense — if you're sitting in Cape Breton.

Mulroney intended to surpass him and he gave it a heck of a good shot. You will recall the extremely generous programs and tax credits in 1984 and 1985. In fact, at one point the feds had a combination of programs that, if you applied to set up a business in Cape Breton, you could actually get funding for 120 percent of the cost. You can't do much better than that. I think that Allan J. never reached that record. This resulted from a combination of grants and tax incentives. At that time, in 1985 and 1986, you applied for a grant at a certain place. Tax incentives were quite separate matters. You applied for a grant and you wouldn't tell that person that you were getting a tax incentive as well, though that person should have known. We discovered after that you could get 120 percent funded. This lasted for about 18 months until the auditor general got a hold of it and it was cut. Policy was made for Cape Breton in 1985 and 1986 so that you couldn't receive more than 80 percent funding. Still, 80 percent funding for your capital costs is a fairly generous thing.

Again, in the short term these policies did good things for the Maritimes. In the long term I don't think so. I think we're seeing the fallout of that. In the short term, sure, it's a good fix. You see activity, you see profile, you see signs popping up. You see 100 jobs announced in the *Cape Breton Post*. In the short term it makes people feel good and there's extensive optimism and so on. But in the long term, if you go back and look at all those businesses that got funding up to 120 percent, there are very few left. And when they leave there's a mental state that sets in that the island is not good enough. Outsiders came, ripped it off and left; so in the long term I don't think it's very positive.

I've talked before of a "cargo cult" mentality. I think it was during the Second World War, when Americans flew in with cargo planes into a South Pacific island, and the natives had never seen a plane before. The Americans came, built an airstrip and all kinds of cargo planes flew in and unloaded good stuff, such as Jeeps and food. The natives were hiding in the trees and looking at this and they hadn't seen a plane before. This silver bird would fly in and bring all kinds of good stuff and they thought that this was how it was done. You go out, clean a stretch of land, put some lights around it and a silver bird is going to come in. That's a cargo cult. The case should be made that in parts of this country we've had a cargo cult that we've put in. We've put in the lights, sewers, water, industrial parks, streets, thinking, now let's sit back and see the cargo come in. But it doesn't work like that. I can show you a lot of parks in Atlantic Canada and Quebec, the rest of the country, that are virtually empty — not a sole occupant. Yet you have beautiful parks with lights, streets, water and so on, but there's no activity at all. That's the link I made with a cargo cult.

Bear in mind that the life expectancy of a politician is four years. He or she must run again. What they really focus on is the next federal election. They don't focus 10 years from now. I think it's expecting a bit too much in asking them to look 15 years from now. If they bring in a park, 10 years later when people see it's empty, they might be sitting in the Senate, a fairly comfortable time to sit and see how it hasn't worked out. It's the longer term that one has to think about and our system is not, and I stress — not — geared to think in the longer term. It's geared to think in the short term. I'm talking politics now.

Radical rethinking in respect to regional development is coming from Bay Street, Wall Street, *The Wall Street Journal* and the money markets. I think those people are forcing Canada to look at its deficit and debt. I think that's the radical thinking. What you do is sit back and chop away, and there's room to do a lot of chopping. Have no illusion about that. What we've seen over the past two or three years is agencies in the West or Atlantic Canada being cut from, say, $500 million a year to $200 million a year. You're seeing them back further and further away. As they back away, they have to focus on a few things that they can do well. You're seeing a fundamental rethinking of regional policy not because you want to rethink it, but because you're forced to rethink it. If you're forced to live with smaller budgets, you're also forced to redefine exactly what kind of programs to put in place.

Recently the government announced they were cutting grants to businesses, but we should be clear about this. There are two programs here. One is called an action program; the same is true in Quebec and in the Western provinces, though they have a different name. Those programs are being put on a repayable basis so they're no longer grants. You feel like they're loans. You'd receive a loan with the interest rate at one percent, but you don't have grants anymore under that program.

There's other programs, fairly generous programs, called federal-provincial agreements, which link money from the federal government with money from the provinces. An agreement is established. It is not at all clear that there are no grants here. I think they've cut grants under the action program, under certain private sector programs driven by the private sector; but under federal-provincial programming there are still grants, in my view.

Secondly, not every region has done so. In the case of Atlantic Canada they've said no more grants. Everything is repayable, whether you get $5,000, $10,000, $100,000, $1 million: everything is repayable. In Quebec it is not at all clear. My understanding is that you can still get a grant, I think it's $50,000, where you don't have to repay it, so it's still a grant. We have to look at that as well. If you let that go, at some point Atlantic Canada is going to say, "Well, just a second now. It's OK to be pure but we'll be pure if Quebec is pure." So you can get Atlantic Canada asking for another grant of up to $50,000 to match what's happening in Quebec. That's how we've lost a lot of regional policy — pure regional policy.

The announcement of these program changes in early December was hardly radical because in the West they've been doing that since it was established in 1988, certainly in the case of WED or Western Economic Diversification. They've had most of their grants to the private sector on a repayable basis. It's radical in the case of Atlantic

Canada. That was a fairly radical and bold move. Bear in mind that in the budget of 1991, as a matter of policy it was established that anything over $100,000, even in Atlantic Canada, had to be put on a repayable basis. It was moved from $100,000 down to zero. This took some courage. Of course if the business fails, it becomes a bad loan.

In terms of regional policy or federal spending, the provinces play a critically important role. First, in this country, contrary to Australia, the United States and other federations, we have stronger premiers mainly because our Senate is not working. It's not doing what it was supposed to do. We have premiers who attend a first ministers' conference or premiers' conference where they have a national camera that stares at them. They can preach to all Canadians about the need to have balanced growth, the need to have the federal government spend more in their province. It gives them a podium. This is terribly important since the agenda is set by what politicians say. Premiers have a stage every so often to get on and grab the headlines and say this is not working. The feds ought to be doing this. Fed-bashing has been a part of the culture in this country. This hasn't happened since Jean Chrétien became prime minister because, if you've noticed, he's never had a first ministers' conference. I think he's probably learned over his 20 years as minister that's not what you do if you want to manage this thing. For the past 20 or 25 years, with the exception of the past 18 months, you've had premiers having a good kick at the can.

Secondly, 80 percent of regional programming is under these forms of agreement, under the form of federal-provincial agreements on tourism, industrial development issues and so on. Up to 80 percent of the funding that the feds do is channelled through a federal-provincial agreement. You have the feds sort of sitting back and the province, take New Brunswick for example, will come forward with a proposal to do something in fisheries. If the feds say no, the province of New Brunswick knows there's enough there so they come back with a tourism proposal. If the answer is still no, they come back in another area. The federal government since 1972 has been turned into a kind of Treasury Board. It sits back to pass judgment and the provinces come forward and badger it with all kinds of proposals, knowing that one of these days one is going to grab and they'll get an agreement. The feds will pay up to 80 percent of their costs, or 70 percent of their costs, and off they go on what is really a provincial program.

We've had problems since 1972 with that, all kinds of problems. One such problem is that the feds have said it's OK for us to pour money into these things but we don't get any kind of visibility. We pay 80 percent of an agreement to do something in tourism, which might cost perhaps $80 million. The province of New Brunswick, because it's a provincial program, gets all the visibility, all of the credit, and that's why, if you travel the roads of Canada, you will see more than occasionally signs saying, "This is the result of a federal-provincial agreement," and the amount. It's the visibility question because of pure politics.

There has been a difference in the degree of success different provinces have achieved with this approach. Nova Scotia has produced more ministers with more clout and that's important — not just premiers. The regional minister has a key role and in Nova Scotia you've had Allan J. MacEachen, in Newfoundland you've had Don Jamieson and John Crosbie, André Leblanc in New Brunswick. Those are pretty powerful cats at the Cabinet table. British Columbia has not produced as many powerful Cabinet ministers, so it doesn't have a leg up, if you like.

I've often wondered if the reason for that is because in the Maritime provinces the real sector that you've seen take flight and grow over the past 30 years has been the public sector. Here, if you're young and ambitious, you look at the public sector with a much more sympathetic eye than if you're in Vancouver.

We, meaning Maritimers, may get the cream of the crop because so much of our economy is dependent on the federal government. We may send our best, whereas in Vancouver the best might stay in business or start a business. I don't know what the reason is but I do know that in terms of politics, pure politics, Maritime ministers had more clout than the ones we've seen from the province of British Columbia.

Secondly, I think people from Alberta and British Columbia come to Ottawa without this notion that you've got to grab and run. It's an unfair tag, I know, but they're not as driven by bringing federal goodies as if you're from, say, Cape Breton, which has got serious problems. You're motivated if you're in Cape Breton, when you have people not working, an unemployment rate of 25 percent. You're motivated to go to Ottawa and grab and run. Whereas in British Columbia, if you're sitting in Vancouver, it's not quite as evident and I suspect that people in British Columbia have a different set of priorities than people in Cape

Breton. So it's not just the 10 premiers that play into this; regional ministers are critically important.

I think the frustrations of the have provinces are starting to show, deep frustrations, and I think part of Preston Manning's success is due to this frustration because a lot of people in Alberta and British Columbia have said we can't put up with this nonsense. The people we send there don't seem to be able to turn off the tap, and Preston Manning has been able to tap into this. I think there are a lot of frustrations that have built up.

Secondly, what motivates a prime minister, when a prime minister chairs a Cabinet meeting and looks around, he looks at ministers that are able to bring in the votes and seats. Allan J. MacEachen was very, very powerful, not just because he was from Cape Breton, but because a whole element of Liberals saw him as the leading light on the left. He had a crowd with him and Monique Bégin had a crowd with her. The prime minister would look at that and decide that it would be much easier to upset a lone Cabinet minister from Vancouver than Monique Bégin, who has a crowd of MPs with her and a number of Canadians are seen to be quite supportive of her. So politics plays at the Cabinet table; that's what it's all about.

I think we've seen a fair number of success stories and I think that hasn't been played up enough. As an example, two or three months ago I was doing a piece of work on regional development and I called a chap in the province of Newfoundland who told me, "I have 90 employees now, high-tech stuff, 90 employees. We're making a profit, we're doing very well. I started six or seven years ago with a small grant and if it weren't for that grant I wouldn't be in business today." That's important. In New Brunswick Harrison McCain, chairman of McCain Foods, a major provincial employer, will tell you, if you ask him, that the reason he's in business is because in 1956 he was able to get a $25,000 grant. Back then it was a fair chunk of money. He got a grant, started in business and today, despite a bit of a family feud, it's going well. So there are success stories. You have to really isolate those and you can see that if it were not for a small grant to get the entrepreneur, to give him or her the edge, to go and try something, it may not have started. So there are success stories. Having said that, we've also spent rather foolishly over the years, so I can't say if regional development in general has been a success story or not. What I can say is that we've seen a fair bit of success.

What I can also say is that we've spent unwisely in a number of areas. Industrial parks are an example, a glaring example. But not just that; we spent money that we should not have spent, although we've had a few success stories that we should never lose sight of.

The reasons behind my writing of *The Politics of Public Spending* are several. I think that a book idea was there for a long time. I wanted to write about the politics of public spending; I also wanted to write about how government works, how it makes decisions about spending. For a number of years I wanted to get my head into that and explain it. Secondly, I became quite concerned, as a number of people have since and some were at the time, that we were creating a monster with accumulated debt. And I thought if I could explain how the process works and why we tend to spend as much as we spend, that maybe I could be helpful. So I had two reasons. I wanted to write the book, it was in me. I wanted to get at how government works, how it operates, how it makes its decisions, how it decides whether it should spend here and not here. I wanted to get into that — what forces were in play. So I had this curiosity to get into that. But secondly, as I explain in my preface, we have a problem. We have a serious problem in this country and if I could, in a small way, contribute to a better grasp of that problem, then maybe I would have done something useful.

When the book was published, within a couple of weeks Jeff Simpson wrote a review in *The Globe and Mail* and said it was the most important book in the past 10 years and people should read this book and so on. That was critical; he gave it flight. After that I got a lot of good reviews. I got 15 or 20 solid reviews; in fact, I don't think I ever got a negative one. I won the Smiley Prize and I think we've had four prints already and it's still selling well. So obviously I got at something there. Government officials — some of them liked it, some of them did not. A number of them spoke to me about it. I remember a senior official who told me one morning, "I'm reading your book. Good stuff." The next morning he was reading a chapter every night, he liked it. When he read the chapter about the public service he came back next morning: "I don't like that book." A number of people liked it. A number of people thought it was unfair in terms of the public service, that I was a bit too harsh. But after it won the prize, fourth printing, and the reviews came in, it was pretty hard for them to keep on being as critical.

Some took exception to what were perceived as pretty serious shots, and a lot of public servants said that it was unfair because the key to all those decisions is Cabinet. If I wanted to take a shot at people it should be at Cabinet. They weren't guilty, if you like, and I painted with a broad brush when I got into the room and accused them. I didn't think that was fair and I told them as much. I think the public service in this town, less today because it's in a state of crisis, but for a number of years, from 1945 to 1985, had a tremendous influence in this town, in chief policy decisions. I don't think that senior public servants can continue to point the finger at the politicians. I think the blame can be spread around. If you look today, for example, in terms of public service we've just seen that they're going to cut 40,000 positions, yet a number of programs are to be kept going. Well, those 40,000 positions could have been cut 10 years ago. Why do we have to wait until we're in a state of crisis? You can't expect a politician to come to the Cabinet table one morning and say, "I think we have 40,000 jobs too many here, we need to cut." A politician will never do that. A minister will never do that, that's not what drives him or her. It's incumbent on the public service to police their own institution. And in many ways they failed and they're paying a high price. So I don't think I was unfair. If I had to rewrite the book, I'd write the same chapters.

As I've said, I had been thinking about writing my book for quite a period of time. I remember a public servant, one of these bright public servants who was totally unhappy but quite bright, young and ambitious, wanting to do good. He told me, "You know, what they're doing to me is giving me a crank that's not attached to anything and saying, 'Keep turning it.' My work is useless. Nobody uses it. I'm turning a crank that's not attached to anything. And for me, what I have to do is keep turning that crank, be quiet and know that at age 55 I'm going to have a good pension. That's the game." In many ways he was right and I wanted to get into that and to expose it. I had been thinking about it for a long time. There were a lot of forces at play that pushed me to scratch and to look into things. I have seen public servants turning cranks that were attached to nothing, and on and on and on. I had a lot of anecdotal experiences of things that I could draw on. That public servant was about 30 years old and bright, really bright, and wanting to do good. I don't know where he came from, Ontario or Alberta, I forget. He did well in university and came to this town. He wanted to go out and change the world, and I could see after two or three years that his life had turned, he was disillusioned. There's nothing in this town that he could really do and he backed away, and he said, "The price for me to keep quiet is that pension at the end of it." It's not fair. It's not fair for taxpayers. And that motivates you when you hear somebody say that — you know that this person is not lying or playing games. He was being truthful at some cost because it was not in his interest to tell me that. So there were a lot of those things that you knew that you had to go and scratch and keep going.

The guardians, or the people charged with holding off the spenders, haven't changed. In Ottawa it's the minister of finance and the president of the Treasury Board. Two guardians since day one and it's still like that. Against those two are all the rest. If you're the minister responsible for tourism or regional development or industry, the last thing you want to do is go home or go to your people and say, "I've done a good job today — I've cut spending. My budget, instead of $100 million, I've got it down to $50 million." No politician is going to do that.

So against that we have a minister of finance. His job is to be able to go to markets, to taxpayers, and say, "I'm not increasing taxes, I cut spending." But he is the only one. He's the only one. There are no other people in Cabinet who have that kind of interest. And so you pit against him spending ministers, 30 of them, and in the case of Mulroney, 41 of them. It's a hell of a battle. Now, the one advantage that he had, has still, though it's been watered down, is that he could grow his budget in secrecy. He could hide for two or three months, come up with tax increases, spending cuts, some spending cuts, in secrecy, and then could blow it open. But to do that, and this is a terribly important point, the prime minister has to be on side. If the prime minister is not with him he's cooked. Because if the minister of finance can't draw on the support of the prime minister against his colleagues, it's not going to work. At critical moments the prime minister has to stand up in Cabinet and say, "I'm supporting Paul Martin or Michael Wilson or Mazankowski." If he does not do that, if he does not say to a lot of spending ministers, "Enough is enough, back off," the minister of finance is cooked. Unless the prime minister is with the guardians it's a non-starter.

Plus, you may have in Cabinet some people who are against spending. In this Cabinet, for example, you have people like Doug Young from the province of New Brunswick who's against spending and we've seen it in his own department. That's rare. Occasionally you have this odd-ball who will be on the side of the guardians, but very, very rarely. It's only in recent months that we've seen spenders turning around and becoming guardians.

In respect to backbenchers acting as guardians, I think they would have more of a say on gun control. More of a say on one issue that surfaces and people know who is on the right side and who is on the left side — who is for and who is against. An MP can go into caucus and say to Allan Rock, who's the minister of justice, responsible for gun-control policy, "Let's debate this thing, you should go farther, you should back off." You can really get into debate in caucus. To go into caucus and talk about a budget that is $152 billion and say let's debate this thing? MPs can't get their heads around that. They can get their heads around something that's in the headlines of *The Globe and Mail* that morning, but getting into program spending, $152 billion, and getting into a debate about what should be cut, what should not, they don't have a chance.

They don't have the knowledge. They don't have the capacity. They don't have the ability. I mean, it's a sad commentary, but an MP who practises law in Niagara Falls for 10 years, arrives in Ottawa, wants to change the world, well, good luck. I mean, there are all kinds of things, all kinds of forces and a minister of finance has a bureaucracy of 800 people, and that bureaucracy's sole purpose is to help him or her. But an MP has got a staff of one or two that helps with his riding, looks at Senate appointments, staff matters; but trying to get their heads around a massive budget, no. They get a budget briefing and the minister of finance will stand up in caucus and say, "Here's what I'm thinking of doing. Here's what I may have to do on the tax side. Here's what I may have to do on spending," in very broad terms, but there is no time or capacity or willingness to get into details of those decisions.

Of the dozens of Cabinet ministers, hundreds of MPs and thousands of civil servants, only a handful have any kind of responsibility as guardians. On the spending side you have all of them.

In terms of fairness, in politics it's if you win the next election that's fair. That matters. Politicians are motivated by going out and winning and getting support. A businessperson is motivated by making a profit. A scholar like me is motivated by having a book out. A student is motivated by getting an A or a B or a C. To a politician, his sole motive is to win. And to do good — I don't deny that. But it's to win and if they can't win, they can't do good, as they will tell you. No sense being pious about this thing, they will tell you, if we can't win, we can't stay here and do good, so let's win. In order to win you have to spend — up until 12 months ago. I think the world has changed a bit over the past 18 months, but one has to bear in mind that up until 18 months ago spending was the name of the game.[1] Hence we've got a debt of $100 billion and some and a deficit of $30 billion because of the spending practice and having two guardians versus a whole slew of spenders.

The guardians were always outnumbered. Though up until 1945 it didn't matter. It mattered after 1945 because the role of the state became so wide-ranging, and prior to Keynes the role of the state was to run the post office, to have an army, some old age pensions perhaps, but that was essentially it. You could run this state with much less. Parliament was simple and spending was simple. You could get your head around all spending programs because there were so few of them. The role of the state was not nearly as important as it is now. Since 1945 it has become a problem. As this thing started taking flight and growing, it became hard to stop.

I think you had a combination of things. Bear this in mind: John F. Kennedy said in 1960 — well, you're too young for that but old geezers like me remember — that by the end of this decade we will put a man on the moon. Hell of an objective, and he turned to a government agency called NASA. Government was asked to put a man on the moon and government put a man on the moon. That's a hell of a thing to put in your mind back in 1961, to think that government could actually take a man from the Earth and put him on the moon and bring him back again safely. That was quite a goal and it was met. If you could do that, then you could solve regional problems, urban decay, all kinds of things affecting the role of government. Barry Goldwater (former U.S. senator and Republican Party presidential candidate in 1964) felt awfully lonely in 1962, 1963, 1964. He was the lone voice saying government can't do all those things. We had a decade or two when we had tremendous confidence in the ability of government to do whatever it set out to do.

So if you created a department called the Department of Regional and Economic Expansion, people on the East Coast would say, "Good, finally they're going to solve this problem. We have an agency. If an agency could put men on the moon surely an agency with $100 million can come here and solve our problems." That was the mentality. That was the culture. In that culture you had spenders who fed on that. That's part of it — a growing positive state and people looking at it in a positive way. If you could put a man on the moon, you can do all kinds of things. Pierre Trudeau talked about a "Just Society." John F. Kennedy talked about a "New Frontier" and Lyndon Johnson a "Great Society." Anyway, they had buzzwords and slogans that they thought would change the world. Government was the arm to change the world and people believed that. And hence it gave an open door to spenders to come in and do things. Secondly, you had a surplus. Imagine, a surplus and you're in Cabinet. You know when the economy was booming in 1969 and 1970 you had a surplus in your government accounts, and you're a minister from Cape Breton. Well, heck, with that surplus we've got things that we need. It was a different world.

In the late 1970s and the 1980s we saw that there was a real limit to the ability of government to do good. There was a limit, so government started to redefine the boundaries, started to think or talk in terms of privatization and so on.

You saw the growth of government because it could do things and you saw that size of government because it had overstretched and overreached it's capacity to do good. There has been a huge time lag in reacting to this realization. We know it now after 10 years. In the meantime you run a heck of a deficit, year after year, as you're learning. And you still have a lot of people, less now after the last 18 months, who will tell you that John F. Kennedy had the right answer — that Pierre Trudeau had the right answer — that if you give money, resources and capacity, the federal government can move in and do things well. There's still a residue of that, no question about it.

At the time people wouldn't have believed warnings that huge deficits would create future problems. Some tried. I think Simon Reisman tried.[2] When the deputy minister of finance resigned in 1975, he tried. He said, "Look, we're pointing the ship toward a serious problem here." But people were in no mood to think of that. And you face a crisis when you face a crisis. When you are in Cabinet and you've got a federal election coming in 18 months, and somebody, a public servant, walks in with facts and figures and says 15 years from now we'll have a problem. Well, we'll see. I mean, there was no real willingness to focus on a problem created 15 years hence.

Government spending became a disease in this country. What I would fault is the thinking behind Minister X who is saying, "It doesn't matter what I bring into my riding. It doesn't matter if it's waste because if you look around, there's more waste in riding Y. It doesn't matter what I bring into Cape Breton because if you look in the province of Quebec, you see politicians like Marc Lalonde and Jean Marchand doing more or bringing more waste into the province of Quebec. So if you are going to solve a problem, don't start with me, start there."

It became a bidding war, a competition between spenders because there is no sense in me backing away on spending, no sense in me trying to cut waste when I know that next door, next riding, next province, next region, they're worse. The worst of the worst, in my view, was to feed on that competition. And it gave rise to a kind of disease, which is the regional disease in this country, that you compete for federal bucks; that was, in my view, the worst of the worst.

A number of people got caught up in that trap, like John Crosbie, a bright MP, very bright. Have no illusion about that; he was probably one of the brightest MPs that walked in here in 1979, and a real guardian. In many ways he lost, and Joe Clark lost the government because of John Crosbie. Crosbie got up and made a very sensible statement. He said, "We have a debt of $12 billion, that's high. We need short-term pain for long-term gain. We need to get this deficit under control." He was a real guardian. In 1984 when he came back, a lesson learned, he was no longer a guardian. Have no illusion about that. John Crosbie brought to the province of Newfoundland many, many billions of dollars under all kinds of programs. Billions. And because he was a force, I mean, he had a powerful personality, bright, articulate, he went into the Cabinet meeting and pounded that table, and the province of Newfoundland got billions in terms of programs — for cod, billions in Hibernia. I mean billions, literally. All this because of the force of personality. And if you pushed Crosbie hard, I'd bet you'd find two reasons that motivated him. He never told me that, but I suspect the first was that he deeply loved his province, which is great. Secondly, he probably looked at the Cabinet table and said, "Why should I cut spending when people like Michael Wilson and people in Toronto, every chance they get, grab whatever is running around; they bring it into the province of Ontario and to the City of Toronto, that rich megacity. Why should I back away from bringing goodies?" That, in my view, was the fundamental flaw in the policy process of this government.

Principled people selling out because they learned that the game was corrupt is a serious charge put in very stark terms, and unfortunately I have to agree with this. Now Crosbie would say, "I didn't sell out. I've got principles. But if you're gonna cut spending, don't come to poor old Newfoundland where we've lost the cod, we've lost the fish. I'm all for cutting spending. Don't do it in my backyard. Do it in some other person's backyard. Don't come to the province of Newfoundland where we have an unemployment rate of 25 percent, where the cod has disappeared, where 70 percent of the economy of the province is dependent on federal transfer payments. Don't come here and do it. If you want to cut spending, go to Toronto where they can afford it, and do it."

He would have been able to play around in his mind to keep with the basic principles that he valued.

It's not in a Cabinet minister's interest to change the rules. Unless you're the minister of finance. If there are tax increases, who gets blamed? Not the prime minister. It's not Cabinet. It's not your local MP. It's the minister of finance; it's Paul Martin. The only one with a vested interest to keep spending under control — so he is not forced to increase taxes and become unpopular — is the minister of finance. Everybody else — it's not a problem.

There's a lot of dealing involved in government. If you want a wharf for your riding, as an example, a small harbour or whatever, you have to trade. You have to trade something. So if you trade a wharf to somebody, you expect something else. If you bring your principles to the Cabinet table and cut that out, you're cutting out an awful lot of goodies. When the MP goes home he or she meets leaders of the community, chamber of commerce, economic council, and they say, "We need this industrial park for this riding to grow." That MP goes back to the minister and if he's convinced, the minister has to go and trade. He has to go and see the Cabinet minister who is responsible for the Department of Industry, who builds industrial parks, and say, "Can you build this park in riding X?" And that minister will say, "OK, fine, you're the minister of transport and I need an extension of airport X in Hamilton, a beautiful airport. So we'll give you that, but give me a stretch of road so that my airport can land jets." There's a lot of horse trading here. And it's not in the interest of those spenders, who are there to satisfy the needs of their MPs, to start bringing principle into this thing. It's not in their interest at all, and don't expect it.

That is why I came up with the lunch theory. Why would somebody not buy scallops and buy a hamburger when he has to pay for scallops? That's what it's about. If you are going to lunch and there are 10 of you, and you know you're going to share the bill — each to pay equally — and you see that the one next to you is buying good wine, good scallops, are you going to buy a hamburger? I doubt it. It's the same in government. If you're going to trade a small harbour for a stretch of road, you better have something; and hence the one who pays is the unknown, intangible taxpayer. He's not there at the Cabinet table while these trades are being done. There's nobody else there. The minister of finance is one person. He's got to go to a lot of meetings in order to say, "Hold it!" because there's a lot of these tradeoffs that take place every day.

I've seen this in my experience in government: an MP often will tell you, "Give me this one thing, this one industrial park, this small-craft harbour, give me this project and I will win. My people, my riding executive, my chamber of commerce, they're all after me. If you give me that I'll win — you'll have my seat." That is a pretty powerful argument.

The unfortunate part, however, is that elections are never won or lost on that basis. They're won or lost because of free trade, because of broad policy areas. But rarely will they be lost because you didn't bring in a small-craft harbour or whatever. But an MP who goes home every weekend, spends Friday, Saturday, Sunday and Monday there — don't try to convince him or her that it's not part of the game because he or she faces the pressure every weekend for an industrial park. The point is that principles belong in the Department of Finance when you talk about spending. They don't belong between MPs and ministers. That's not part of the game. The small community that gets the industrial park gets a bit of a fix for six months, and then eight or nine years later they say, "Well, there's a nice industrial park, beautiful lights, beautiful water — but there's nobody there." However, that's eight years from now. The immediate fix is pretty powerful stuff. It is like a drug. They get a fix: they get an industrial park.

Do you think that people in Yarmouth, say, are worried about the debt? They're worried about their community. They're worried about getting this thing that they've been after for 10 years and getting their

MP cranked up to bring in this thing. That's what motivates them. The debt is buried in some building, pretty big stuff, but surely somebody in Ottawa has got to worry about that. We can't worry about that. That's part of the problem. It's an intangible, I mean, Canadians don't understand that debt of $550 billion. They just do not understand it. It's really expecting too much to expect somebody that gets up and wants to do well for the community of Yarmouth, who every morning runs a small business, teaches at a local school, a school principal, to worry about the debt of $550 billion, knowing that your community is in trouble and you need this one project. That's asking too much.

I must tell you that at one point I was prepared to give up; hence I wrote that book. I was thinking, this is not going to work. There are too many powerful forces at play, feeding this spending frenzy. There's too many powerful forces that played there in competition to bring more spending into communities. So I wrote a book saying that the system is not working and we can't make it work, and here is what we have. Here is why we have this problem. I think what has happened is that the international market, the global economy, has changed the way we think, has said, "Just a second now. You want to keep on spending, go right ahead, but your dollar is going to be worth 50¢ and your interest rates are going to be 20 percent." Now people go, "Whoa, just a second now, if we do that and if I'm selling cars in Moncton, it's terribly important because at 20 percent interest rates I can't sell cars, so government get your act together." Thus we're starting to see the fallout of that and so on. That's what drove it more than anything else.

I think we should blame ourselves and this community disease that I talked about, that people are in competition to outspend between regions — that is us. It's us when we see the local MP say, "Get this thing, get this grant, get this industrial park." We are part of the problem. Seriously. We are part of the problem.

But I think the world is changing again because when Paul Martin was preparing his last budget, at a critical moment when caucus was meeting in Toronto, *The Wall Street Journal* ran a piece saying that Canada is a Third World country. Now, people would think they might be right, or think somebody put *The Wall Street Journal* up to this. I mean, *The Wall Street Journal* just did not say this is a Third World country — the timing was delicious and it couldn't have picked a better time. For two days there was a caucus meeting, where Paul Martin was asked to go in and explain what was happening, and the fallout of that piece in *The Wall Street Journal* was that the Canadian dollar started to slip and slide. There was a crisis in the making. So Finance and Paul Martin could walk into Cabinet and caucus and say, "We've got a problem," and MPs for the first time realized that there was a serious problem. It cut the urge of spending, if you like, because this was a serious problem. I'm told, as obviously I was not there, that in the two-day Cabinet meeting that they had, every hour or two somebody from the Department of Finance would walk into Cabinet and whisper in Paul Martin's ear and say, "The dollar is down point three or the dollar is down point two." That gave Paul Martin quite a hand in telling his colleagues, "Look, we've got to get a handle on this thing." But that never happened up until a few months ago. I mean, 10 years ago, 15 years ago, one would never have thought that *The Wall Street Journal* could play havoc with public finances here. Nobody would have thought that. We've reached the stage where it's havoc and I think that if you see any discipline, that is where it comes from.

Are there flaws in the system which could allow this situation to happen again? Well, the flaw in the system is this: it's called a general election every four or five years. That is a major flaw in the system. That is terribly important because come election time, people tend to lose their nerve and *The Wall Street Journal* can take a hike if it means losing. But so long as they keep Canadians' feet at the fire by saying you've got to get spending under control for the international community to have confidence in your currency, I think we are on the slope of getting our deficit back under control.

The world has changed, in the sense that if you have $10,000 now and you want to invest, the opportunities to invest in the world are much, much greater than they were 10 or 20 years ago. Even if you don't know anything about investment, you go to a mutual fund, and there's such a thing as a global mutual fund, or an American fund, or a European fund, and you say, "I'm going to gamble on Europe or Asia; you can't gamble on this country anymore." The world has changed, the money market has changed, and nothing is overseas anymore. You can send $10,000 to Europe like that. Fifteen years ago you could not.

Even as long as 40 years ago those charged with being financial guardians didn't play any more of an active role. The big difference is that the role of government was much smaller going into the 1960s, and the role of government has expanded. As the role of government expanded it became much more complex, and as it became much more complex it became harder for guardians, the Department of Finance, the minister of finance, to get a handle on spending and really get to understand what was at play. It was much easier for a guardian to look at a budget of $10 billion and 100 programs than it became when you looked at a budget of $150 billion and 1,000 programs. You lost control because there are only so many hours. As government grew, guardians lost the edge, if you like; but when it was smaller, they could get their hands on it. You know that 40 years ago at a Cabinet meeting, at a Treasury Board meeting, you would see ministers sitting down saying, "Electric typewriters. All right, this year we're buying for the Government of Canada, what — 5,000." Nobody talks in those terms anymore. Typewriters or computers, that's something decided much lower down.

And so ministers, guardians, Treasury Board, the Department of Finance had a capacity to get at spending, at programs, at the administrative structure because they could understand. They could get their heads around it because it was much smaller. As it grew, they lost control or they could not control it as much. They could not get their heads around it. They could not marshal solid arguments why things should be cut or why you shouldn't buy more than 5,000 computers or 5,000 typewriters because you bought 6,000 last year.

I don't think Pierre Trudeau ever felt that he was threatened by anybody, including God, if you like. I mean, Trudeau was not the type to be frightened. He might have had a few problems with the Department of Finance but he sure took care of them. As an example, in 1978 when he came back from Bonn, he said, "I'm cutting $2 billion in spending. I'm going on TV speaking to Canadians and I'm going to announce where we're going to spend." Jean Chrétien was minister of finance. This caused a crisis because the minister of finance thought of quitting. Trudeau was never intimidated or frightened by the Department of Finance or by anybody. There is always a bit of tension between politics and finance. But if the prime minister, any prime minister, wants to control the Department of Finance — no problem. And certainly Trudeau had that capacity; have no illusion about that. If spending grew under Trudeau, it's not because he was against it.

A senior Cabinet minister under Trudeau told me after he read *The Politics of Public Spending* (and he came from a very poor region of the country so you can guess where he's from), "I read that and you know, only Bay Street wants to cut spending. Poor people don't want to cut spending. If we ever have a crisis in this country, poor people are not going to be paying taxes to resolve the crisis; it's going to be Bay Street. You're making the case in *The Politics of Public Spending* that we have to get the deficit and debt under control. So as long as there are people from where I'm from, who don't have enough food to put on their table or who can't give to their kids what the kids need, the children need, to go to school and grow with some confidence, I don't buy your thesis whatsoever. I'm going to keep on spending, come hell or high water, because the ones who draw any benefit from that are poor people. That is who I worry about. I don't worry about Bay Street. If they want to worry about deficit and debt, let them worry about it. Let them resolve it. It isn't going to be the poor people."

That was his argument. There was a matter of principle there — a matter of self-justification for all the spending that he promoted over the years. But also a bit of a moral question there, that he felt that his role was to help people in regions that couldn't be helped, that needed public funds to go to school, to feed, to put clothes on children and so on. He made no apology whatsoever. Quite the opposite. If he had the same opportunity, he would outdo himself, I suspect. On the question of morality or principle it works both ways.

I think that if we were ever forced into any kind of situation where we have to cut and slash — where we have to cut spending because the international market says your dollar is worth 20¢, get it under control or else — if we ever get into that, and we're getting there, the people who will pay the highest price are the poor people.

So people living in Rosedale, don't worry about them. They'll survive. I mean, their money is probably in the U.S. by now, or Europe. I wouldn't worry too much about those people. I wouldn't worry too much about Bay Street. They'll survive any financial crisis. The people who are vulnerable are precisely the people that he thinks that he was protecting. It's a good debate. He didn't buy what I was saying and I didn't buy what he was saying. Nice, pleasant dinner, good wine, but we never agreed.

That's the point I make. The most vulnerable element of society in the end will pay if we face a financial crisis. Not Bay Street, not the wealthy. They won't.

In fact, in every course I teach I end by saying to my students, "Give me a vision of where you want Canada to be 10 years from now." What I would like is to see Atlantic Canada much more self-reliant. I would like to see the province of New Brunswick, for example, being able to contribute to a net flow of funds rather than draw from it. I happen to think that a lot of the things we've done over the past 30 and 40 years were well intentioned but were wrong. They hurt us. I think that we must come face to face with reality and know that there is a limit to the ability of government to do things well, a very serious limit. If we could come to terms with that, we'll have a much better country.

To be a cynic and to be an academic are not quite compatible, and I don't think in *The Politics of Public Spending* I was being a cynic. I really thought, and I still do, that when you have a debt of over $500 billion you have a serious problem. When 40 percent, 30 some percent of your revenue, all of the taxes that you take in, immediately, before you can spend it on one program, you have to service a debt, I think we have a serious problem. I hope that I didn't come across in my book as cynical, but I wanted to make the case that the forces that have led us here are very powerful.

Do you think it's lacking in principle or lacking in good intentions to come to Ottawa, if you decide that your role would be to bring things to your riding and to your community, and to do whatever you can to act as an advocate, as a lobbyist, on behalf of your riding? Those MPs over the years, I have no doubt, view that as a noble role that they do and did. If you were to talk about discipline, they would say we have a national problem called deficit and debt. It can't be resolved in Yarmouth. It has to be resolved at a national level. Don't look at me. I'm just a little MP. I go to Ottawa and I don't know how that big town works. There's bureaucracy, there's Cabinet, there's ministers. I haven't got a clue. What I'm here for is to speak on behalf of my region and I'm going to do that, and I'm going to knock on whoever's door I need to knock on to get things done down here. That's what motivates that MP, and in fairness our system is built around that. Our system is built around an MP coming from Yarmouth and not knowing how the system works. I mean, you don't go and take a course to become a politician. It's like motherhood; you're supposed to know it immediately. You arrive in this town, a big bureaucracy and a complex system. You get lost. The most brilliant of persons will get lost in this town. It takes years to understand Ottawa and to be able to know how it works. In the meantime, in your learning curve, you're going to worry about your riding.

So I don't think that it was bad intentions or those people were acting in bad faith. I think they came and did the only thing they could possibly do in Ottawa. The only thing they were allowed to do in Ottawa was to squeeze and scratch and hunt for things for their riding. They weren't allowed to go in the Department of Finance and roam around and fix things. Public servants don't want an MP there. God forbid, you don't want an MP there! So they were left on the periphery looking in, doing what they thought they were here for. What they think they're here for is to bring things back home.

If I were 20 years old I'd be awfully frustrated, and I think there are people in their 40s who are very frustrated with what's happened. The situation is bad but it's not hopeless. It takes political will. It will require political will to see us through, but it's not hopeless. That's point A. Point B, and I think I'm right in saying it, is that the generation that did what it did — I really, honestly, in my heart of hearts, don't think that they were acting in bad faith or wanted to hurt this generation — grew up in an era where government was the answer. When a 20-year-old in 1963 or 1964 finished university, the ultimate challenge was to go into the public service and serve.

I've just finished a book, if I can digress briefly, on Thatcher, Reagan and Mulroney. It took me to Britain, Washington and here in Canada to do a number of interviews, and I met a number of public servants. It's amazing the number of public servants that I met. It started in the 1960s. Public servants were fresh out of law school from Alabama, from Washington, from all over the place, and they came to serve. What is truly amazing, when you talk to them now, is the sheer frustration of those people. As more than one told me, "I told my son and daughter, 'Don't make the same mistake I did. Don't become a public servant.'" So that tells you. You know, it's 30 years in a public service career for them. It's not wasted, but close, and they feel the same frustrations. The ones who were guilty, if you like, in doing what the younger generation may think lacks moral principle don't feel terribly good about it; that's my sense. And so it's not hopeless. Yes, we did wrong. Yes, the younger generation is paying for it. Yes, they're getting it right in the ear, more than any other generation, but it's not hopeless. And it will take people like you to get the situation right again. So find yourself a good riding, run, become an MP and say, "I'm here to stop spending." Tell your constituents back home, "Don't ask me to spend, I'm against it." That's what is going to be needed, other than the market and Wall Street, Bay Street, playing with us. Other than that, it's the only answer.

There are several reasons that make me question whether we're on the slope of cutting back. I don't think we cut back, notwithstanding all the speeches from 1984, until a year or two ago — those speeches by Michael Wilson, Brian Mulroney and so on. The public service was not cut back but it is now being cut back. Why was it not cut back? Because if you don't have the discipline to call a bottom line, and I hate to overuse that because it's been overused, but if you don't have that kind of discipline, and if you are a manager in the public service, what interest do you really have to cut people? You don't. It's tough. Nobody wants to look a person eyeball to eyeball and say, "Sorry, but I'm cutting you, go on, goodbye, take your pension and run." Nobody wants to do that, and if there is no bottom line forcing you to do that, you will bob and weave.

Secondly, we have a Public Service Employment Act in this country that makes it incredibly difficult for a manager to get a non-performer and to cut him or her. It's extremely difficult for a manager to cut a public servant. Let's say I'm cutting you because you're not performing. It requires several months of work, documents, memos, putting it on paper; it's quite an elaborate exercise. For that manager, at the end of seven months there's no thank-you note. There's no promotion because he's done that. You've got a smaller office. You've got a smaller staff and so on. But why go through that when you can play with other things that you can have more fun on. That's the essence of it. I think we are now seeing a process in place where you will see a smaller public service for the first time.

I think another point about the public service is, as an institution I think it lost its way over the past 25 years. And by that I mean it was not able to police itself. It was not able to say, instead of 240,000 people, we can do this very job with 180,000. I think we can accuse it of that and I think it would be fair. Hence we have a crisis. Hence the 10, 15, 20 years of bloated bureaucracy and the inability of the institution to say enough is enough and cut it back. We've landed this institution, which is a terribly important institution for the good of the country, into a state of crisis. And for that reason I say it didn't police itself.

If I can digress briefly, in 1979 Margaret Thatcher came to office. The day she arrived in office the clerk of the Privy Council, or the Cabinet secretary in Britain, arrived with briefing books and said, "Prime Minister, we need another 40,000 civil servants to do the job that's expected of us. We're short staffed and we need more public servants." Margaret Thatcher said, "My dear friend, you are not going to get 40,000 public servants and I'm asking you, over the next 18 months to two years, to cut 140,000. Now just go and do it. Tell me how it's done. You're not getting the extra 40,000." Subsequently the secretary of Cabinet said it was a wise decision, that he felt that it was needed. But he and the institution did not bring it to the attention of the prime minister. It had to be the prime minister that told them to do it. Quite the contrary, he arrived saying we need another 40,000 public servants. The point I am making here is that the institution failed itself in terms of being able to control its growth.

We now have a crisis of such proportions that I worry deeply about it. It's a crisis where we have a public service which has lost a lot of credibility. A lot of Canadians just don't believe it anymore. And lest I make the point again, the public service is a critical institution for the good of this country. If you look at countries who are modern, competitive, the public service is modern and competitive. If you look at countries that can't get a leg up, often — invariably — we will look at a country where the public service is corrupt, not transparent but lacking. So if we get our public service going through a state of crisis, if we don't worry about it or try to solve it, we are asking for a problem 10 years from now. Much like we were asking for a problem in terms of deficit and debt 15 years ago.

That is a critical element. And the way we've been trying to solve it for the past several years, I think, is wrong. It's wrong headed. What we are trying to do is bring private sector management techniques into the public service: notions of empowerment, quality of service, all this kind of stuff. It doesn't fly, doesn't stick — it's crap. It's not going to work. We are going to end up with a public service lacking in confidence, unsure of itself, with tools that don't fit at all.

I mean, you can talk about empowerment if you're in the private sector because you have a clear way of knowing. You make a profit, yes or no. If you make a profit, you are empowered. If you don't make a profit, you have problems. Public service, that's not the way it works at all. This notion flies in the face of reality. It flies in the face of Parliament. There are all kinds of examples where it was tried, to empower public servants, and it blew up. The public service is there to serve the public, to serve and assist Canadians, the private sector included, to be competitive. That's its role. Its role is not to make profit. It can't and so to bring in private sector management techniques is wrong headed, dead wrong. I think that this measure of success has proven to be a disaster. No, I think the measure of success is this. It is to have programs that operate well. And you may ask, how do we know the program operates well? You look at a program in Canada, say social services. You look at the program in Britain or in the U.S. and you say, "In Canada on a per capita basis we spend X billion. In Britain they spend Y billion; in Canada we have 10,000 people working the same program that they have in Britain, except in Britain they do it with 8,000 people." There are measures that you can look at. But look at it from a public service point of view. Don't try to compare it to the private sector because it's comparing apples and oranges and it's wrong headed.

As for a financial boundary in which the public service operates, well, it's got a limited budget but let me come back to that point. If you run, say, the UI Program, the Unemployment Insurance Program, you have $16 billion to spend. Month 11, you've already spent $16 billion; you're not going to turn off the tap. You're not going to say for the next month nobody will get UI. You go back to Parliament or to Cabinet, really standard stuff. You get supplementary estimates and you get new money. If you're looking for that kind of discipline, you're not going to find it, sorry. You had better have a fairly solid case. If you go back and say to Cabinet ministers, "Well, my case is that we've been able to sustain this program, UI, for 11 months, but at month number 12 we have to close it down. People who are on UI won't have a cent for a month." That will focus the mind in Cabinet.

I think the consultation process has been oversold. I think we saw it in the constitutional process, where you consult and consult and then, once you've gone through a charade, you come back and make decisions. I think consultation is often a lack of leadership. You don't have the courage and the will to move so you go and consult. I mean, a lot of it is not necessary and I don't buy this participatory democracy and all this kind of nonsense. As for lobbyists, I think we've reached a point in this country, and the Americans did much earlier than us, where government is so complex that it takes a professional who understands how it works to get clients in the door a lot easier, a lot quicker and with more success than a person who does not.

Companies like IBM or General Motors have lobbyists here to understand how this town works. And so if the president of IBM says, "I want to talk to John Manley," who is the minister of industry, he just picks up the phone. John Manley is going to call back. If John Black from Yarmouth has got a little business and wants to talk to John Manley, he may have a problem. The little businessperson in Yarmouth won't have a lobbyist but the presidents of IBM and GM will. We have a serious problem here, and it makes the point that an MP who arrives in this town who doesn't know how the system works — can you imagine what he or she is up against? So I think lobbyists have been part of this town because the government is growing so complex that you need a professional, you need expertise, to make sense of this town, and they make it a lot easier for the private and large private sector firms to access whatever program is going around.

I think the private sector, frankly, has been guilty of many things over this. It's not just ministers and bureaucrats or have-not regions. I think the private sector has in many instances been a fraud, a complete fraud. They will argue, businesspeople will fly down and argue to cut spending, but they'll be the first at the trough. In one of the chapters in my book I wrote about the private sector grabbing with both hands. It's amazing what the private sector can do in this town. I mean, they grab grants, they grab programs, they sell things to government. They take advantage of situations and frankly they've been part of the problem. What they say and what they do are vastly different things. A successful businessperson, if he or she can make the case, can come in and open the floodgate. Don't play games anymore. Anybody can make that case.

Finally, we can look at the provincial claim that there has been an encroachment of provincial powers by the federal government. They, particularly the province of Quebec, have made the case time and time again. Premiers in fact have opted out of a number of federal programs to get compensation. Alberta has made the case time and time again that the feds have moved in; so has British Columbia. So much so, that if tomorrow morning, and forget the Constitution totally, the federal government would say, "We are no longer willing to spend $1 in fields of provincial jurisdiction," you would remake this country from top to bottom. You would have a totally different Canada, a completely different Canada in 12 months. The Constitution debate would be nonsensical compared to what would happen. Imagine for a moment if the federal government were to back away from health, social services, education, regional development, on and on. You would not need to worry about a sovereigntist Quebec. They want more power — take it, it's yours. Use taxpayers' money, *your* taxpayers' money, but do it.

Since 1945, though lately they are starting to try to back away, the feds have moved into every field of jurisdiction that moves and does not move; they've encroached all over the place. We even see the feds building roads. I mean, if there's one provincial area of jurisdiction, it's roads, small roads. The feds are in there building roads. Hospitals, schools, building schools, they've been there. They've been all over the place. So I don't think you need to play with the Constitution in this country. If you want to reshape this country, look at the Constitution and play by its rules. Quebec's rationale for trying to regain that power has been, well, "master in their own home," René Lévesque's theme; that so long as the feds are in there, they are not free to set programs, policies, initiatives to fit the requirements of Quebecers. It's a special society — a special case. They've made the case that only if they are free from the feds interfering in their field of jurisdiction can they shape their province and their society. They don't hesitate though, having said that, to come knocking when there's federal bucks around.

I think the point I was making about the private sector, the point I'm making about Quebec, is that everybody's guilty. Everybody's guilty. It's not just Cabinet ministers and MPs. Canadians can all look at themselves. If you are a Roman Catholic say, "Mea culpa, mea culpa." We are all guilty.

NOTES

1. Savoie is referring to the election of the Liberal government under Jean Chrétien in 1993 and also the economic recession of the early 1990s.
2. Simon Reisman later became deputy minister of finance and was the key negotiator of the North American Free Trade Agreement.

DEFICITS, UNFUNDED LIABILITY, ENTITLEMENTS

The Monsters We Create

ROBIN RICHARDSON

Mr. Richardson, who is involved with the Fraser Institute's debt awareness project, discusses unfunded liabilities, including government loan guarantees.

The work I'm doing at the Fraser Institute is called debt awareness. It's an education where I have taken the most comprehensive view of Canada's government debt and it comes to about $1.75 trillion. If you compare this with other countries you'll see we've joined the Third World. If we don't start getting things under control there are consequences, as has happened in many, many other countries. The hit-the-wall experience where people simply stop lending money to government will happen if your financial figures are as out of line as they are here in Canada.

Increasingly young people are beginning to understand the implications of this debt. With the government's record, if I were a younger person, I would not be willing to make a sacrifice for a public pension plan; but you don't have any choice because it's a government program. You don't have any choice whether you belong to the Canada Pension Plan or not. Your only alternative is not to work.

Even I am recognizing the implications of the debt and I'm a few years away from getting my Canada Pension Plan. We have the attitude that we can't count on that because the debt is just so large. It would be unrealistic to really expect to have the same kinds of pension benefits that our parents have enjoyed. So we have to make provisions through our own personal savings for our retirement. Don't count on the government. In fact some would say don't even count on any of it to be available, let's say, 20 or 30 years from now.

Italy, one of the represented countries at our Fraser Institute "Hitting the Wall" conference, recently reported that it had a crisis situation. They too have a large unfunded liability in their public pension plan. So they increased the age of eligibility by five years and they reduced the benefits. Now Italians will get pensions like our Canada Pension Plan, which pays to Canadians at age 65, but they will have to wait until age 70. They also get less than they would have before. They're just out of luck if they were counting on it. Don't count on it.

This problem affects all generations except the current generation which is enjoying the pension benefits. They're not likely to have it taken away from them but for younger people it's just an unsustainable situation. When you get unfunded liabilities of that type, you must be willing to have the government take more and more out of your paycheque to go into forced savings, to go into the Canada Pension Plan. That's basically the approach that the government is taking. They're projecting that the contributions that they're taking out of our paycheque will have to more than double over the next 20 years.

An unfunded liability means that there's a promise to pay. Let's take the pension plans, for example, the Canada Pension Plan and the Quebec Pension Plans: they're promises to pay in the future. But the CPP is not properly financed; at least there's no provision for the financing from taxes or from something else. In Canada's case, when you take the Canada and the Quebec pensions into account — because Quebec runs their own pension plan separately — that unfunded liability comes to $650 billion.

So what it means for the future is that the contributions that people put in, and which are taken out of your paycheque, have to increase dramatically or they're not going to be able to deliver the promises to pay the levels of benefits that they're currently paying. This is a real problem because in Canada's case it's $650 billion in total. When you relate that to the size of our economy, that's about six times higher than the similar measure for the United States, where they have a partial, but still largely unfunded, pension or social security system.

A number of the public employee pension plans, that's the civil service pension plans and teachers' and municipal workers' plans, have large unfunded components. A very extreme example is of course the members of Parliament. Members of Parliament, for every dollar they put into their pension plan, taxpayers put $6 in. They have a very generous pension plan. It's fully funded, but more so by the Canadian taxpayers, which is grossly unfair.

On an international level, with our unfunded liability, of the G7 countries Canada is the worst by far, that is, when you look at the unfunded liabilities in relation to the size of our economy. Italy's sort of in the middle and they're in a financial-crisis situation, which happened in 1992 when they had to make those changes I was telling you about. The United States is the lowest. Some countries are more exposed than others are, but Canada, of the G7 group of countries, is the most exposed in this regard. This comes from a study that was done by a working group at the OECD in Paris last year, and I quoted it in one of my reports from the Fraser Institute.

When you take our total debt, including these unfunded liabilities and some other obligations we have, we're in a Third World category, quite frankly. We're worse off than many countries in the Third World, let alone in the industrialized world, and one of the worst in the industrialized world. Unless we take action, financial markets will likely force us to take action.

The solution in the whole area of unfunded liabilities is to move gradually. I should stress that because you can't move from where we are now to get to fully funded overnight. It'll take over several decades, if in fact we want to continue to have those kinds of benefits. Either that, or the public may decide that we're not going to have those kinds of benefits in the future.

Another element contributing to our public debt is government's practice of making loan guarantees. A loan guarantee is made when a government entity, let's say a Crown corporation, wants to borrow money. It will have to make a presentation and go out and try to raise bonds or get a loan from the bank. But the guarantee that goes with it is that if they can't make their payments, then the government that's backing them up will make those payments. That's where the guarantee is. It's also like the student loan guarantee program. If the student can't repay that, then the government would pay the bank because you get the money from the bank.

Examples would be a Crown corporation that is looking to raise some money or a hydroelectric utility that wants to build a new dam. They're going to have to go out and borrow some money, in this case probably bonds. They'll sell some bonds for that particular purpose, then the guarantee would come from the provincial government, say the Government of Ontario and Ontario Hydro. The guarantee would make it more attractive for a person to loan money to that utility to buy their bonds. If Ontario Hydro couldn't pay the interest or defaulted in some way, then the Ontario government would back that up. Presumably they could raise taxes or whatever. So this gives some comfort to the people that are loaning money.

It's insurance and it's something that government shouldn't be into at all. In my opinion this is one of the problems leading to excessive government debt in Canada at the federal as well as at the provincial levels. Part of this, not all of it by any means, but part of this is related to these loan guarantees. Most of the Crown corporations in Canada, for instance, the hydroelectric utilities and others, are self-supporting. They charge for whatever they're producing and sometimes they can show a profit. Sometimes they don't, but basically they're self-supporting. They can pay the interest. So there's absolutely no reason why the provincial governments, or the federal government for that matter, should give loan guarantees to them.

If the governments dropped their loan guarantees then it would cause those that are loaning money to those utilities, these Crown corporations, to really take a second, harder look at the project. Unfortunately I think people have been willing to give money to some projects in Canada because of these loan guarantees, knowing that they can't really lose. It's what a guarantee means. It's up to the government, federally and provincially, to simply say, "No more loan guarantees." They've stuck with the loan guarantees they've already done, but from this point on no more loan guarantees. That would be a good signal to the financial marketplace that the government's serious about getting its house in order. The market would continue to work but basically they would take a much harder, more critical and analytical look at the costs and the benefits of any particular project. Those that are financially sound would still be able to get their money and get it at a good commercial rate.

I don't think they have to pay anything more if they're sound projects. Those that are unsound, that have just been going along —

people have been loaning money to CMHC (Canada Mortgage and Housing Corporation) or any of the other Crowns because they know they're going to get their money back from that guarantee from the taxpayers — those kinds of projects wouldn't get started. I say let the market sort it out but let the government first of all do its homework. If the government truly wants to subsidize something, if they feel from a public policy point of view that a project deserves a subsidy, they should be up front about it. Otherwise it's a guarantee and if the project fails, they get their money back; but who pays it? The taxpayer, the taxpayer of Alberta or the taxpayer of Ontario or wherever, gets stuck with the bill. I don't know the rationale. The project should stand on its own feet or they shouldn't be into it at all. Loans are too easily given out. The government of New Zealand, since they hit the wall 10 years ago in 1984, has a new policy to stamp every document that goes with a bond subscription. It says, "This bond is not guaranteed by the government of New Zealand." That should be our policy here, provincially and federally too. If a hydro-electric utility, I keep using that example but you can think of a whole lot of others, wants to go out and borrow, then right there on the first page should be, "This bond issue is not guaranteed by the province of Ontario."

In terms of CHMC, a Crown corporation which issues bonds or borrows money publicly and is backed by the federal government's guarantee, I don't think that guarantee is necessary. If they were into housing projects, then development would primarily be housing projects for which there's a market. If they've done their homework on it, then it should fly on its own. In fact that holds true for all of the Crown corporations. The loan guarantees are entirely unnecessary. Private companies have no such guarantees. They have to sign on their own merit when they're out borrowing money; they have to make a financial presentation that shows that their project has got a reasonable chance of making a profit and it's going to be sound. Then, as a good investor, you would look at that, bearing in mind that you've got lots of other places to put your money, and then decide if that's a reasonable return for the kind of risk that you're taking. There's no guarantee for the future. If anything, the economy could go down. A project could fail for a lot of reasons, but the investor is putting his good money out there and they'll assess these sorts of things.

Other types of government involvement, joint projects with private industry and regional development projects, need to be reconsidered. St. Clair is a private company in Cape Breton and they put in $3.5 million and the federal government put in $13.5 million on a project. Often the government will give guarantees on these types of projects too. Sometimes they'll give an outright grant, but usually it's a loan with some type of guarantee. Regional development programs may well be on the chopping block when the federal budget comes out.

I think the government should get out of those as well as student loans. I mean, there's over $1 billion of unpaid student loans out there that have accumulated over the years that the taxpayers of Canada have to pay for. If you want to give a grant or a subsidy, then make it right up front, don't do it through a loan guarantee. In my view they should just make the subsidy right up front. They should set it right out in their budget and say, "This is the money that we're going to go with and this is the reason we feel we need to subsidize this particular area." I don't know why they won't do that. It seems reasonable to me to do that, but basically it may well be that they don't do that because they like to keep things hidden and it's very well hidden from the taxpayer. The other thing with the student loan program, and this would be true with business loan guarantees as well, let's say it's a bank that is lending the money out: they don't really look at it quite as hard with the guarantee as they would without the guarantee, and there have been some studies, particularly with the student loan programs in Canada, that had demonstrated this.

There's a terrific risk to the taxpayer of Canada with these guarantee structures. The taxpayer, you and me, our money is going down the drain when these loans aren't paid back. I would think there is a pretty good prospect of eliminating all of that, the students loans, and then the loans to government-owned entities like the Crown corporations, which is the largest category. I say they're totally unnecessary. All these add up to a contingent liability, in the sense that if the person that's receiving the money can't pay it back, then the taxpayer has to pay it.

There is plenty of hiding going on. Most of this information, things I look at at the Fraser Institute in the area of government debt, is available but it's really hard to get hold of. You have to really dig, be a financial analyst and dig in there and get things out, but where these things should be recorded is in the budget, right up front where people can see it and where Parliament can debate it and vote on it. And that's not being done in a lot of areas unfortunately.

I've just heard that the Alberta Natural Gas magnesium plant is costing taxpayers about $1 million a month yet it's not written down. I'm surprised to hear that. I'm not familiar with that particular project, but I would think that the auditor general of Alberta would insist on it. If you wanted to check with him, you'd probably find something in the public accounts documents. The information is there but you have to become a debt detective to go and dig it out. In some cases it really is hard to find. But in that particular project or others that have failed, I would suggest to you that if there were no loan guarantee to start with, there would have been a much harder look at the project. It might not have got started in the first instance.

As I said, it's hard to find information on this. It's there but it's not readily available in the sense that when a government brings out their budget it's not really right up front. You have to go through the public accounts, which is another set of documents, and find that usually it's hidden in footnotes and it's all over the place. What I've done in my work at the Fraser Institute is collected all this information for each province as well as for the federal government and then documented it. We update this annually.

I think originally information was deliberately stashed away. You get into habits, I guess bad habits, but provincial auditors constantly are coming out with reports every year saying that there should be fuller disclosure and there should be more up-front disclosure of these things. Take British Columbia, for example. We have an excellent provincial auditor and auditing office there, as in all the other provinces. But I'm a little more familiar with that one. The provincial government has consistently, for several years now, not followed through with certain things that the auditor general's recommended. All he can do is recommend. He's not in the position to do more. It makes sense and so why don't they? Well, bad habits die hard. I would think that's the charitable view. Deliberately hiding it? Possibly. I called it deceptive deficit practices and so I guess "deliberate" is partly in there too, depending on which government you're talking about.

They're protecting themselves from full disclosure, from the light of the day, from the taxpayers' wrath and people saying no. Take British Columbia again as an example. But it's true in other provinces that the deficit itself and the budgetary deficit is where all the focus and the media attention and everything is. But the government hides things. They take things off the budget and they put it into other areas, into the Crown corporation area.

You need a much more comprehensive picture of the government as a whole. The government departments in many provinces only account for 50 or 60 percent of the total government as a whole. When you take all the Crown corporations into account, you've got a much more accurate picture of what the government is. Look at what's happening there in terms of the deficit or the surplus. You'll find that a lot of things get pushed off, in British Columbia, into Crown corporations that should be reported in the line departments. They're hiding it deliberately, putting it out there, spending borrowed tax dollars, which eventually have to be repaid. And that's going on in the billions of dollars in British Columbia right now.

When you take all of these liabilities into account, including the unfunded liabilities of the Canada and Quebec pension plans, Canada has a total debt of $1.75 trillion. That's over $61,000 of debt for every man, woman and child in Canada. That's more than what most people make in one year. For a family of four, that comes to about $244,000. So it's a tremendous amount. There are other contingent liabilities. Aboriginal land claims are one. Sometimes it's hard to get information on these items, to know what's being demanded and what's finally settled.

When it gets right down to it, I hope governments will follow through and avoid this type of hit-the-wall experience. But when you look around the world, to New Zealand and Italy and other countries that have had that experience, the consequences are dramatic. In Mexico and Latin American countries they generally don't take these actions until after the crisis has occurred and it's very painful for everyone. If governments don't move, then the consequences are that the Canadian dollar goes straight through the floor. Interest rates get extremely high. It becomes totally impossible for people to buy homes and you get a recession. Your business investments go down too. It affects consumer and business confidence, so these are really unfortunate consequences of procrastinating, or worse, continuing to move along the highway leading to higher debt, which is what's been happening for the last 30 years in Canada.

DOUG DAVIS

A Bay Street investment dealer attacks government profligacy and financial irresponsibility.

Canadians are the best-educated group of totally naive people in the world. What I mean is that Canadians who are intelligent with an extremely good academic background, generally, as a group, have not really come to understand what's going on with their government. Principally in that area I'm referring to, the fact that the government has seized control and has not permitted the people to participate in spending decisions.

It's gone off the track in virtually every way. We are at terribly high levels of debt. The interest expense is increasing on a daily basis — have you seen these debt clocks that show the debt just piling up? And to service that debt we have to cut programs. Each time you cut a program you provide less service for the people. So on a regular basis the programs are being taken away from the people but the taxes are not being taken away because the taxes are needed to cover the increased interest payments.

The financial community is really to blame for what's going on here. To put it in terms of an alcoholic, the government is the alcoholic and the investment community is the facilitator. The investment community finances the debt on behalf of the government, and it does so willingly because it's collecting very large fees for doing so.

Essentially the investment community is really the whole community. It's all of the brokerage firms. It's all of the people who buy the securities from the brokerage firms. It's the credit rating agencies that rate the debt. Basically these institutions, the issuers, the governments, are bankrupt. They're financially bankrupt. If they were corporations they would be deemed to be bankrupt. They're insolvent. They can't meet their obligations, and if these people in the investment community were selling you the debt of a company and the company were to be bankrupt, they would suffer legal problems; they could be sued. So we have a double standard here. We have a standard for the government, which is abetted by the investment community, and we have a standard for corporations and private industry, which are not aided by the system and by the investment community.

The financial community is partly to blame for this, but the financial community is a revered group. Typically they do well financially. They're leaders in society. They appear to be making a valid contribution. I think that people have really not reflected on this, but the government could not issue this debt without the financial community being there. You need the people who will sell the securities and also the people who will buy them. So when someone calls me with an offering of a province or the federal government, whenever that government is not balancing it's budget I tell them that they're being unethical.

I say, "Look, you're wanting me to buy for my clients the debt obligations of bankrupt institutions and I won't do that. And I would like you to know that I think you're unethical and I would like you to go back and tell your bosses that they're unethical because it's absolutely not right that I buy this paper and put it into my portfolios." I would far rather buy the debt of a nice corporation that is profitable and earning money and paying it's way, where I know the assets aren't going to go away. Where I know the corporation is being well managed. Where I know that my clients are going to get their money back. Which is what I do in most cases, such as the province of Alberta, where I believe that my clients will get their money back.

The investment community gains by participating in financing groups. These groups are put together to share the risk and also to share the rewards on the financing. To the extent that you're part of such a group, you gain rewards and the government controls the selection of the members of the group. It's like a club. So first of all they have to select you and secondly they have to decide what percent you will have within the group. If you're not in the club, you try and join. If you are in the club, you try and increase your participation because the fees are virtually guaranteed once the issues come out.

To a certain extent the government gives special preference to a select group of financial people, and they're not going to fight too hard to call government on their debt and borrowing obligations. Where they've gone wrong is that they have failed to inform the general public of the dire straits that these borrowers are in. The public needs to know how bad it really is, and they don't put it down in black and white and that's wrong. They really have to come to that. And when they do come to that, fewer people will lend money to these institutions and we'll get a more honest playing field. Some will take the risk anyway. I mean, some people still loan money to countries in South America but that's a risk they understand.

It's absolutely a question of honesty. It's an honesty question that even they, the investment dealers, do not understand. It's not conscious dishonesty; it's subconscious dishonesty. They're my friends and colleagues. They're my best friends in many cases and I tell them just the way I would tell you, and basically they laugh. I have one banking friend who said, "Look, Doug, Ontario's still a double-A credit. In other words, because some credit rating agency put a double-A rating on this, it was OK to buy the debt. Of course that's just not right. Ontario is bankrupt and we all know that. It's going into the hole at the rate of $1 billion a month. Therefore, because it is bankrupt, it is unethical for me to buy Ontario's debt and put it in my clients' portfolios. I feel that that's wrong.

The government has this wonderful power of being able to adjust who is in the financing syndicates and what their share will be. To the extent that you're not in and you're an investment dealer, you're trying to get in. To the extent that you're in, you're trying to increase your position in the syndicate because just to be in the syndicate is to produce this wonderful flow of cash by way of fees on these issues. They have a tremendous power.

Moody's or Dominion Bond's rating services are overranking the Canadian debt. Moody's recently reduced the federal rating to double-

A-plus from a triple-A, which it had always been. Well, in actual fact a triple-B might be a more reasonable rating. The government cannot meet its obligations. If it ever ran into a time when it couldn't float more debt, it would be bankrupt on that day. Effectively the correct definition is that the government is insolvent. It's not able to meet its obligations on a day-to-day basis.

The financial community gets a very large benefit. They collect big fees every time one of these debt issues goes into the market, so they definitely benefit. The big banks now own the big brokerage firms, so the whole community is involved here. The banks are not only effectively sellers of the securities, they're buyers of them too; and the insurance companies are there buying the debt, as are the big pension funds. You'll hear talk from time to time that pension funds should be obliged to buy a certain amount of Ontario government debt. Well, that would just take it one step further, make it even worse. Not only would the sellers of the debt be doing something unethical but the government would force the pension fund manager to do something that was very unethical too.

Not very many people are talking about this in the financial community. I talk because I'm a Canadian patriot. This is my country. I love it. I was born here in Toronto. I don't want to have to leave Toronto. I don't want my children to have to leave Toronto. I don't want their children to have to leave here. If things are corrected, they won't have to face those sorts of alternatives. If they want to stay, they can stay. But the future for them looks very bleak. And it looks bleak because reality has not been faced.

My advice to the younger generation is to be honest. For instance, if a government came in and the government looked insolvent, it seems to me it would be logical that the government should have to issue a prospectus to the buyers showing that they are insolvent so that the buyers at least would have an opportunity to judge whether or not they should participate. If they don't issue that prospectus, then the buyers are buying without knowing all the facts. So I would ask them to make sure that, to the extent they were selling such paper to the general public, the general public be informed as to the financial status of the issuer.

Companies have to present audits to potential investors because if the company is not financially sound, that has to be recorded. If it's not recorded the directors of the company are liable. So it's very serious when a company does a financial issue and directors of companies pay very close attention to that. In the case of the government there is no statement, and the government is doing something that corporations would never be allowed to do.

It is a double standard for government because the government makes the rules. They have made the rule to suit themselves. The government is principally composed, at the parliamentary level, of people from the legal profession. Most of them have never studied Economics 101. So effectively they're making rules around an area that they don't understand, and that is serious. It's a real problem. If they understood better, they might make better rules. Of course, there's the problem that politicians really are there to get re-elected and so their number-one focus is that of maintaining popularity, and what is popular is not always right. So they make the rules to suit their objective, which is to maintain popularity.

Government buying into the debt is not legally fraudulent. It's ethically and morally fraudulent. In other words, the way the rules are set now, it's legal. Therefore it's not fraudulent. But in actual fact it's morally fraudulent and ethically fraudulent. They are cheating people. Canadians and the financial community and the government have all bought into this — every single one of them. This tells us something about Canadians that takes us back to my first statement: Canadians are naive. In many cases the Canadian voter does not understand what's happened here. They know that they're worse off. They know that their standard of living has gone down. They just don't know why. And they're going to have to come to understand why in order to change it. If you can't define the problem, you can't change it. I don't think the problem has been defined in their minds. So somehow they have to come to understand what the problem is. And I don't think that's happened yet.

I think it was understood a lot better right up to the early 1960s. We had in those days both democracy and responsible government, and the governments of St. Laurent and Diefenbaker balanced their budgets. Robarts in Ontario balanced his budget. But something went wrong in the 1960s and it stayed wrong. In fact, the problem has increased rather than decreased. The problem was created and the country went off the rails during the leadership years of those who were in power in the 1960s and 1970s.

Correcting the mistake is too painful, politically. I believe the Canadian people would accept it and I think we're seeing that in the jurisdictions where politicians have at least tried; I think that Alberta is a nice example of that, New Zealand is a nice example of it. But the politicians in recent years have managed by polls. They take a poll and decide what the people want and if the people want something, they give it to them, so there isn't very much leadership here. What we need is for the leaders to have more confidence in their own talents and abilities, to understand that the country needs them to do what they know is right. When that happens we will get change. The politicians leading by polls always seem to worsen the situation.

The massive debt accumulation during the 1970s and 1980s constitutes a moral problem. What the decision makers failed to do was to do what they knew was right — to not create a burden for future generations. Now, in the beginning they thought they were following Keynesian economics: borrow in the tough years and pay it back in the good years. But it never worked that way. The way it worked was borrow in the tough years and borrow less in the good years. It never got to the point of repaying anything. It was not a theory that worked. It was a wonderful theory but it didn't work, and they all bought into it. There wasn't a North American politician that didn't buy into it. My friends and colleagues are still buying into it simply because it is a business interest that they're pursuing and they benefit from it. So they do buy into it.

If a politician were to declare himself a one-term leader and go for broke — go for the right solution — then maybe we could break away from this sort of system. I think there is a small number of people over the years that have been willing to do that. They seem to get shot down very early by another group that's in on this. That is the press. They have a vested interest in the spending part of government and in pushing liberal concepts, and I'm not talking Liberal Party concepts, I'm just talking about the concept of being nice. Every Canadian likes to be nice, so the way to be nice is to spend money on people who appear to need it.

The press shoots down people very early who make noises about trying to do the right thing here, so they are very definitely in on this. I don't know how you get them to stop but any politician that expresses concepts like balanced budgets immediately becomes an enemy to the popular press. John Crosbie is an example. The press destroyed John

Crosbie by making fun of the fact that he couldn't speak French, even though he had wonderful solutions for the country. So he's a definite example. He's the last guy who's tried at the federal level. Yes, he appears to be the last one.

As an investment counsellor, I manage portfolios for corporations, non-profit organizations and individuals. In that role I make the investment decisions as to what we should be buying and what we should be selling. Typically we will have portfolios that will have bonds in them and common shares. To the extent that we have bonds, we try and make sure that the bonds are going to be able to be repaid at the end of the term and also that the interest payments will come in on a regular basis. As part of our selection process we measure risk, and we feel that the risk associated with the offerings of certain provinces, including Ontario, are very high. Those risks are there because some of these provinces, the ones in question, have not paid attention to the flows of cash in and the flows of cash out and they're borrowing to plug the hole.

I'll tell you a story. Years ago when Darcy McKeough was treasurer here in Ontario, I was at a meeting of financial analysts in which he spoke. He was talking about the province and how it was doing and so on, and he was talking about trying to get the budget into balance. I said, "Well, that's fine Mr. McKeough, but when do you intend to start repaying the debt that you've already built up?" And he said, "Probably never." He said governments don't repay debt. They only borrow. So it was really interesting because the rest of us all have to pay our debts back. When I borrow money from a bank, the bank wants its money back. It wants interest. If I don't pay the money back, they seize my assets and sell them and get to pay themselves back that way. Why not the government? What's the difference here? You know, it's really, really wrong. It's too bad for the country.

WALTER SCHROEDER

The founder of Dominion Bond Rating Service explains the urgent need to cut deficits and government debt.

The basic thing that happened in terms of Canada's national debt was that government just spent too much. It started small and just crept up on them. They had very little deficits in the first decade, 1965 to 1975, but then it was a just a continuous round of more benefits, expenditure and small deficits that were not addressed. So it was these small deficits that weren't addressed that ultimately, through the compounding interest route, just grew and grew and grew. Over the last decade, the 1985 to 1995 period, governments were successful in slowing down the program expenditure but they couldn't contend with the compounding interest. So there was a series of small deficits over the past 30 years that just kept growing because of interest costs. Eventually compounding interest took over and now it's essentially compounding interest that's the problem.

The degree to which government overspent on programs compared to interest in the last 30 years is slight. What the numbers here show is that the total amount of program deficit was relatively small over the past 30 years. It might be somewhere very close to about $40 billion. The remainder of the deficits accumulated a shade very close to $500 billion over the past 30 years, and the bulk of that was compounding interest. But what government did, expenditure and revenue, taxation, and expenditure on welfare and everything else, was minor. That was only about $40 billion of the total outstanding debt today. The rest of it was all compounding interest.

We call compounding interest the silent killer because it creeps up on you. The first stage of interest is a slight deficit on the program expenditure basis; where expenditure exceeds revenue you have a small deficit. What happens then is the deficit has got to be covered somehow with borrowings and the borrowings attract interest. That's the first stage. It starts very, very small. Then the deficits continue as well as the interest. Gradually you develop into a position where higher interest costs require more borrowings and the borrowings require higher interest costs, which raises the deficit and you get a spiral. You get what we call a debt spiral with the higher interest costs compounding. And gradually your problem is this interest factor, not the expenditure on program services that the government does at all. That's the stage the federal government is in today and has been for the past 15 years.

Let's put it this way: the government debt today, March 31, 1995, is of the order of $546 billion, give or take a billion. Of that total amount of debt, 90 percent is due to compounding interest. The remainder, this other percent, is due to program expenditure being higher than program revenue. The things that government does, that's about seven percent of the debt. The other three percent is the debt that was outstanding as of March 31, 1965 — 30 years ago. So then the debt levels break down roughly 90 percent compounding interest, seven percent of the debt due to government expenditure exceeding revenue and three percent of the debt roughly equal to what was outstanding March 31, 1965, to start off this 30-year period. It's scary what compounding interest has done to us, but it's that interest component right now that's driving the deficit because the government is in balance and has been for the past 12 to 13 years.

Understanding compound interest is fairly easy and straightforward but initially the government had the feeling that it was just a small deficit. It was a small thing and it just got away from them. That, plus the fact that economists kept saying, "It doesn't matter what the deficit is, it's the relative size of the deficit to GDP. Don't worry about it if it's a low number." What they forgot about was compounding interest. That $1 today is going to be worth a lot of money in about 200, 300 years, and unless it's corrected in the future by cutting program expenditure below revenue, you're not going to correct the situation. So we're in a very, very unhappy position today. To overcome this interest problem, we've got to cut our social welfare and program expenditure down to levels below the revenue figures that are actually coming in. So we're cutting now on the program side to save and pay the interest.

All this happened during a time of relative expansion; however, the surpluses weren't used to pay down that debt simply because it was too easy. Basically the politicians didn't want to make the hard choices and they didn't think they had to. Perhaps I can relate a story about one of the premiers that happened a few years ago. We had breakfast with one of the premiers of this country and we congratulated him on obtaining a surplus on an adjusted basis. Later on, the bureaucrats we were with said to us, "We wish you wouldn't have said that to the premier, congratulating him on the surplus." They said one of the greatest problems with politicians is showing them that they have a surplus because in that case they're going to spend the money. "What we, the bureaucrats, are doing is using accounting conventions because we're hiding the surplus, not letting the politicians know. By not letting him know, we're able to help contain the expenditure level of the greedy politicians. We wish you wouldn't have congratulated the premier because if he's got a surplus, he's going to spend it next time." Basically the politicians are one of the main problems. They have not been willing or able to cut back. When they see a surplus, they'll spend it. Now that sentiment is changing a bit today with people just getting fed up with paying taxes, but that sentiment prevailed until at least about five years ago.

Canadians don't care until there's a crisis and the crisis now is the fiscal situation. Generally speaking, to truly understand what the government does requires a combination of accounting and economic skills. And it requires time. Most people couldn't care less. They just worry about their present tax situation and they leave it at that. So to really read and understand what the government accounts mean requires knowledge which goes far beyond what the general populace has. Not having that knowledge has put this country in hock. If people

116

knew and could have seen the situation developing sooner, they would have reacted sooner. That's a fair comment. However, people don't understand until their tax levels start to keep rising to such levels that they've got to react.

In the 1960s and 1970s taxation and spending were basically going up exponentially. The Canadian public's role in all this was one of great ignorance. One of the favourite questions I have in the many speeches I give is when I ask the people, "How many people here read the public accounts?" Sometimes we see an economist raising his hand, but there are so few people that read the public accounts or that understand the public accounts. This means the politicians and the bureaucrats and whoever can get away with murder and can simply hide things. They can overcome any inhibitions that they, the politicians, have. If I asked you, for example, if a deficit of $10 billion for Ontario is bad or good, if I asked that to a typical person, most people wouldn't know how to react or how to indicate if that was bad or good. So it's public ignorance of the size of the deficit and what it means. That is probably one of the great problems. People just don't understand it, and people are generally selfish. People look after themselves, so if there's a tax increase in the budget, they look at a budget in terms of what's in it for them. That in turn has prompted the politician to do what he does.

You can't point blame at the person or the politician. It's probably both. The politician does what the people want and the people look at the politician for a free lunch and that's been the basic attitude. That's why we are where we are right now. In speeches I give, if I want to get a reaction, all I have to do is look at the people I'm talking to and gauge what their position is on a taxation basis. If I direct the speech in that theme, I can direct it to the mood of the audience very much, and usually that's the basic selfishness. If the people are going to benefit from a certain move, they're all for it. If it's going to be a revenue benefit for the people, they're for that. If it's going to be a tax reduction for that crowd, they're for that and they'll support that.

If the audience is mostly a business crowd, you can very much get a reaction in the people for tax reduction and government control because that's basically what they're after. If you talk to welfare groups that know very little about taxation or the economy, they'll be looking for the welfare and other benefits that government gives out as a main theme — don't cut them. Fundamentally the crowds are kind of two different camps and they're each looking after themselves. It's probably wrong to totally blame the politician because selfishness usually takes the reins when it comes to anything relating to revenue or expenditure at the government level, and very much so.

In Canada we don't have any way to stop that sort of behaviour, until you get to the extremities. Canadians don't react unless they get hit by a two-by-four 15 times. We've had such high tax increases over the past 20 years, especially in Ontario, that people are basically getting fed up and that's why we're getting a reaction now. The irony is that as people pay higher taxes, all they're doing is paying the interest on last year's borrowings for the deficit. That's what is getting people fed up now. The skyrocketing interest costs are now getting so high; there are decreases in benefits too because it's all going into interest costs. I think that's why we're finally getting a reaction from the people.

It's reached crisis level and the crisis is twofold. One is that taxes help to pay the interest. The second element of it all is benefit cuts also help pay the interest. So it's hitting them on both sides. People are waking up now and saying, "Hey, our benefits are getting cut." Or if it's on the tax revenue side, they can see their taxes going up. So it's kind of getting hit on both sides at the same time and not being very happy about it. Yet they can only blame themselves. The period when it happened was what we call the "bad years," which is the period roughly between 1975 and 1985. That is when the debt levels accumulated so badly in Canada at the federal level. Then in the 1985–1995 period, nothing was done about it.

If you wanted to get very, very political you can't really blame any one party for it either, which is kind of a sad thing. The Liberals, between 1975 and 1985, kind of caused the problem with the huge deficits and especially the three budgets between 1982 and 1984. Those were the three big budgets that really broke the bank. But then you can turn around and chastise the Conservatives for not doing anything about it between 1985 and 1995. They just ran what we called "balanced expenditure budgets." In fact, in that time period during the Wilson budgets he ran an actual surplus of about $13 billion in all the budgets that he presented. I think there were about nine of them. He ran a surplus of $13 billion but it was interest of about

$313 billion that killed Wilson and the Conservatives. The point is they did nothing about it.

We asked the government and they did some work with us as to what happened within the Wilson/Mulroney years. They said it was very, very simple. On June 19, 1985, Mulroney got beat up by an old age pensioner. This intimidated and in fact shaped Mulroney for a few years. In 1985 he backed down on the indexing of pensions and that was the 1985 story. In 1986 Mulroney was concerned about the sudden drop in oil prices in January of that year because there was a collapse in oil prices. And so that stopped his cutbacks. In 1987 he was concerned about a recession, so he didn't cut back because of the recession. In 1988 he had to get himself re-elected, so there was no cutback then. So Mulroney actually did a reasonably good job in his second term, starting in 1989, but by then it was too late. The compounding interest had reached too high a level.

Over the last 20 years there's just been an unwillingness of anyone to admit to the problem and/or do anything about it because it meant cutting, and cutting expenditure meant raising revenue. Although the attitude has changed. A very senior politician took me aside one time when we were chastising him on expenditure and he said, "There's limited benefit in cutting expenditure levels. It's far, far easier to tax." That was the sentiment for the past 20 years — much easier to tax. Expenditure cuts breed demonstrations by the poor and it's hard to justify that. When you raise taxes you can base it on greed. It's easier to sell greed than poverty. So we'll raise taxes. And that was kind of the sentiment of the time.

Let me tell you an anecdote relating to Stalin that was told to me by one of the politicians. I guess the reason the politician was talking to me about this was the fact that we were relating this whole question of expenditure and revenue. He said that many, many years ago, around 1946, Stalin was advised by his advisors to go very easy with the Catholic Church. He was advised that if he was too tough, the Catholic Church was going to take avenues that were later going to hurt the Communists. Stalin looked at his advisors and said, "How many battalions does the Pope have?" and proceeded to slam the Catholic Church. This politician looked at me and said, "On the basis of cutting back expenditure or raising taxes, if there's going to be a taxpayers' revolt today, how many battalions does the taxpayer have?"

I guess the taxpayer now has spoken because there's some outright hostility, there have been cutbacks, and there's probably been tax evasion through the goods and services tax and other things. That's the way the taxpayer is fighting back right now. The analogy is that there was absolutely no benefit whatsoever in fooling around with expenditure cuts at that point in time because it was so easy to go after the taxpayer since he had absolutely no power. What was he going to do? I mean, how many battalions did he have, how much scope did he have? Was he going to demonstrate? I mean, the taxpayers were so divided. This could also sell on the basis of greed — to avoid taxes is greed. To cut back on expenditure, that's poverty. And as I said, it's harder to sell because you're hitting the poor there. It's always easier to hit the rich than tax the poor. Robin Hood proved that. Robin Hood wouldn't have been a hero if he stole from the poor. He stole from the rich to give to the poor and was a hero because of that. That's how the modern-day politicians saw themselves.

A politician is not an economist. The reason the politicians didn't really care about interest costs was because economists were advising them that it didn't matter what the deficit was. It was more about how large the deficit was relative to GDP. What the economist forgot was that as compounding interest took over, the deficits were going to be driven by compounding interest. So the politician to a great degree was just reacting to what the economist was saying. As we all know, 18 economists have got probably 34 opinions and 29 topics. So they could always find the economist who would support their position. Basically it was the politician listening to economists and reacting to the fact that deficits didn't matter. It was how high the deficit was relative to GDP that mattered.

Now we're dependent on third parties. And the third party now, to a great degree unfortunately, is a foreign investor, because Canada, unlike Italy, did not borrow domestically. We borrowed our social welfare abroad. Today Canada, with a net foreign indebtedness of 46 percent of GDP, is in a class all by itself. The number-two country of the G7 is Italy at 11 percent of GDP. So Canada at 46, Italy 11, and then it goes down from there. The United States, I think, is at 10 percent and Germany and Japan are negative: they've got more foreign assets than they've got domestic liabilities. So Canada is in a league all by itself in the world today. Even Belgium and Sweden, which are always cited in relation to Canada as having a lot of debt, are in good shape because just about every country in Europe you can think of has got the debt owed to its own citizens. This makes it easy. Canada has got its debt owed to foreigners, which means we've got a current account deficit that's under constant pressure. The interest cost to pay the foreign debt is what's driving our dollar today.

I think politicians and other people like to cite the young 25-year-old traders of Wall Street as establishing Canada's future direction, interest rates and currency by speculating against the currency. But speculators usually don't get anywhere unless there's a reason to get there. The reason that they're speculating against Canadian currency is because there's so much there to speculate against. We've got such a massive level of interest cost to pay in our foreign indebtedness now that it exceeds roughly $30 billion a year interest, so we've got to borrow, generally abroad, to pay.

Canada's got the same problem on the foreign-interest side that we've got on the debt side. The fact is that with a trade surplus we can generate a net foreign currency from just goods and services that we export, but it's the $30 billion in interest costs right now that keeps driving our current account deficit down. We're in a position right now where we've been borrowing abroad to pay our interest. That's the second part of this component. Governments have got to borrow to pay the interest on the government debt. Canada as a country has got to borrow abroad to pay the interest on its foreign debt. So we're getting double-whammied here and that's what's driving the currency down today. That is what's causing pressure on interest rates. Rising interest rates today are causing all the problems in housing and consumer borrowing to spend; this is one vicious circle that probably all starts with this big kind of benevolent type of deficit that we had about 20, 30 years ago, and that just grew.

Through the media, foreign lenders are very quickly understanding exactly what's happening in Canada. As far as the sophisticated investor goes, I think they're very much starting to see what the fiscal problems are in Canada, and the size of them, and that's becoming understood in the investment area. The unfortunate thing is, the image the rest of the world has of Canada, I think, is probably false. This image is aligned also with the fact that Canada was often considered to be the most livable country to come to and stay in, and was so generous to the minority groups.

What's happened in Canada is we went abroad and borrowed our deficits to finance all our social programs. So of course it's a great place to live when you don't have to pay the pain. You go abroad and borrow the money to pay the interest on the borrowed money. Nobody's got to ever pay the bill. So of course it's a great place to live. You can give terrific benefits if you borrow abroad and then redirect the money into benefits to the populace. But you can't keep doing that forever and that's what's breaking right now. That's why Canada's running into the crisis that it has. It's done too much of it. Finally, the size of the problems are so big we can't keep doing it. So I think the image of now having to pay the piper is possibly going to change things very quickly over the next decade.

Over the last 30 years benefits have been going up, taxes have been going up, we've been borrowing all this time during times of substantial growth, and the younger generation is going to pay for it. My generation's going to pay for it. The people over 60 today are the ones that took the benefits, that benefited from this period of borrowing, and generally were architects of this great run-up in indebtedness that occurred.

It's the present young generation that's going to have to pay for it in various ways. The ways they're going to have to pay is, first of all, the interest rate levels in Canada are going to be much, much higher than they would otherwise have been. So these people are going to have to pay the differential if they want a house or anything that's capital intensive. If they want to borrow money, they're going to have to pay the price that way. Secondly, they're going to have to also pay the interest and someone's going to have to pay that interest in the future. The younger generation is the one. That's also going to mean they're going to have to pay higher taxes; so it's the present young generation that should be pretty frustrated from all this because they're going to be the ones that are going to probably be asked to pay the price.

Until this generation puts more pressure on the politicians to stop the freewheeling, they're going to end up paying a higher and higher price, and not only them; their sons are going to have to pay for what the generation that's 60 right now started. The other choice is to leave the country. Otherwise you don't have a choice. Someone's got to pay it, or Canada goes into default. Before they go into default they'll raise taxes and they'll do everything they can. Otherwise they're isolated from the world community. So there's no choice. Well, one choice — you can leave the country, go somewhere else.

I don't think you will be facing a moral question in the future — between looking after my parents or my kids. The benefit right now is the potential that you may ultimately inherit your father's house. Or you may also inherit your father's estate and maybe that'll help ease the load and help you pay the interest costs somewhat. You're going to be paying higher taxes right throughout the rest of your life because of the problems now. But the politician is also looking at means of stopping you from getting your father's house and estate. The way things are moving right now, possibly by the end of this century we'll probably see an inheritance tax, so they'll try and take away the estate and stop you from even getting that. So you're going to have to contend with that as well. You may not get your father's estate.

I don't know if it's a moral question for those who took those benefits and burdened the next generation. What I find, especially when it relates to money, is that people are extremely selfish. People look after themselves and those people don't think there is a moral issue here. They think they're just going on living day to day and doing things that they did yesterday and enjoying it: I don't think there's much of a moral issue here at all. Besides that, anything relating to taxation and government is purely not a moral issue. People cheat on taxes and they don't have any moral misgivings about that. So anything relating to government, taxation, your relative position to the state, I don't think there's any moral issue there at all. It's just an issue of selfishness. People look after themselves first. I suppose selfishness could be a moral statement to a degree, but if the people don't recognize their selfishness, it's not a problem for them. For there to be a problem you've got to define it and recognize it, and people don't really think or recognize it to be a moral issue for themselves.

It's not as though they didn't think beyond today. It snuck up on them. They don't think they're responsible for it. They think the politician's responsible and the stupidity of politicians is that they don't condone or take responsibility for it. To sum it up, I think you're flying on your own in the future when it comes to the debt. You either leave or you help pay for it. You don't have any other choice. But there are two ways to fix it. First of all, limiting the expenditure and the benefits, and that goes for all programs, right through to social welfare.

That's the first way. The second way is probably to deregulate the economy and let the economy go. Get out of the way of business. Let them run and let them try and turn around the economy by growth, which is by far the best way. It's the least painful way to try and fix the problem. You generate enough jobs and enough future GDP, you can pay the bill. But to do that is going to take quite a few dramatic changes in the attitude of government toward business. Also, business has got to have the incentive to invest, which I don't think exists right now, today.

The problem and question of Canada defaulting comes up from time to time. In the present 1995 crisis, the whole problem of Canada's default relates to the net foreign indebtedness position. Because our deficit is so high, we've got to borrow the interest now. We have to borrow to pay the interest on Canada's debt. The degree to which we can keep doing that establishes whether or not we default. So questions relating to Canada's default generally relate to the fact that Canada's got so much foreign indebtedness that if the foreigner doesn't lend us more money to pay the interest, because of the sheer size of our deficit, we could default. We've got to keep the foreigner interested in Canada and assure the foreigner that we're creditworthy. And then he'll keep lending us money.

Governments are starting to cut back. The 1995 federal budget was a step in the right direction in the sense that it changed attitudes. I can't believe, as a quasi-insider with all the governments for the past decade, how much Ottawa moved in the past year. If you look at it from outside you don't notice it, but looking at it from the inside the move was quite dramatic. It was a total change in attitude and the left wing right now, the Liberal Party, has shifted its thinking a lot and the centrists in the present federal government have shifted. So it's been a total change in attitude in Ottawa. The free lunch is over and I think they realize it now.

Provincial debt can be described as kind of a two-six-two exercise, when you look at the provinces. We call it a variation of the Clint Eastwood theme. It's called the good, the bad and the ugly. We've got two good provinces in Canada today that are unquestioned from a level of debt, from the economy, from the way the deficit there is trending. The two good provinces in Canada would be British Columbia and Alberta. We've got what we call the two ugly provinces, which are

Quebec and Ontario, totally in a league all by themselves with massive deficits. Yet even though the economy today in 1995 is not at the top of the cycle, at least it's driving a pretty good economy. We've still got massive deficits. But the ugly component of the 10 today are Quebec and Ontario. They really stand out.

Then we've got six other provinces, the so-called bad-middle-ish provinces. The ironic thing about these six provinces in the middle is that they've got the same problem that the federal government has got: the deficits they're running are virtually totally equal to debt and interest that was put on the books before 1981, 1982. The six provinces also have much higher deficits than they should because of this compounding interest that occurred when it was put on the debt in the 1970s. So the provinces are facing the same dilemma that the federal government is facing with interest payments and debt generally, even though eight of them today are close to balancing their budgets. They've done that through a massive combination of expenditure cuts, and in some cases selective tax increases have helped too. But eight of the 10 provinces are close to balancing their budgets doing exactly what the federal government's got to do.

The provinces generally are much better off than the federal government in the sheer size of the debt. If you measure debt, you measure it on the basis of debt dependent on tax revenue and you relate that to the gross domestic product of the country. GDP is what pays the interest and pays the principal on the debt. So you relate the debt to the GDP of the time. If you look at GDP and the debt, the federal government right now on a net basis is sitting on debt in the area of 75 percent of GDP. So think of the number 75 at the federal government level.

The typical province today, if you take a province like British Columbia or Alberta, they're about 24 percent to the federal government's 75 percent, so they're one-third as bad. Ontario right now is roughly running at about 36 percent, so they're about half as bad as the federal government. The only province that's really in the federal government's league today is Newfoundland. They're very close to the federal government — they're in the 70s. And Quebec is in the 50s. Quebec is a high average for a Canadian province, yet it's about one-third better than the federal government. Ontario is about twice as good as the federal government.

125

The best two provinces, Alberta and B.C., are three times as well off as the federal government. So that kind of puts all the provinces in perspective. The attitude of the premiers changed much earlier and quicker than the federal government simply because the provinces are poorer. They didn't have the tax base of the federal government and they didn't have the tax-revenue generation capacity of the federal government. So the provinces cut back sooner. Most of the provinces started to cut back in about the 1987, 1988 period, with the exception of Ontario, which was booming right throughout.

Ontario had a basic problem that started between 1985 and 1990, when it taxed and spent its way through a boom. In between 1990 and the present the bureaucracy took over. They bureaucratized business to death in that time period. Employment equity, pay equity, Bill 40 on labour legislation, things of that nature, the bureaucracy of it all just stymied business. We had a problem with David Peterson in 1988. I was actually banned from any contact with the Ontario government and the budgets in 1988 and 1989, on the simple basis that we put the province of Ontario under review just before the budget in 1988, on the basis of the expenditure pattern.

You could see exactly what was happening in Ontario. The expenditure was starting to skyrocket. They were taxing their way through the period. And as soon as the recession hit, the simulations we ran showed that the deficit was just absolutely going to explode. As soon as there was the first hint of a deficit based on the expenditure patterns they were setting up, which were so high that they couldn't possibly sustain them, we warned Ontario, in 1988, and got into a free-for-all with David Peterson in the process. But Peterson didn't think that we were accurate. He thought that he could keep spending and that the economy in Ontario had the capacity to keep generating enough tax revenue to keep that expenditure level and finance it. That was our basic disagreement. What happened, of course, was that he had to keep raising taxes.

That's what happened in Ontario. In the past seven or eight years there have been massive tax increases here. I don't think I was the Lone Ranger in calling his bluff. I think the electorate called his bluff in September of 1990 when they threw him out of office. We had two, three booming years. When you look at Ontario, and we've spent a good time with Ontario, I think what put Ontario in its present dilemmas were the budgets of 1988 and 1989. They substantially raised expenditure and kept taxation moving right through the boom period, and that's something that Ontario still hasn't recovered from.

At that point in time the economy was so strong and Ontario's deficits to that stage hadn't been that serious. I don't think too many people believed it could happen, that there could be such a thing as a severe slowdown in Ontario or that the expenditure levels, raising benefits in the different programs, could possibly skyrocket to the levels they did. Social welfare, for example, in the 1988–1989 period was rising at about 14 percent a year. The question we were asking then was, if welfare rises 14 percent to 15 percent in a boom, what is it going to do in a recession? Well, we got our answer very quickly. It started to rise at 45 percent a year. That's what got us into this dilemma. Under the definitions we use, welfare rose so quickly it surpassed education costs in Ontario as a major expenditure category, which is absolutely awesome. It started to happen about 1991, 1992, and just came from out of nowhere.

The way we define welfare costs includes housing subsidies. Welfare costs exceeded education costs in Ontario in about 1992, 1993, just through the increase in benefits that occurred starting in about 1987, 1988. It took awhile for it to come, but they couldn't possibly have handled it worse. They raised the benefits just before one of the worst recessions since the 1930s. They couldn't have timed it worse if they had a computer to time it. It was absolutely perfect timing because it just coincided. The benefits increased at the same time that the economy dropped like a rock. We got our answer of what would happen to welfare costs in a recession. Instead of rising 15 percent as they did at the top, they rose at 45 percent annually.

The investment houses really don't see calling one's bluff as their role. They've got a good relationship with the government. They sell government bonds. It's not really their role, and they don't see it to be their role, to warn about the deficits. They're in there to sell bonds. They're in there to market. It's not really their function. If selling bonds or whatever the focus is, is the main interest of the investment houses, the other interest is the fact that there's really no benefit to them to get the government angry. That really doesn't benefit anyone. They don't feel they can do very much about it, so why get the government angry at the same time? It just doesn't make any economic sense to them to do anything. So what the investment houses do is stay quiet in a period where they see the deficit rising. A few of them will speak out, but generally it's not their sentiment that they should go and raise any alarms because they're making money off it and there's no benefit to them to criticize the government. It really doesn't benefit them at all.

We establish ratings for government borrowing on an objective basis. The rating cut is established by looking at the debt levels, interest costs and growth potential of the economy, and putting it all together and comparing it to other countries of the world. Once that's established, and once the trend has been set, you can try to measure degrees to which the principal and interest on that debt can be paid, generally without printing currency. The federal government has got the capacity to print currency, so before they print any currency, we measure the capacity to which they can pay the interest and principal on that debt. That capacity relates to things, the most important of which would be the economy, and the strength and weakness of the economy. It also relates to the level of debt they've got already outstanding, which is an important consideration. We put a high stress on expenditure levels and revenue levels, and how much they've taxed in the past and what their tax capacity is. The stress is on how well they've controlled expenditure.

What differentiates Dominion Bond Rating Service from the American agencies is that basically we've taken a much harder position on what we call fiscal responsibility. Through all the years that we've rated for the past decade, government debt tended to be lower than the American agencies for the simple reason we've put a greater emphasis on fiscal responsibility, which we define to be the expenditure and revenue patterns of that government. The American agencies have put a far greater stress on the economy. That's why they're higher than we are in the ratings because the economy is stronger than the fiscal capacity of the government.

We should also discuss the public accounts committees of the legislatures and Parliament. Well, the so-called public accounts Committees look at accounting issues as they relate to the provinces to keep the provinces and the federal government on a generally accepted accounting basis that's consistent with what's happening in the corporate side. The federal committee makes recommendations as to proper accounting techniques that should be followed, and basically the wants and desires that the provinces follow. But they've got no power to enforce it. The provinces still can do really what they want when it comes to presenting their public accounts.

Some do; some don't. Right now we've got at issue four provinces that don't. There's Ontario, British Columbia, Quebec and Prince Edward Island. As a rule of thumb, for example, to get the true deficit in Ontario you take what they publish and you add $2 billion to $2.5 billion. With Quebec you add roughly about $1 billion to what they publish, and British Columbia is also at $1 billion-odd. They can do that. They can understate the deficit. The main method is through the way they treat capital expenditure. What the provinces do is instead of expensing funds spent on hospitals, they create an agency that does that sort of work and they extend the money to the agency in the form of a loan. A loan is an asset. It doesn't go through the budget. So it understates the budget deficit because what the province does is in effect create accounts receivable assets to itself. It doesn't expense it. By doing that they understate the deficits consistently and that's the main way they do it. There are other ways, but none as major as that.

I'm not sure our private lives have one code of behaviour and the government has another. I do think the government wants to present things in the best possible light, so to do that they'll use whatever creative accounting they have, to get that idea across. They'll do whatever they have to do to get themselves re-elected. I don't think there are any evil thoughts in government or that they're necessarily trying to hide something, but they're just trying to put their best forward. They like to do that just before elections so the third and fourth year of budgets are usually the most accounting-creative, and it gets more creative as election time comes by.

To understand this entire issue, it takes more than just plain accounting. It takes accounting; it takes knowledge of public accountants; it takes knowledge of economics. Then different groups have got different degrees of interest. If you look at the stock market today, there are a lot of equity analysts interested in companies and they report on them. But governments are not stock markets, so right off the bat that cuts out many of the people who would normally follow and report on government financial activity. So beyond that you've

129

got your different left- and right-wing think tanks that report on it and the rating agencies. The rating agencies are possibly a bit more independent than some of these right- and left-wing causes, so they may have a bit more credibility reporting on it, in that sense. To make a long story short, there are not very many entities that have got really an economic interest to report on it or the ability to do it, and it takes both. Thirdly, they don't have the independence that it takes to be objective. So rating agencies right now are one of the few objective analysts in this field, and that's probably why they're being vilified by many of the people who think they've got too much power. Basically they are the umpires and that's the role of a rating agency. They're the umpires of the capital market. They call the balls and strikes. When a company's got too much debt or when the government's got too much debt and bills, it's the rating agencies that call the balls and strikes. By cutting the credit rating, they're in effect the umpires of the capital market.

I'll conclude by again talking about interest rates. From an RRSP standpoint, compounding interest builds interest revenue very quickly. The interest just compounds and grows. The longer the timeframe, the bigger the compounding component. And it doesn't take long. There are old stories of IBM and the way it was growing in the 1960s and the 1970s. Given the way it was growing, people predicted that by the year 2040 it was going to be bigger than the gross domestic product of the United States. Ultimately that of course was impossible and reality stepped in and IBM slowed.

The same thing with the interest problem the governments have. It's the interest on the interest that is the problem — overcoming that is a problem. The way it works is when you start cutting back and you start paying down debt. The compounding interest has got the negative effect and it can very quickly work in reverse. So in 20 years if we handle our fiscal side correctly, we can solve the problem. But I think we're looking easily at 20 years because it's going to take the reverse compounding-interest effect: pay down debt then you pay less interest and that starts to compound and the savings start to compound instead of the other way around.

So it's your best friend or your worst enemy but right now we've got to make it our friend. To do that requires the worst of all worlds, which is going to be the pain for the next 10 years. The pain will be cutting expenditures, welfare, education, roads, everything that government does has got to be cut now, and cut below the tax revenue level enough that the difference can pay down the debt. That's going to be painful. We're in for 10 painful years. I just hope people like you stay healthy because someone's got to be around to pay that interest.

DAVID SLATER

A respected economist looks at deficit spending, unfunded liabilities, the CPP and QPP.

A number of years ago I encountered something very illustrative of this whole issue of the debt and deficit, not just concerning pay-as-you-go pension plans, but in other areas. In about the mid-1960s Ruth Smith, the wife of the second chairman of the Economic Council of Canada, got into the oral history business. Assembled at a dinner party one night were, among others, Rasminsky, John Deutsch and the architects of the post-war application of Canada's social welfare policy.[1]

At the gathering they talked about the benefit of 20 years of hindsight, as it relates to the debt. The universal opinion was that it's easy to have deficits and never easy to have surpluses. The principal error of post-war macroeconomic policy was that when there were high points in the economy, governments simply couldn't bring themselves to build up adequate surpluses to compensate for the deficits that would occur when the economy was soft. I think this is a very wise observation. The point is that when governments have money in their pockets they almost inevitably find ways to spend it. There are more good works around on which to spend your money than there is money, even at the best of times.

The Americans now are debating a balanced budget amendment which was defeated in the Senate just this last week. One of the things that defeated it was this: the American public pension system, the social security system in the United States, by design tended to be, if not a fully funded, a nearly fully funded system. Out of the benefits, the contributions, the investment fund and the investment returns, it's supposed to be able to meet the future obligations. And there's a big fund there. Well, in their government budget in recent years, the Americans have been using the so-called surpluses in the social security fund as a source of finance.

They say, "We don't have a deficit of $1 trillion, there's a surplus of $500 million in the social security fund and we just sweep those things together." So here you've got an example of, even with a program intended to be funded, a government in effect using and drawing on and postponing to the future, therefore drawing on the resources that are supposed to be meeting the future retirement system. The general point is the terrible temptation to anticipate that your surpluses will be larger than they will be and your deficits will be smaller than they will be. The terrible temptation is to put obligations under the carpet by using guarantees instead of actually having to borrow loan money. They are endemic in the system. The single most important lost opportunity is saying, for the benefits of a kind that your fathers got, you can expect less benefits and you will have to pay more for them. And that's the outcome of this process and these policies.

At the time of debt accumulation in Canada, there was pressure that eventually the debt would burden our children. But they were thinking it was going to happen in 2000 or 2010. At the time they were concerned with the present, thinking about the poor children, underfunded education, our deteriorating road system, etc.; those were the urgent issues to be dealt with. The other issues, such as the debt, they thought they'd be able to take care of later. I don't know if it's naive; I think it's human nature, particularly if it's easy to do.

Let me go on a bit about the part of the pension system of the country that is not the government system but is up to us or our employers, such as registered pension plans, RRSPs and so on. Actually these programs are at least as important, in the aggregate, for the income of retired people as the old age security, the GIS (Guaranteed Income Supplement), the CPP and QPP taken together. For the most part the intention of these programs is that they're to be fully funded. Also, they're subject to actuarial evaluation and supervision as to whether they're funded or not funded, adequately supported or not.

But all of those programs are given very large tax incentives and tax privileges. If you were into an RRSP program, you would deduct, in calculating your taxable income, your contributions to your RRSPs so that you get a tax deferral. The investment income earned by your RRSP is not counted as part of your income as you go along, so you're getting a tax deferral on that. Those tax deferrals are really quite large. The last time the federal government counted them up, which was about three years ago, they amounted to about $15 billion a year.

Over and beyond that, because of the way our personal income tax is structured, the provinces were giving another $6 billion or $7 billion. So even then there was $22 billion of tax deferrals to encourage you, and me when I was a little younger, to save for my own retirement income. There's a certain amount of attack on those privileges now, the argument being that those are too generous. They are things that the better-off people are getting, we're relying too much on that sort of thing and not enough on Canada Pension Plan and so on. So there are arguments there. But a fundamental point about those tax privileges is that they are tax deferrals, significant encouragement and incentives to us to take care of ourselves, to a large measure, for retirement income.

When you retire, the tax deferral you've had in a sense kicks in reverse because then you pay tax on everything you draw out, such as the investment income and all that sort of thing. On the whole I think that has been a very good and healthy part of the Canadian retirement income system. It doesn't help the poorest people in the country, but it cuts well down now, into the middle-income ranges. But the question being raised now is, "Aren't we being too generous in giving those tax incentives?"

Of course, if they cut back on those incentives and discourage taking care of ourselves in retirement, what's going to happen is the pressure for expansion of the Canada Pension Plan program and Quebec Pension Plan program will increase. We've got a difficult problem now with the Canada Pension Plan and Quebec Pension Plan, but I think that would add pressure. Put it another way: it may be that as much as

40 percent of Canadian government financing by borrowing is really being financed out of pension programs and RRSP programs now.

The size of the unfunded liability in the Canada Pension Plan right now is close to the size of our national debt. I think it is surprising that it wasn't faced up to sooner. To some extent the explanation is, as long as the visible part of the national debt was not so large, it wasn't quite such an urgent matter. The visible part of our debt is so large and it combines with the invisible part, arising out of these unfunded liabilities. It's really the invisible part that is creating, if not a crisis, an urgency for action that just didn't exist 10 years ago.

There are reasons why we see the debt of the pension plan. The first thing is that any estimate of that debt is something that comes out of an actuary's and economist's model. There are different ways you can calculate that, and there are different ways you can come up with the sums and what it will take to change these things and so on. Indeed, in the auditor general's last report, Chapter 34 speaks about the evaluation of the Canada Pension Plan. It notes that there are at least two or three different ways that it could be looked at, urging that the Department of Finance do the different calculations and make them available to the public so the public can get a better understanding.

Let me put it to you this way: I don't think I could tell you within a margin of 20 or 25 percent what the unfunded liability situation of the Canada Pension Plan and Quebec Pension Plan is at this point. I simply don't have enough information on all the bits and pieces to evaluate them. Let me give you a specific part of it. Do you realize that about one-third of the outlays of the Canada Pension Plan and Quebec Pension Plan are not pension benefits? They're disability benefits and they're benefits to widows and their children, etc. They are a kind of life insurance eligibility benefit. Not only that, the disability element is growing more rapidly than the pension outlays. As this morning's paper indicated, the disability elements in the Canada Pension Plan vary enormously from one province to another in this country. I mean, I just do not have enough information on the disability elements.

The term "latent deficit," or "hidden" or "invisible deficit," is really an actuarial estimate. It takes into account what assets a plan has, what its future contributions will be, what the future benefits will be, what the future mortality will be, etc. It's an estimate of the amount of resources you would have to put in to have the thing fully funded. It's the difference between all the income and assets you've got now and an estimate of the outlays you will have to make in the future, taken as of this point in time. It really is based upon a view of the future outlays and deaths and births and everything else; it is an estimate — it can't be anything other.

But estimates can be calculated within certain margins of error. In fact, in a recent World Bank report, a special research study they published last year, they calculated the social security deficit, as they call it, of Canada and a whole series of other countries. Certain estimates of about a $500-million or $600-million or $700-million deficit in the Canada Pension Plan I'd say are compatible with the World Bank figures, but they are estimates. They can't be anything other than that, but they're worthwhile estimates.

I think the people who are going to pay for reduced benefits in the future should absolutely know about them. Just as in the reform of pensions that took place in the early 1980s, it's really a very important matter for us to have a full analysis and a full exposition of this sort of thing in terms in which the public can understand the matters. Unfortunately, often reports have the kind of impact of royal commission reports. They may be wonderful but they're put on the shelf and other more short-term concerns are just so much more urgent. I'm talking about the defence of the country, the problems of regional underdevelopment, the high levels of unemployment of this country, the organization and ability to finance the health-care system. There are lots of urgent problems around at any given time, and this one just didn't seem to be that urgent. But the urgency of it has just enormously increased.

The reports are available. If you went to the Ottawa city library and looked up in the card catalogue, or now in the computerized catalogue, publications on pensions, you could be in it two hours. You could pull out a dozen things that have appeared, including at least four major pieces of publication by the Department of Finance on the pension system of the country. It's there, so there is accountability in the sense of there being numbers that are reasonably well laid out with the methodology explained and all that sort of stuff; but that doesn't produce action.

What generates action is a sense of crisis. In dealing with the Nova Scotia government and teachers' union, when I confronted them with the fact that they had all the existing pension obligations and they were going to have 5,000 new pensioners come on their scene — that produced action. It was so clear that if they did nothing, disaster was going to happen. I don't think the Canada Pension Plan is a disaster in that sense, but the dimensions of the problem are large. What our younger people are going to have to pay in benefits, in comparison with any reasonable expectation they would have based upon the experience of their fathers and mothers, that's an enormous wrench to the policy in this country. I think it's a sufficiently dramatic problem that people will simply demand that something be done about it.

I think it's too harsh to say that our budgeting and spending in Canada is essentially based on crisis management. Not all of it is, but there's a large element. Just to give an example of something that was not short term, consider this. The corporate tax arrangements in the United States and Britain and so on were based upon a narrow base, a lot of exemptions and high rates. All of those countries, after careful study, recognized that broadening the base and lowering the rates made a lot of sense. That's a longer-term kind of thing. It doesn't produce results overnight but it was done in the United States, done in Canada, done in Britain, done in Germany. So it's not all short term, but there is a strong bias in the structure of the agenda toward the shorter term.

Any major action that's undertaken in a crisis is bound to have some winners and losers. Action on the Canada Pension Plan in particular is going to be partly based on the reduction of benefits and partly on increased contributions and changing the disability arrangements and so on. There are going to be people who are losers compared with what they thought they were going to be. The spectre of the losers is a terribly retarding factor in taking hard, tough decisions. Secondly, and I have no expertise in this, my impression is that the television age tends to focus a bit more on the shorter term. The development of interest-group politics has also been a major deterring factor. It's probably done some good things but people in interest groups are either promoting their own thing or trying to see that nothing hurts me in my backyard. It's an enormously powerful force.

I'll give you an American example. American tort law, product liability and so on has been a scandalously rich and unfair kind of system, and tort-law reform is now once again before the U.S. Congress. Somebody noted that the largest single lobbying contributions in the United States to presidents' and congressional campaigns come from the defence attorneys' organizations. In this country the influence of interest groups is enormous and that would be a major deterrent to reform.

We used to say that in Canada there was a prime minister and one anti-spending minister. If there was a Cabinet of 27, there were 25 spending ministers. The one anti-spending minister was the minister of finance, and the perpetual job of a ministry of finance and the Treasury Board is to try to beat off this incredible pressure of caucus spending, trying to get things for their good works. It's just very difficult to appreciate how enormous and how subtle and how complex the pressure is that is imposed on the spending ministers in the country. I don't know how you overcome that or lessen that, but it is very difficult to undertake major changes in policy. Particularly if you think it might be a little less serious in the future or your ability to meet that policy is going to be greater in the future.

The best illustration of the 25:1 ratio of spenders to finance guardians, without telling tales out of school, comes to mind from when I was in the Department of Finance. About February every year there would be something called the fiscal framework established that went through Cabinet. It would have in it a certain amount of reserve money, you know, five percent of the reserve money. For two or three years running all those reserves were committed before the fiscal year started. The spenders had got to the prime minister, and if the prime minister is soft, the finance minister can't stop them. You've got to have a prime minister with sufficient power and control over his Cabinet and his caucus to say no. And they don't always have that power or choose to use it.

There were specific examples two or three years running, under the regime of John Turner and Donald MacDonald, when the fiscal framework was blown before the fiscal year ever started. That gives you an idea of how strong the pressure of the spending side is compared with the prudent limitation to control that spending side in governments. The same thing happened in Ontario. When I found that the public service and teachers' pension funds were so far in the hole in Ontario, we dealt with the ministers. The minister said, "OK, we'll pick up all the past service unfunded liability. You make sure that that pension plan can stand on its own feet in the future. Never come back to us and we'll do it." That was $7 billion of debt put on the province's books right then and there, which they undertook to fund over 35 years. And that's still being paid off now.

It's just another example of the government, in that case the Government of Ontario, being clearly culpable. They were the principal reason why the unfunded liability built up. They had put off corrective measures, they'd increased benefits and not increased the contributions, including your own, and that's where it ended up. It goes on over and over and over again. I suppose spenders have always been powerful. They do good works and therefore they are a kind of hero to their constituencies. So the people supporting you are an enormously powerful force.

NOTES

1. Louis Rasminsky was governor of the Bank of Canada, John Deutsch, a leading economics professor and public servant.

PAUL McCROSSAN

Actuary and former MP describes unfunded liability with particular reference to the CPP.

Let's start with the term "unfunded liability." If you had accrued or earned certain benefits to date, you can calculate what those benefits are worth. And that's the actuarial liability. If you paid in a certain amount of money over your working lifetime, that's the assets backing that liability. The unfunded liability is just the difference between what you've earned to date really costs and what you've set aside. So it's the amount that hasn't been funded yet.

The unfunded liability means practically nothing to the worker if this situation doesn't become fully funded at some time. If you're in a private pension plan, it means a lot because a private company can go out of business. So it's very important, if you have a pension with a private company, that it be funded over time because if the company goes out of business, you want to have enough money. Practically speaking the government can't go out of business. There's not going to come a day when the government just ceases to exist. At least we hope not.

Government plans are funded basically on a cash-flow basis, which is, how many taxes do we have to raise this year to pay for this year's benefits? So the really important thing with government programs is what's called pay-as-you-go costs. How much does it cost to pay the benefits each year? The costs have not been keeping up with the benefits that people are receiving. The value of the benefits has never been charged to the taxpayer.

The Canada Pension Plan system was introduced around 1965. The contribution rate that was set at that time was 3.6 percent for the benefits. The value of the benefits in 1965 over a worker's lifetime was just over five percent. So it was anticipated that people wouldn't contribute enough and the contributions would have to rise. The original plan was set up so that the contributions would be fixed until 1986 and then they'd rise thereafter.

So when you look at people who retired after 10 years, my father's a good example, he paid 3.6 percent of his salary each year for 10 years, which was 36 percent of his salary over the 10 years. He received in return 25 percent of his final salary each year, indexed to the cost of living. And my mother continues to receive a survivor pension today. Now, you don't have to be God's gift to the world to figure out that if you pay 36 percent in once, and you get 25 percent out each year, that's a heck of a bargain. So for the people who were born around the First World War, what they got out, on average, was worth about 15 times what they paid into it.

Now skip a generation. I'm a war baby, born in 1942. I will pay on average about five or six percent of my covered payroll over my 35-year working lifetime. The benefits I'll receive on retirement are worth about 13 or 13.5 percent of my covered payroll. So I'll pay almost one-third. Contribution rates are now going up, but they're not going up fast enough to make it worthwhile for the benefits that I earn.

Switch to my daughter. My daughter finished university in 1995 so is now entering the workforce. She's going to pay probably an average of 11.5 or 12 percent for something that's worth about 13 percent. And the benefits will probably be scaled back, so she'll probably pay 11 or 12 percent for something that's worth 11 or 12 percent. So she gets no bargain out of this. She'll pay for the benefit she earns. What's happened is there has basically been an intergenerational transfer. If you think of today's graduates, their grandparents got a great gift. Their parents got a good gift. And they pay their own way.

The 20-year hiatus was given to those who would benefit from the system because it was funded as a pay-as-you-go system. Nobody who retired before 1965 got any benefits. If they retired in 1966, they got one-tenth of the benefits. In 1967, two-tenths, and so on until they got ten-tenths, graded in over 10 years. So they needed very little cash to pay the benefits. The 3.6 percent of payroll they collected was far more than they actually needed to pay the benefits. That's where the so-called CPP fund comes in. The excess money was turned over to each of the provinces and the difference between the taxes collected, the 3.6 per-cent, and the money spent on pensions was turned over to the provinces each year.

All of the provinces except Quebec basically spent the money and wrote non-negotiable government bonds back. And that's the so-called Canada Pension Plan. Quebec decided they wanted to re-industrialize. They viewed themselves as needing to have an industrial base, so they cre-ated something called the Custodie Poli-Placements, which took the excess money and invested it in building up Quebec infrastructure and investing in the stock market. What happens now is that the Quebec Pension Plan has real assets. They invested in the market and all of the rest of the provinces just have notes saying, "We'll pay you in the future." But of course those so-called assets are just promises to tax in the future. So the money's been spent and what's been given back is a promise to tax.

All along the government absolutely understood that this was hap-pening. It was part of the deal. Pensions are a provincial issue and the federal government did not have the power to bring in the Canada Pension Plan. In order to bring in the Canada Pension Plan they had to get the provinces to agree. Mr. Pearson's initial proposal was to charge taxes below 3.6 percent and raise the taxes as the money was needed. The province of Quebec said, "If you want our signature on the agree-ment, let's set a contribution rate that'll be good for 20 years. Give us the money to invest and we'll sign on to bring in the national pension plan." So it was on that basis that the federal government had to obtain the provincial governments' consent that they set up this program of over-charging for 20 years and handing the excess over to the provinces.

In terms of what the provinces have done with their money since, they argue they did lots of things, such as building schools, roads, what-ever. Essentially they spent the money. But they argued at the time that they were going to make lots of social investments. So the money basi-cally went into infrastructure or was frittered away, depending on your political point of view. But it was spent, in every province except

Quebec. In Quebec the money was invested and is clearly set aside in marketable securities.

When I was in government they introduced the plan. They didn't know that it was going to head for trouble. They introduced the plans — both medicare and the Canada Pension Plan were developed around 1964. That was essentially just before the pill was introduced to society, and birth rates had been very low during the Depression. During and following the Second World War they jumped to a very high level and they stayed up from 1948 right through to about 1964.

So when they were planning the Canada Pension Plan and when they were bringing in medicare, they were thinking in terms of the nuclear family. You know, father working, mother staying home, two or three kids. That was going to be the norm for society. They were thinking in terms of the birth rates they had then, and given that sort of environment, the plans are reasonably well designed. But of course it hasn't quite turned out that way. Just starting in the middle 1960s the pill was introduced. Sexual mores changed. Birth rates just dropped out of sight, well below zero population growth.

So the environment that they planned for just isn't the one that came out. By the late 1970s it was apparent that we were headed for trouble. We had seen the population birth rates fall from 1964 right through 1976. We knew if they stayed at 1976 levels we were headed for trouble. In fact they have continued to fall since then. In 1976 it was apparent we were heading for problems so the Senate started studying it. The House had started studying it. They did studies galore. The government studied it, the Economic Council of Canada, Ontario formed a royal commission and Quebec established a system review. There were all these studies going on looking into how to cope with this problem. The issue was studied from about 1976 to about 1980. Most of the reports were in by 1980 or 1981. In 1979 during the brief Clark government, we were going to bring in pension reform. We had a national pension conference in 198l, so all of these studies came together then and we started examining how to redesign the pension system.

At the conference people came and gave their views and interpretations. Then the government wrote a report on the consensus arising out of that and proceeded to have parliamentary cross-country hearings. An MP called Doug Frith had a parliamentary committee on pension reform and he went across the country for about a year seeking views.

In Mr. Trudeau's very last budget in 1984, he brought in proposals for changing the pension system in Canada. Of course he was defeated, or he resigned, and Mr. Turner was defeated almost immediately. So the actual pension-reform legislation came in 1985.

So far we've just talked about the Canada Pension Plan. The Canada Pension Plan is funded. I mean, if you go out today and buy a Canada Savings Bond, you think of it as an investment. What it really is, is a promise that the government will tax somebody to give you the money back in the future. So the CPP funds consist of bonds issued by each of the provinces. They were handed the excess money each year from 1966 to 1986. They spent it. They signed IOUs back and that created the Canada Pension Plan assets. So that's where the money came from — from the excess contributions because the 3.6 percent tax-contribution rate — 1.8 percent from the employee, 1.8 percent from the employer — was higher than what was needed to pay the pensions.

One of the things that I personally found out in 1979 was that the Canada Pension Plan was the only social program for which we had any estimates in the long term at all. Old age security had never been estimated for more than a year and a half in advance, as far as I can find out. The Guaranteed Income Supplement was never estimated until the late 1980s. To my knowledge, the cost of medicare has never been estimated to this day. So we've brought in a lot of social programs figuring they were self-sustaining, but nobody actually prepared the figures to determine if they could be afforded in the long run until 1986.

In 1986 I introduced an act in Parliament called the Public Pensions Reporting Act. It required the government to table in Parliament cost estimates for every social program that it had, except medicare, on a three-year cycle. It had to bring in costs for old age security, Guaranteed Income Supplement, Canada Pension Plan, the MPs' pension plan, the public service pension plan, the Mounties, the judges, the whole lot. None of those things had ever been published before 1986. We'd always gone on the basis that we can afford them.

We had a situation in Canada where the growth of these social programs in the 1960s and the actual long-term costs of programs were never estimated, apart from the Canada Pension Plan. They set the contribution rate at what they thought the Canada Pension Plan would cost 20 years out, which proved to be a really good estimate because the cost in 1986 was just about exactly what they estimated it would be in 1964.

But for old age security, there were no cost estimates. The MPs' pension plan — no cost estimates.

The MPs' pension plan was approved in July 1981, in one day; the first, second, third reading all in the House without even a bill being printed, so it was brought in with no cost estimates. It was approved in the House and in Senate on the same day. There were people who objected at the time but there was a feeling that we were a wealthy country, we could afford these things and there wasn't a real concern about the long-term cost, until we started to run into real economic difficulties after 1980. Budget deficit didn't exceed $10 billion until 1980, and then between 1980 and 1984 it ran from $10 billion to $40 billion as we went through the recession. So it was really during the early 1980s that we dug ourselves into the economic hole.

When I suspected the system was actually working in this way, that's when I got into politics. I was the chairman of the Education and Examination Committee for the Society of Actuaries on designing social programs and I had pretty good suspicions that this was going to happen. I wrote a letter to Joe Clark saying as much and they asked to talk to me and encouraged me to run. Then I got elected to Parliament. Once I was there I tried to find out what the costs were going to be. The Conservatives came to power in 1979.

As soon as we became the government, within a month we asked for all the cost estimates for all the social programs to be given to us. We wanted to figure out what the long-term estimates were and that's when we found out that none existed except for the Canada Pension Plan. So we ordered them immediately. We ordered that all of the studies be prepared. We ordered the Treasury Board and the government's chief actuary to prepare all of the studies of the costs of the social programs, but we were defeated before the studies were completed. We were only in government for nine months. None of the studies were released in the next four years, so it was only when the Conservatives were re-elected again in 1984 that we went back. At that point we asked them to hand us the studies that we'd asked for in 1979 and we tabled them in the House of Commons in 1985.

I think what was going through the minds of Canadians at the time were the needs of people. If you go back to the predominant social ethic of the 1960s and 1970s, it was about helping out the less fortunate. People thought we were a rich country with essentially all the resources that you could ever imagine and we could never have debt problems. Indeed, we never did have any debt problems until the very late 1970s. We ran balanced budgets for 100 years. So when the plans were developed no one ever conceived of the fact that we could ever develop the large debts and no one conceived of the rapid shift in the population because of the changing lifestyles.

The other thing that has happened that undermined the social programs is the breakup of the family, what with so many single-parent-led families now. The single largest element of poverty now is female-led families where there's no male in the family. That didn't exist, really, in the 1960s. The second biggest element of poverty is single women in retirement. You have to understand that going back in the 1960s, women's and men's life expectancy was in the early 70s. Now men are expected to live until the late 70s and women will live until their early 80s on average. Because of increased medical technology and better nutrition, there are a lot more single women around in retirement. And a lot of them have serious poverty problems. Those problems didn't exist in the 1960s. There was much more tradition of looking after your mother and grandmother, you know, helping out in the family. Now we're much more remote.

At that time I think both the citizens and government asked that these programs be instituted. The old age security that was introduced in the Depression was on a means-tested basis. It was made universal after the Second World War. The last thing the St. Laurent government did was increase the old age security by, I think it was, $10 a month, and the finance minister was called "Ten Buck Harris." During the election they sneered at him, saying, how dare he increase the pensions only by $10 a month? We were a wealthy country and living standards were going up. Why shouldn't the retired senior citizens participate in the wealth? That was very much the thought of the day.

From the 1930s to the start of the 1980s, living standards increased dramatically and so it was a question of sharing the wealth. At that time Parliament saw that sharing the wealth was part of its job. To protect the elderly against the costs of medical diseases that were going to catch up with them sooner or later, bring in medicare. Protect the senior citizens through increasing old age security. Bring in the Canada Pension Plan. There were so many problems to be dealt with and we were a very rich society with no debts and it was a question of "Let's share the wealth and help the less wealthy."

It went off the rails because we started spending more than we were collecting. The deficit sort of accumulated bit by bit. For better or for worse, the public didn't realize that it was a serious problem. So in 1972 the budget was essentially balanced. During 1973–74 we started to have our first deficits. They weren't very big. From 1974 to 1979 they increased from a couple of billion dollars through to $10 billion a year. That was cause for alarm. When Mr. Crosbie said the budget deficit was a serious issue and proposed increased taxes, they proposed a tax to raise the price of gasoline from 18¢ a litre to 22¢ a litre. That sounds laughable by today's standards, but at that time there was just a massive rejection of doing anything like that. The taxpayers just didn't want to have anything to do with taxes to control the deficit. They didn't want to have anything to do with cutting back the benefits either.

Of course, the Clark government was defeated. By the time Trudeau came back to power, the annual deficit quadrupled over the next four years. By that time it was pretty apparent that we were getting into difficulties. There still was not a realization that there were serious difficulties. When Mr. Wilson brought in his first full budget and it proposed even partially indexing old age security — basically indexing it by a couple of percent less than the increase in the cost of living — there were demonstrations on Parliament Hill. People were saying, "We're cheating the senior citizens, everybody should be sharing the wealth. Why are we taking it away from the seniors?"

The purpose of the 1985 budget was to reduce government expenditures. They were being reduced in all sorts of areas, including old age security payments. There was no realization that the debts could be very high and would get out of control at that point. I can very well remember, as a member of Parliament, coming to work and having demonstrations with senior citizens carrying placards blockading the entrance for the MPs. Even though the amount involved might only be a couple of dollars a month, there was a feeling at that time that it was an unfair cutback, so the government withdrew the measure. They withdrew it because it was tremendously unpopular. Sure, the senior citizens still felt they were entitled to the full cost-of-living protection with the full benefits, and they demonstrated very vigorously to maintain that.

LLOYD FRANCIS

*Economist and former MP criticizes overgenerous govern-
ment programs and outlines the role of politics in the CPP
and UI programs.*

I was trained as an economist. I have a Ph.D. from the University of
Wisconsin in the United States. I graduated at Toronto and worked
for nine years in the Department of National Health and Welfare. I
worked with Paul Martin when he was the minister and set up a long-
range planning group.

An accounting deficit between one generation and another is a
very academic thing. Today's young generation is going to inherit
knowledge, skills, capital equipment, hospitals, schools; and all of these
are the things that give you a standard of living. It's not what's on the
books. But having said that, the debt is a very serious matter. And looking back I feel that two individuals are responsible for no small part of
that, and they were both members of the party to which I belonged in
my political career.

I'll start with Walter Gordon. The universal Old Age Security
Program was put on the books in Canada in 1950. It was novel to pay to
everybody at the age of 70 so many dollars a month. I think it was $40
or $50 a month then. Without any test of means, you just proved your

age and residence in Canada and you got it. When Walter Gordon became minister of finance in the 1960s, he wanted to do something; he wanted to lower the age. And just as he was leaving office in 1965, he announced, no doubt with the approval of Prime Minister Pearson, that there would be a reduction of the age of eligibility in the future, by one year at a time. It would go from 70 to 69 to 68 and so on, down to 65.

Everybody believed in Walter Gordon. He was such a nice guy, you couldn't help but like him. His personal integrity was beyond dispute. But there were no demographic studies behind that plan. It was just an act of faith. It flew in the face of the fact that people were living longer and were healthier. No other country in the world ever paid everybody at the age of 65 a universal pension without any testing of resources. If you'd projected an aging population, with more older people living longer and a scarcity of a younger generation coming up in the labour force, then I think you would have said, "This is a very foolish thing to do." The age of retirement shouldn't have gone down, it should have gone up; not only because people were healthier and living longer, but because there weren't as many young people to replace those who were retiring. The fall in the birth rate meant that we didn't have as large a number of young people coming up to take their places.

For both reasons it was wrong. But it was done, and you had to be the Grinch that stole Santa Claus to go against that. Everybody thought it was great. Walter Gordon said it was fine. Well, it wasn't so good. I support health insurance and welfare, but a universal pension paid to everybody at 65 is wrong. I'm in pretty good health at 75. I like to think I could still carry a job; I don't particularly choose to, but I did carry a job into my late 60s. I think many people are able to do it and want to do it. That's what's going on in the contemporary world. But Walter never even thought of that. They didn't do any long-term studies of demographics. So the policy was wrong. Those of us who had done some preliminary work in this field (and I had, when I worked for the Department of National Health and Welfare as an economist) knew that this was wrong, that retirement policy could not be based indefinitely on reducing the age of retirement. Nor could it be based on the assumption that we'd always have an indefinite number of fully skilled young people waiting. In my time, instead of a golden handshake at retirement, there'd be a golden incentive to stay another year or two, especially if there wasn't a well-trained younger person available to take your job. And I think we'll see that.

But when an elected representative can go to his constituents, meet people who are turning 69 and say, "Vote for me, and next year you'll get your pension at 69," it's a highly compelling argument at the polls. I spoke in the caucus and to my colleagues and to some members of the Cabinet. I expressed my views, but I couldn't really persuade anybody to take them seriously. A lot of people in Parliament were looking to votes and getting re-elected. They didn't want to listen to anybody who said this plan wasn't a good thing and it was very hard to persuade someone otherwise. "Walter Gordon said it was OK. Who are you to say he's wrong? Walter's a great guy." He'd been minister of finance and chairman of the Royal Commission on Canada's Economic Prospects. His credentials were impeccable. People tended to take his representations on faith.

It wasn't common at the time for program changes to be announced without long-term projections. I worked in the Department of National Health and Welfare from 1951 to 1960. We did the planning for hospital and health insurance, and there were elaborate projections of costs. As it turned out, the costs were much greater than we anticipated, but there were attempts to form realistic projections. The group that did that work was later dismantled. After the introduction of health insurance in the late 1960s, that kind of study was not done, and in its place were detailed studies of actual costs instead of projections.

Now, the second individual was Bryce Mackasey, the minister of labour. He was responsible for unemployment insurance, a scheme designed on fairly conventional social insurance principles. In 1974 he decided to extend it to seasonal workers. The question was, who was a seasonal worker? He talked to the Atlantic caucus and they were all in favour of fishermen being seasonal. He spoke to people who were in favour of forestry being seasonal. He wasn't that quick on agricultural workers, but Alf Gleave has told me that he and the rest of the NDP lobbied to get the agricultural workers of Western Canada in there as seasonal. One after another, they all got in.

At the time the chairman of the Unemployment Insurance Commission, the body responsible for administering the program, was Clifford Murcheson from Saskatchewan. Clifford was a very rugged individual whose integrity was beyond reproach. And he advised

Mackasey, "Don't do it!" He said it would subsidize the seasonal industry, keeping too many people in industries where they shouldn't be. They should have shifted to other kinds of employment; not easily done, I know, but in the long-term interests of the country it had to be done. It would also subsidize the employers and it was a regional welfare transfer: a transfer from central areas with high employment to other areas with low employment. If you wanted to do that, you should do it through welfare, not through unemployment insurance. It would add enormously to the deficit of the program.

Murcheson was right on. Everything he said turned out to be true. But Mackasey paid no attention to his representations. Clifford came to me and told me about it. I went over his documentation. Then I went on the committee studying the revisions, and I objected to the changes. I felt that they would destroy the fund over a period of time. When I started to talk up about it, the chairman of the committee, David Weatherhead, who was a good friend and still is to this day, took me aside and said, "You know, you're not being very helpful, Lloyd. Why don't you get off the committee? We know what we're going to do. You're just making trouble." I was taken off the committee. It was as simple as that.

You couldn't talk to anybody. The Atlantic caucus was solid for Mackasey. He had carefully lobbied the caucus in favour of "Santa Claus," giving people in these constituencies fairly substantial sums of money out of the unemployment insurance fund. It was no longer an insurance program. Bryce Mackasey destroyed it. If it was a welfare problem, it should have been handled within a welfare context. There was nothing you could do to stop it. You couldn't go to the Atlantic caucus and oppose the fishery workers; you'd be in fear for your life before you got out of the room. You couldn't go into many of the other caucuses. The fact is that it was immensely popular with a large number of elected representatives; Mackasey had very skillfully lobbied them.

The program became a boondoggle from that point on. Abuses crept in and we now have the situation that is very difficult to correct. I've spoken recently to a man who was a member of Cabinet at the time and now has misgivings and recognizes it was a mistake. He said, "Mackasey lied to us. Things were said that were simply not true." That's all I got out of him. He's reluctant to discuss what took place within the Cabinet, but he did say that much. I don't know. I wasn't in Cabinet.

And I couldn't cope with him, I just couldn't. Clifford Murcheson, who was his senior pubic servant, couldn't cope with him. And what was done to the act just about broke Murcheson's heart. He really was hurt.

The amendments to the Unemployment Insurance Act have come back to haunt us today. How do you cut back? Once you've given something, you can't take it away, just as taking away a pension from somebody on their 65th birthday is politically not a nice thing to do.

These two events and these two men are, by my rough calculation, responsible for close to one-quarter of the current federal deficit on a yearly basis. And if we have a $40-billion debt, you're looking at $8 billion or so from these two events, maybe one-quarter of the debt from these two decisions. I'm subject to correction in detail, but that's the order of magnitude we're talking about.

Looking back on these two issues, they were so important. I probably should have gone to the prime minister, but I doubt I would have been able to persuade him. That's a judgment call. Who is so absolutely confident that they're right and everybody else is wrong? You'd have to have a lot of confidence in what you were doing. From my economics background I had confidence that what I was saying was right. But I couldn't really get to bat in the caucus. I was hooted down. The avenues are not that great to fight a lone cause within a party and survive. I fought the changes because I thought they were wrong. On many fronts I got into differences of opinion; these were just two. I had the reputation in the Liberal Party of being a Cassandra. I didn't like what they were doing, and when I said so I became very unpopular. I said it and I got into trouble. That's the way life is. You don't win 'em all.

Also, I represented the English-language public servants of Ottawa West, and there was a great deal of dissatisfaction among them about the language policy at that time. I voted for the policy and supported the government, but I had a real problem with many of my constituents.

Between my representations on the language policy implementation, and those on unemployment insurance, and those on old age security, I found myself "odd man out." Occasionally I felt like a nuisance. That didn't bother me then, nor would it today. One reporter said, "Why didn't you resign?" And my comment was, "Did you ever hear of the epitaph of the fellow in the cemetery? On his tombstone they inscribed, 'He had the right of way.'" You can be very right and very dead. You can be very right and totally out of the picture and not have any influence. I chose to stay within my party and see what influence I could have, and in some areas I did have success. For example, I was chairman of the committee that rewrote the Veterans Charter. I look back on a few things and feel they were worthwhile, but on these two, old age security and the amendments to unemployment insurance, I regret that I was not able to persuade more people at the time. In the course of events there are many people who fight for things they believe in. But if they're implemented, they don't get credit for them, if they're not implemented, that's later seen to have been a mistake.

Jim Richardson had a difference with Trudeau on policy, and he resigned as minister of national defence and literally went off the scene. There are many such cases of members of Parliament. Politics is survival; if you're not in there, you're nothing. You have to be in there and somehow carrying some weight and credibility. And some people manage to do these things better than others. Looking back, I might have done more. Who knows? What if I had gone directly to the prime minister and made a forceful representation? It wasn't easy to see the prime minister in those days. I rarely asked to see him; in the course of my career, maybe only four or five times.

I remember a decentralization move to take Mines and Technical Surveys to Quebec, which made no sense whatsoever. I went to Mr. Trudeau three times over it. And eventually they did not move, but Mr. Charest told me at a reception not long ago that when he was the minister, he got some of them moved into Quebec. This was an issue where I was positive that it was wasteful and destructive. It would take people out of the area where they're most effective. By going to the prime minister, I was able to achieve a certain success with it. But you can't do that too often. You can't go to the prime minister every day.

I didn't always lose and I didn't always win. No regrets. I probably wouldn't have done anything any differently. I probably couldn't have.

I don't think any member or any Cabinet minister gave me more than the time of day on the issues. I think that in the case of Walter Gordon, his overwhelming prestige was such that when you started to ask questions, people dismissed you. They all thought it was a great idea. "Why, think of the votes in it!" Sometimes you see what you want to see.

In the case of Mackasey, he did a very effective lobby of the caucus. You couldn't possibly counter him — there was no way. He had that capacity of lobbying, wining and dining key people and setting up a situation. You couldn't rally a group of people to go in with you and fight. "Well, no, Lloyd. I'm kind of busy. I don't think I'll make it." You say, "This is wrong," and they say, "Now just a minute, Lloyd, how do you know?" There we are. Sometimes people believe what they want to believe.

It did affect my credibility in the party at the time, but not over a longer period. At the time I was just a difficult character. There were a few others protesting; four or five I found who should have been able to carry some weight. But the power of party discipline in Canada is enormous. The congressional system gives more independence to elected representatives. Under our system you don't get on committees, you don't go on trips, you don't become a chairman of anything, you have to fight to get a spot to speak in debate; there's just so much that can be thrown at you by the party.

In 1972 the party sent organizers in to deny me the nominating convention in Ottawa West. Four paid organizers were sent in to support another candidate because of my reputation as a Cassandra, but they didn't defeat me. I still won the nomination.

There are one or two famous party outlaws. Ralph Cowan was one. Ralph defied every rule in the book and enjoyed doing it. After a while there were pictures of him on the front pages of the Toronto press — "Ralph Cowan: Renegade." In a way maybe that did him some good, but it totally discredited him as a credible spokesman.

The executive has a great deal of power. The prime minister has an incredible amount of power in our country, more than the president of the United States has. But Parliament still has a role. It can be essential when there are crises, when there is a balance of power within Parliament, when a government is a minority or even when a very basic issue comes up.

I would think, for example, that in the British Parliament today, Mr. Major is having great difficulty reconciling his belief in the European Community and the fishermen on the coast who sympathize with Canadians for what the Spanish trawlers are doing. This is splitting a party. Under such circumstances, when there's a basic split on principle within a party, Parliament emerges as the arena in which real decisions are made. But most of the time it isn't.

Parliamentary government has been around for a little while. It evolved out of a fight with the Crown in the United Kingdom. It was a concept where the government has the confidence of the elected House of Commons and the role of the Crown is restricted. I think that this basic concept is going to be with us for a long time, even if we replace the monarchy (and I'm not advocating that, but I conceive that it might happen). Whoever is the head of state has to recognize that the elected representatives choose a prime minister who is the seat of authority. If you have effective opposition in Parliament, that sometimes helps.

An MP does his or her best. You serve the people who vote for you. And sometimes when you're in an "odd man out" situation you have a difficult time. Some MPs combine the skill of saying something that's very unpopular and not getting too much odium on them when they say it. They tell it with a joke. They manage to polish it up and quietly make their suggestions. It takes a great deal of skill to do that. I tended to be a little more emotional in reaction, and I didn't always handle things as smoothly as some people did. And, as I said before, you can disagree, you can resign and you can go down into oblivion. People will forget you. If you stay and try to fight another day, you might win on one or two other fronts.

It's not a matter of selling out your principles, it's just a matter of your being there. And you're not a single-issue person, you're there to represent your constituents on a broad range of things. On some matters you're able to prevail and carry your opinion; on others you can't. But that's the way democracy is. It's compromise; it's not a clean "everything this" or "everything that." Every MP has to balance his or her judgment. You meet a lot of people who say you let them down, you didn't do this and you didn't fight for that. Sorry. I did what I could and what I thought was right.

It's always a moral struggle. Your constituents may not always be right. Politicians supporting gun control might sit in constituencies today where there's an organized, determined pro-gun lobby. And yet I'm satisfied that the overwhelming majority of Canadians are saying that we've had too much unrestricted control in the handling of guns, and that guns should be registered. I think the majority of Canadians support that bill. But there are many MPs in this Parliament, especially those representing northern and rural areas, whose constituents do not support the bill, so they have a problem.

I'd say to the younger generation, don't be mesmerized by the accounting. The accounting is just figures. The standard of life you're going to enjoy comes from what you inherit: the capital stock, the knowledge, the schools, the hospitals and the factories that produce your automobiles. All of these things physically are going to be there, and they'll provide the services for your standard of living. If there are some accounting problems in regard to past generations, well, a country like Brazil wiped those out by the device of inflation. There are all kinds of ways in which a society makes its adjustments. But keep your eye on the fundamentals: what you inherit in the physical stock, knowledge and skill of your people. They're going to give you your standard of living.

I don't want to say that budget deficits aren't serious. They're very serious. But somebody is spreading rumours about the Canada Pension Plan, that you might not live to draw a pension. Have you heard that the pension plan is broke, that it's not properly funded? Well, do you know what an actuary does to make that presumption? The actuary tells you what the interest rate, the productivity rates, the average retirement age, the labour force participation rate, the numbers of women and young people in the workforce, and the number of people working part time at home with their computers will all be in the year 2010. He has to make all of those assumptions before making a global projection of the income and outgo of a pension fund 30 years from now. God bless him, I just don't share his confidence in taking that to several decimal places.

The budget process is changing. This budget had more consultation than any in my recollection. Before adopting it the minister invited the members to say what they felt about tax increases, spending cuts and a number of very specific things. Members had every opportunity to make a presentation to the minister on their point of view. I believe more than one of the caucuses did so. I suspect groups of other MPs in the House of Commons also expressed their views before the budget was adopted.

Budgets are cut and dried and hammered out and people vote the party line. Rarely do you get a budget revolt in our history; I can't think of one. I've voted against a couple of things. I wanted escalation of public service pensions because I represented a public service constituency. While we didn't get it that time, we got our way later; we did get escalations.

Even with my background as an economist, I could only cover a small part of the budget. I couldn't begin to cover a whole budget. Most

MPs take a certain section where they're particularly involved. The budget development process has always been mostly out of MPs' hands, but it's more in their hands now than it ever was before. When I was first elected, you had nothing to do with the budget. It just came out and there you were. You were as surprised as anybody else, when you read it, to see what was in it. The situation has improved a great deal. I think Paul Martin, without actually giving away the precise details of the budget, went a long way to indicate the direction and thrust of what he was going to do.

There's no question we have to take a harder line on spending and there's no question we have to build restrictions into the process of spending money. Looking back, there were some easy years in the 1970s when revenues rolled in. We even had periods of surpluses, though it's hard to believe. When there's a surplus and the country is prosperous and revenues are high, there are always proposals for spending and this is when the discipline that prevailed before disappears. You go through certain periods when there's a great deal of optimism, and you think the future's going to be like what you've had in the past. Well, it isn't.

Maybe out of this rough period will come a sense that there is always a day of reckoning. If you spend a lot, there's a day when you have to pay for it. And maybe we can build into the parliamentary processes a sense, or some rules, that we don't just spend, that in years when things go well, we tackle that debt and get it down. We must get it down, and somehow do what New Zealand and some other countries have done. This isn't very popular; it doesn't win you votes. But we don't really have an alternative.

BILL MACKNESS

A critique of deficit financing and entitlements from an economist who has played key roles in both the public and private sectors and in academia.

The Mulroney government in the 1980s, through Michael Wilson, thought it would be useful to put expert individuals into ministers' offices on a short-term secondment basis. I was the first and, I believe, the last such appointee. Much of the regular civil service didn't find it too helpful to have someone in the minister's office, if you like, second-guessing what was being done. So I don't have an awfully strong opinion on that matter. It's really a taste of what the government would want to do and my experience was that it didn't make a great deal of difference because ultimately governments are very much captives of the bureaucracy, unless they have an extremely strong ideological focus. But regular bureaucracy has a momentum that carries the ship of state down the centre-left column.

When I arrived in Ottawa I went with Mike Wilson to the Department of Finance. My principal interest, although I was involved in any number of items, was the fiscal matter. At that time there was a growing recognition that something of crisis proportions was brewing on the fiscal side and that something would have to be done about it.

The statistic that comes to mind most immediately was that spending was then 54 percent in excess of revenues. Even a committed Keynesian would have to know that something had to give.

I held the view that the situation was considerably more serious than it was generally perceived to be, particularly than it was perceived to be in Ottawa. The basic policy put forward by the bureaucrats, which had been worked up over the summer when Parliament was shut down and the election was going on, took a very soft line toward the fiscal matter. It was strong on rhetoric and, in fact, quite soft in terms of action. In its wisdom the government chose to adopt that particular document.

It actually was quite well received, and in the business community too, because, as I said, the rhetoric was excellent. But the basic arithmetic was wrong. The deficit was roaring at such a pace that I believed, short of some draconian movement to get the fiscal situation back into balance, that the ongoing economic expansion would simply fund an inexorable rise in the debt load. That would then develop into an even worse crisis at the next business cycle, which I think is a fair measure of what happened.

I believe that those offering the advice were very capable people and very well regarded, and the advice, incidentally, was politically very attractive. It said that rather than taking some very difficult spending cuts up front to deal with the problem, that the problem would sort of go away if you nibbled at the spending side over the next seven years. So that was really quite attractive. Indeed, if it had worked, it would have been a much superior program to taking the tough type of medicine that we're into now.

Financial problems tend to get worse unless you deal with them up front and quite dramatically. The lack of will to cut spending forced the debt outstanding to continue to grow much faster than the economy. That means that the debt load, relative to the economy that had to sustain it and finance it, was growing much faster. The predictable consequence is that five or seven years down the line there was a much more serious problem. My recollection is, in 1983, 1984, the federal debt outstanding was about 40 percent of the GDP. I think we're now up to about 80 percent. So what we've done with this gradualist policy is simply let the debt run so that it is now literally twice as large a problem as it used to be.

The Conservatives did run some program surpluses, but to my recollection the debt continued to grow each year and grow more rapidly than the economy. The issue was, once the debt gets large enough, to regain control of the situation you have to run very large program surpluses. Politically that's not easy to do. You have to be either a true believer, or the second alternative is that your bankers on Wall Street tell you there will be no more money unless you do it. In fact it is the latter alternative that is driving the process. I don't believe the fiscal reform in Canada is a cerebral exercise. We are moving toward fiscal reform, but I think that it's based on a script written on Wall Street.

In terms of the program surpluses the money is fungible. All that it meant was that the deficit was a little smaller than it would have been otherwise. But the issue was that the size of the interest burden was so large. I don't recall the numbers right offhand now, but the program surpluses would have been a faint image of the debt interest charges. I've never really felt that this idea of a program balance or surplus is really very helpful because it's the deficit each year added to the outstanding debt that is the operative mechanism. The split between interest and programs is rather academic because that's not what's driving the system. It's the size of the debt load that is driving the system.

By Christmas of 1984 I was pretty dispirited with government. I thought a great opportunity was being missed. There was a major review of the unemployment insurance system and that put us off track for a long time. The excesses and abuses there were obvious. There was no need for a year or two of study to deal with that. The Nielsen task force held out great promise and was staffed by some very able people. A great disappointment was a prime ministerial decision. I think there had been quite a row about some tax measures with respect to the elderly and I think the prime minister was a touch gun-shy at that point. He volunteered that any savings from the Nielsen task force would be directed not toward reducing the deficit, but toward more necessary social and public spending. And I didn't feel that that was a very good philosophical structure from which to run a deficit-reduction program.

So I completed my commitments and stayed until the following fall. I'd made a commitment to go up for one year. You know, with the blinding light of hindsight, one can't be positive at the time. It's also a little on the unnerving side if you get that far out from the rest of the pack. I think in general the fiscal approach of the Conservative government was relatively well received. There were two opposition parties railing to not be so harsh and to be more liberal and sensitive and so on. It was a serious political problem. I believe that the government and Cabinet did believe the projections from the Finance Department, which consistently said that this is a manageable problem that will cure itself over time with some very modest restraint.

That was basically the message of all the budgets going forward, and not surprisingly it didn't work because there had been nearly a decade of that type of wishful thinking under the Liberals. There was essentially a little more pro-business, pro-market rhetoric tossed in but the basic formulations were the same. It was a classic gradual solution to a financial problem that simply said, rather than taking painful, disruptive and politically inconvenient disciplined action up front, the resolution here is to draw a trend line out for seven years and at that point somehow the deficit will have disappeared. Those lines, of course, are drawn on the assumption that there are no surprises, no upsets, and everything works out just about right.

I wouldn't exaggerate my degree of surprise that the system is perhaps stymieing because I'd been watching the process for quite some time. I would say that I was disappointed that there wasn't firmer action on the fiscal front. It was also disappointing in that the other policy actions of that government were right on the mark. I mean, it was very much a pro-market, free-market government. They did move toward privatization and deregulation and they were doing those things quite properly. I was not privy to any Cabinet views on the matter but standing back and looking, I believe that they were honourable ministers who believed that they could get from here to there without inconveniencing themselves, and in the process regain control of the fiscal situation. It didn't work out that way but there you are.

Again, the power of assertion has much to do with convincing the public that this gradual approach was the right thing to do. I do believe that the rhetoric in the document was very strong and I think that to an uncritical eye or an uncritical ear, the programs looked pretty sensible. It is amazing that after more than a decade of these year-by-year budgets purporting that a gradual solution will work, that we then had a brand-new government that immediately adopted the same basic stance. I'm really at a bit of a loss. I guess the learning curve doesn't slope up quite as sharply as some people would like.

Middle-class entitlements are essentially the universality arrangement. When medicare came in, for example, there were any number of private or provincial plans working in that area that had the disaster-type arrangements connected with them. It also left people who are better off to look after themselves more. The view of the social activists who wanted these universal social programs was a little perplexing because they would say that you must ship this out to everyone. I guess one of the examples was postal employees wearing out the shoe leather while lugging baby-bonus cheques around Forest Hill and other neighbourhoods where it's not obvious that they were required.

There is a political justification for universality that tends to co-opt opinion leaders in the middle classes — the media, the clergy, school-teachers, university professors and so on, if you like, the ambitious middle class. What happens is that when universality is spread out, the result is there is proportionately much heavier use of education subsidies, for example, by the middle class. They get a wonderful deal. People down below are shipping money up to educate middle-class children. Work at the Fraser Institute indicates that the middle-class and richer populace consumes a disproportionate amount of medical services, presumably because they're better informed and more interested in looking after themselves. Who knows? But these studies were quite conclusive.

The education one is pretty obvious but the medical care one was really, I thought, quite interesting and it was quite a significant difference. What it did was expand the universe of people who were actually getting more from the government than they were putting in, and that has an important effect on the electoral process. That's why the middle-class opinion makers that I spoke of have such a disproportionate influence on public perceptions in these matters. Certainly the CBC would rank high on the list of those who are not only proponents but also the defenders of these entitlement schemes. Essentially I think they are a major bribe, if you like, to bring the middle class on side. They're very expensive.

I'm so far away from the numbers so I really would hesitate to say what percentage of the budget covers middle-class entitlements. That particular study I referred to would still be available from the Fraser Institute and it's quite a clear and very exhaustive study done by absolutely impeccable researchers. It was really interesting; a senator, who can remain unnamed, a Liberal senator, once confided something to me. Indeed, when these programs were being brought forward I asked the obvious question: why would you not have done away with universality and saved an immense amount of money? The reason, he said, was that if you did that, you wouldn't maintain the support of the middle class for the expansion of the programs. If these programs were restricted to the poor, the middle-class opinion makers would have been much less vocal in their support of the programs.

Government can spend more than they take in by the amount of the deficit. That's what makes this politically so attractive when you've got a good clean balance sheet, as we would have had in the late 1960s. You hit a crossover point, as we did in 1984, where the interest on the previous borrowings then becomes so large that it consumes more than the deficit, so that although you're running the deficit and it's taking some of the sting out, you are running operating surpluses. That inexorably means that the citizens are getting less government spending, interest excluded, than they're putting in.

How you get into the mess, I believe, is that the government is literally able to spend on ordinary taxpayers significantly more money than they are putting in during the early stages of this process. After the crossover point the issue is of getting a majority of the electorate in the position where they're literally getting more out of the system than they're putting in. The Fraser Institute's study indicated that something in the order of 58 percent of the electorate were getting more from the system than they were putting in, and in that particular matter the swing factor is the middle-class entitlements. These programs are sacred cows for Canada — I guess because our foreign lenders have such a great commitment to us consuming more than we produce. Literally it's a question of getting away with it. I think that's turning now.

I don't know why the government never talks about middle-class entitlements. I think there still is a very major commitment to universal social programs on all political levels in the country. What we're engaged in now is damage control. I don't think there's any philosophical shifting away from the universality. If you don't think about it very much, universality has a nice ring. It is, however, very much an income-redistribution scheme that carries with it some quite untoward results, such as major subsidies from lower-income Canadians to middle- and upper-income Canadians.

Certainly the university educational system would be a classic example of a system that draws almost exclusively from middle- and upper-income families, whereas the bulk of the tax funding is coming in from people at the lower end of the scale. So the individual who drives the bus to get the middle-class children out to university in the morning is also contributing because he's paying a great whacking tax bill to underwrite the educational institution, you see. I don't believe that upper-income Canadians should take major subsidies from lower-income Canadians, which is the case with education and medical care. I think that's an anomaly and I think there's a strong political motivation for keeping that system in place because it keeps the opinion leaders on side, if you like.

There is a political dimension that the first rule of health care is that if you'd like to lose an election, just try fooling around with health. Even Premier Filmon in Manitoba had a very close brush with disaster for doing nothing more than taking modest and very important reforms in the health-care area. It takes on a dimension and it allows opposition politicians to run on a system of fear. We have an aging population and any perceived threat to ready access to medical care is just a nuclear disaster for whoever suggests it. That's not to say that we have an efficient or effective system. I think that these reforms will be brought in slowly, very slowly.

I personally believe that the medical-care system would work better with an element of price discrimination or price allocation within the system. I think we will be driven there by demographics by the early years of the next decade. I think that the system has an inexorability about it, not unlike the cuts that are coming in social security. The system's bankrupt. The issue is that those of adequate means aren't going to get paid. It's already happened in Italy. I think that these things tend to be resolved by crisis rather than by a cerebral advanced-planning system.

We can't afford the level of waste that's inherent in many of the programs. The non-life-threatening, minor procedures and doctors' visits and so on, they burn up an awful lot of the resources that could be better allocated to life-threatening areas. Any system that operates with no price mechanism is inherently less efficient. One of the problems with our health-care system is that two men and a boy could have designed it in the 1960s because it wasn't a problem then. We had the youngest population in the Western world. Running health-care systems for young, healthy populations is really easy. Now we're starting to see the rubber hitting the highway because the demographics are running the other way.

That's also happened in the social security system. What it means is that we will have to put in more efficiencies. For all the moaning and groaning, the hospital system is running much more efficiently now than it did five or 10 years ago. There are plenty more efficiencies left in that system. I also believe that much of the health-care system could be farmed out on a private-tender competitive basis, hospitals included, and certainly the armies of bureaucrats who manage the system and so on. You could cut those requirements up into discrete lumps and put them out to competitive bidding. I think you might get some quite surprising results from it.

Frankly, the level of financial expertise in the Department of Finance disappointed me. I perceived a lack of appreciation of the seriousness of the problem and the risk of the problem spinning out of control, as indeed it has done. It was handled at two levels. The thinking focused mostly on the deficit, which was the politically visible issue. The thinking, in many instances, was a rather petulant view that the markets think this is just fine. They're buying this stuff up like there's no tomorrow. We have no difficulty whatsoever issuing the paper, ergo, there can't be anything wrong with issuing the paper or the market would figure it out.

I would take a different view. If you're willing to impoverish yourself and still able to pay what people are prepared to loan to you, it is your responsibility to ensure that any borrowing you're doing is within your means to accommodate it. But probably the more serious problem, in terms of both the Cabinet and the population at large, is a lack of appreciation of the balance sheet or the mountain of debt that is building up. When you're dealing with a clean balance sheet, namely little or no debt, the degree of latitude and flexibility you have is really quite exceptional. Indeed, in Canada we ran major deficits for 15 years before the system began to bite. I think there was a mind set that, goodness, you can just make this debt structure grow and grow and grow and it just basically looks after itself and there aren't any problems.

It's 10 years on since that period when I was in Ottawa and it's only now that the system is beginning to bite in earnest. One of the reasons it's taken so long to bite in Canada is that we're a very wealthy country. We're politically very stable, certainly by international standards. So there is a very high degree of confidence in Canada. If this were a more ragtag and poorer country, we wouldn't have gotten away with this. So to really ruin the balance sheet you have to start with an excellent reputation. You'd find that also works in corporate circumstances. Marginal corporations just can't pull off the full disaster financially, whereas if you happen to be a world-class, renowned developer, you could probably get enough debt onboard to go down in flames. So there is an ironic aspect to this, that you really need a good reputation if you're going to ruin yourself financially.

The irony is that a lot of the corporate entities that have done that are Canadian. We have a full record there. We're not alone, though. The difference of course is that in the private sector when these disasters occur, they then rebound to the expense of the owners and the investors and the lenders and you wipe the sheet clean. The problem when you get into one of these disasters in the public sector is that the debt's just piled on for future generations to look after. There's no equivalent of bankruptcy or default. We're still rolling the First World War debt, and it can still be identified, as the government borrowings roll forward and as outstanding bonds mature. So it really is quite different in the public sector.

The private sector is basically self-correcting. You don't find bankers as willing to loan to certain classes of people as they used to be, but with the governments, until your credit rating is devastated, basically nothing happens. Every time there's a mistake and you run a much larger deficit or a string of deficits, you simply put the debt on the shelf and continue issuing more to finance it, you know, borrowing money to pay the interest on money you borrowed before. And that doesn't fly in the private sector. It's an important distinction in that although the justice is a little rough in the private sector, it is self-equilibrating. In the public sector it just goes on and on until you are into a full-blown financial crisis, which we are skirting at this point.

Canada fell behind by the 1980s, I think because there was some element of having led such a charmed life for so long. We'd never had a major financial upheaval. We went through the 1930s much better than the United States. We kept our banks intact and the American banks went up in smoke. There was a higher level of confidence. Also, the generation of leadership from the 1970s forward were basically people with no close experience of the disasters of the 1930s, so you had a more carefree and less concerned aspect.

One thing that's often forgotten is that up to the late 1960s Canada had a worldwide reputation for financial rectitude. We developed in this small country world-class banking and insurance operations that operated worldwide. You don't get into that business if you have a reputation of being a financial village idiot. We had a wonderful reputation. The debt that had built up during World War II was basically worked off with the growth of the economy over the 25 years following the war. The average fiscal deficit in Canada between 1945 and 1955 was zero. Any small deficit was offset subsequently by small surpluses and we really were straight arrows. It gave us an exceptional financial sector, an extremely strong balance sheet. Then someone found the balance sheet and also found some lenders on Bay Street and Wall Street and the party began. Now the younger generation has to clean the mess of that party.

The most visible sign of that mess is our foreign indebtedness. In Canada since World War II, private sector savings have almost perfectly balanced the private sector investment. On that basis there was no need to borrow any money abroad. As Canadians we were saving enough to finance all of our commercial activity. What happened was that when we began to run these massive government deficits, we began to dip every year into the savings pool in Canada and take one-third to one-half of Canadian savings into government and use them for current consumption spending. The legitimate borrowers in the private sector who still needed the money were then driven abroad to borrow. We have an international debt now of about $375 billion, largely put on since the late 1960s. This country had no need to borrow abroad; we were a very rich country. The reason we borrowed abroad was because we insisted on running government deficits, which cannibalized our savings and drove our legitimate borrowers abroad; often the borrowers were Crown corporations, who should have been perfectly well funded in Canada. There's nothing that says you have to run to Wall Street to finance your utilities and so on. Of course the reason we had to go there was that the government had a prior claim on the savings to use for more socially sensitive programs.

If I had to clean up the mess, I would get rid of the universality. I would put a short leash on the political establishment with some form of balanced-budget legislation. In terms of getting rid of the universality, certainly the upper-income earners in the country are going to be quite hard hit, as universality can't be justified when a generation such as yours has to pick up this size of debt burden. You're going to have to be quite discriminating on where you throw your money around.

FILIP PALDA

An analysis of universal entitlements and taxes from an academic and member of the Fraser Institute.

L et me tell you about middle-class entitlements. You're looking at one of the biggest beneficiaries of those entitlements — me. I've been feeding off the government quite heavily for most of my life, and I'd call myself middle class.

My education has been almost entirely paid for by the government. I did a Ph.D. in the United States, paid for largely by the Canadian government. There was no reason for them to pay for that education; it paid for itself.

I haven't even begun to count all the entitlements that I'm grabbing. I take the train between Montreal and Toronto about once a week, and that train is subsidized; the Canadian government picks up half of the tab. I'm not complaining. I must pick up several hundred dollars' worth of subsidy every year, and it goes on. If I became unemployed, I'd pick up something like $735 a week for the length of my unemployment.

I'm not the only one who benefits from these middle-class entitlements. Students going to university are beneficiaries of a subsidy. They think their $1,500 tuition is paying for their education, but they're only paying about one-tenth of the cost. The rest is picked up by taxpayers. That's a middle-class entitlement because the people most likely to go to university are children from families with incomes above the national average. And we know, again, that an education pays for itself, so they don't really need this sort of subsidy.

You might call subsidies to the arts a middle-class entitlement, probably even an upper-class entitlement. There are subsidies to the CBC, and who listens to those radio programs? There are subsidies to all sorts of film production companies. Those theatre festivals at Stratford are consumed by people in the middle- to upper-income range. Any subsidized Canadian arts are largely consumed by the middle class.

Now, those entitlements are not a big hit on the budget. But there are lots of other examples in subsidies to business. Subsidies to farmers are probably a middle-class entitlement. If you want to be a milk farmer in Ontario or Quebec, you need to get a daily quota. That quota, just the right to produce milk, will cost you several hundred thousand dollars, not to speak of all the equipment you need to buy. To be a farmer is for the most part a big business. So that's another hidden middle-class entitlement.

I must mention unemployment insurance because it's geared to the amount of income you make. The more income you make, the more UI you're entitled to. It's funny; unemployment insurance goes mostly to families with incomes above the national average. There's also health care. We're starting to find out that middle- and upper-middle-income families tend to have better access to the Canadian health-care system because, through their social connections, they know doctors and people in the community who will get them to the front of the line. So health care is another middle-class entitlement.

I guess I could go on listing categories. I use the word "entitlement" because when people get something for a long time, they start getting used to it, and they figure, "Well, this is mine now." It becomes part of their background and they make all their plans around it. And when you build your life plan around something, you don't want the government yanking it away all of a sudden. That's why governments have so much trouble cutting these entitlements. I think of a recent federal budget, when my mother was very concerned that the old age pension was going to be cut. She figured it was her entitlement, even though she is from a middle-class family that has earned an income slightly above the national average. The thing is, her savings plans were set years ago. She decided to save less because she knew the government would take care of her. So when you start taking that away, you're upsetting people's plans.

We think that these entitlements go to the poor and that they should be directed toward them, but it's not the case. The idea wasn't really to take money away from the middle class and give it back to the middle class. This is really a shotgun approach aimed at the whole population. I ask myself, "Why is this happening? What's going on here?" And I think what's happening is a separation in Canadian politics between people's actions — and the consequences of those actions — and their entitlements. People don't pay up front for their services. And if you don't pay up front for your services, you're going to demand too many of them. When going into a grocery store or supermarket, people consider very carefully what they're going to buy because they know they're paying for it out of their hard-earned savings. The cost is right up front. But now imagine that you're an interest group, and you go into a government department store where you say, "I'd like to get an education at no cost." Of course you're going to lobby directly for it.

Somewhere down the line some taxes are going to go up, but you don't feel or see that immediately. Something is being cut there, the link between your demand for the service and your payment for the service. And when you cut that link, when you cut those nerves, you get irresponsibility. We teach children to be responsible. We tell them that their actions will have consequences. They also learn by direct experience. If you put your hands on the stove when it's burning, you don't do it more than once. You say, "Ow, that hurt! I'm not going back there."

That's not the case with the government and a lot of its programs. Another way to think about it is like a feast. If you go to the restaurant with 20 friends and everything's on a common tab, what's the point of holding back? You say, "Should I get a beer?" And if you do, the cost is spread evenly across 20 people. Everybody's sitting around this table, and they only pay a minute fraction of the costs of their actions because the costs are spread out. So everybody gorges, everybody overfeeds. And that's what happens in a country of 26 million or 27 million people. You're an interest group and you go ask for your subsidy. The costs, in taxes, are going to be spread wide over the whole country, so you're not going to feel the immediate cost. And everyone's acting like this.

Roughly 70 percent of government spending is taking from one portion of the population and giving to another. Government waste is probably just a very tiny part of the services budget. That's not where the hits are being taken. The hits are being taken in the transfers that make up 70 percent of the government's budget, that part that doesn't go to pay for interest on the debt. I'm thinking of welfare, old age security and unemployment insurance; and I should probably count things like education, which is considered direct government service. The activity of taxing and giving the money makes up that 70 percent. Middle-class entitlements make up as much as 40 percent of that.

Canada is a different case than the U.S., where they target the poor a lot more precisely. Here this notion of compassion exploded, so that now everybody's included. It's what they call "universal social services," everyone's entitled to the compassion. It's part of our caring way. But I'd argue that this isn't caring at all. This is actually the opposite of caring.

When I got my money to go to university, you'd think that was a noble thing. A student gets money to go further his education. But that money was forcibly taken from someone. Some hard-working man or woman out there had to earn that $40,000 or $50,000 which I pulled down to pay my way. I think we'd get a very different result if people could actually see the consequences of their demands on the government. Suppose that the government had told me, "OK, you get $50,000, but you're going to meet your designated taxpayer. You're going to have to say, 'I'm here. The government has given me a right to take so much money from you. Fork it over.'" If I were to meet my victim face to face, I'd think twice about doing this sort of thing. And if my victim could see me, they'd probably rebel at the thought of a middle-class boy being paid to get an education at one of the best schools in the United States. So the subsidy doesn't encourage compassion; it creates confusion and removes us from the consequences of our actions.

I think of this as warfare. We're not compassionate; we're at war with each other. During the Second World War we had bombers, decent, young Canadian men going over there and bombing Germany, killing hundreds of thousands of people. They could never have done this if they'd had to go over and face to face shoot every individual. All of modern warfare has evolved to remove the victim from the aggressor, and that's made it very easy. We've seen the result: mass destruction. In a sense we're getting mass destruction in our political system because the people asking for the services don't see the people paying for them. We can think of them as predator and prey, warrior and victim. And the people paying have a hard time knowing who's throwing that bomb. "Who's firing on me?"

Our government is like a veil that comes down between us. People aren't really satisfied with the political system, but they can't put their finger on it. What we need is some reform that will bring us that information, lift that veil, let us see whom we're firing on and who's firing on us. That's not to say that government is bad. Government doesn't have to be bad. It can be a fantastic instrument for preserving the law, for helping the poor. It's a very potent invention, but we're abusing it, we're not using it the right way. And who in the end pays for this?

There's an argument that we eventually pay for our entitlements through our own taxes. People say, "You benefited from those education subsidies, but you're going to pay your dues." And it's true, in the end you're going to pay. But no one's going to hold you to pay. Nothing says that after my education I have to live in Canada. Nothing says I have to work; I may decide to go on the dole for the rest of my life. There's no direct, gut-wrenching link between the service you get and the amount you're going to pay. So I don't even have to sit back and calculate it. When you remove the cost of my education to 15 or 20 years down the line, it's almost as if it didn't exist in my calculations. If I'm not serious about an education, the government is still out there, ready to fund me, even though I don't have confidence in myself. But if the government didn't fund me, I'd have to think really hard about my options, and I'd have to make a choice that was probably more in line with my abilities.

Credit cards came in big 10 or 15 years ago, and what you see is that people don't quite understand the link between what they're doing at Christmas, the shopping extravaganzas, and the bill that's going to come next month. There's just this separation. Psychologists have found that whenever you separate an act from its immediate consequence, people behave differently. They behave less responsibly. Take a lot of people reasoning like that and what you get is everyone demanding services from the government. And that's what's happening on a massive scale.

In Canada the top 40 percent of income earners, roughly, pays the majority of the taxes. The bottom 60 percent of income earners pays less than 60 percent of the taxes. This means that the bottom 60 percent, a majority, is getting, on paper at least, more spent on them than they're paying out in taxes. Some of those people would be upper-middle class. The top 40 percent probably starts at $70,000 to $80,000 per family. So the other people benefiting are by no means poor.

This is the sort of war we're in with each other, where there are all sorts of different groups in society putting forth demands and getting government services in return. What a lot of people don't see is that if somehow everyone could just settle down and make fewer demands on the system, the services would be lower, but their taxes would also be lower. It's like low-level warfare on a static front. I think of World War I, when the front didn't move more than five miles one way or the other for four years. The only things moving were bombs across the front. At the end of the war, the armistice, the bombs stopped flying, the front was still the same, the borders were still the same. The only thing that changed was that the destructive efforts halted.

We're throwing bombs on each other when we go out and demand services from the government, and that government has to turn around and forcibly remove money through taxation. So in a sense we're using the government to throw our bombs for us. In the end we're not doing ourselves any good because it's a closed community. We end up paying the cost of our mortar fire. The real war that we should be fighting is the war to help the poor, the people who can't help themselves. And we're not really doing that. We're focusing all of our firepower on the wrong targets, ourselves. We shouldn't be doing that.

How do we stop the middle-class entitlements? In the end it's the middle class paying for its own feast. And they're feasting too much because they don't understand. And it's not in any one individual group's interest to cut back. Suppose the students say, "OK, government, go ahead, cut our subsidies." The benefits aren't going to come back to them immediately in lower taxes. They'll be spread wide among the whole population. Chances are there's another interest group, maybe businessmen, who'd lobby to pick up the students' surplus, and who'd get it in a subsidy for their businesses. So they could give up their billions, but it's not necessarily going to be devoted to lowering taxes. It could pay for some other interest group. So we're in this bad holding pattern. How do we break the holding pattern?

Another problem with the current system is the loss of funds through transaction costs. I can give you the example of a business subsidy. For every dollar a business gets, it takes about 20¢ of government administration in collecting that dollar, deciding who gets it and administering the grant. So on every dollar you pay, 20¢ immediately disappears. The government collects the taxes, which siphon through this sort of filter back to you in the form of services, but there's less there in the end. This keeps circling.

Compassion is a great excuse for extending these services. There's this new wave of the last 20 years of everyone declaring themselves victims. Everyone's saying, "I'm entitled," to this and that. For example, farmers have a very powerful emotional appeal. Canadians believe farmers are worthy of support, and as a result they get it. Few people realize that many of these farmers are wealthy. A silo costs several hundred thousand dollars. It's a big, capital-intensive industry. So one of the reasons we're compassionate in the wrong way and to the wrong people is that the messages about the objects of compassion are wrong. A lot of people do not deserve the compassion they're being shown.

Another reason is that we've been promised a lot of good things from the government, a lot of services that are paid for by debt. It's very easy to accept that a universal social program is compassionate, "Let's be good to everyone," if foreigners are paying for it. The Italians, the Japanese and people in Latin America are lending us money so we can be compassionate to middle- and upper-income people. It's easy to be compassionate with somebody else's money. But the resulting debt means we're living beyond our means.

Our government is not confronting the entitlement problem. The silence is deafening. Even the most gung-ho political parties in Canada who are for cutting government spending will not come out and say that everybody has been feasting, getting kickbacks from the government and enjoying unemployment insurance, education, health care, subsidized arts and everything. All the little goodies we're getting are very hard to take away from us because we've gotten used to them. I don't want to say it's our candy; it's something we plan our lives around.

Imagine that a politician comes around and says, "Wake up, folks. We're going to end subsidies to education, we're going to end UI to anyone whose income is above some destitution level." Well, you're taking a lot of money away from a lot of voters doing that, and they don't have any guarantee that the government is going to lower taxes as a result. Politicians would have less problems confronting voters and telling them, "Cut this, cut that, everyone has got to tighten their belt" if we had some mechanism in our democracy that allowed everyone to suffer the same pain at the same time. For example, if we could have an across-the-board spending cut, where everyone is in the same category and is hit the same way, along with some rock-solid guarantee in our Constitution that the government will lower taxes, people could believe in the political system. Then they might be willing to say, "OK, cut back our services; we know you're going to cut back our taxes." But currently there's fear in every single group. Politicians divide and conquer. They create fear in certain groups: "You're going to lose your entitlement and you won't be compensated." I shouldn't say "politicians"; a lot of interest groups do that and whip up those fears. We can't really band together and act together if we don't have the right mechanisms in our democracy.

We need more sense of the connection between our tax dollars and the services we receive. To trace your dollar through the government would be a devastating exercise. The first step would simply be to see that you're paying that dollar. When the GST was introduced in 1990, that was an excellent tax because everybody hated it. Everybody could see they were being taxed. Brian Mulroney and his party were kicked out in part because people realized they were being taken. A recent example, which doesn't relate to tax, was the cable rate increase. For the first time people were made aware that they were being ruled over by cable companies who had a monopoly on them. And the cable monopolies went too far. They asked for too much, too fast. People stirred.

So the first step is simply making people aware that they're paying something. Then, in terms of tracing where it goes, the next step is giving people more power to decide how their money is spent. One way to do that would be to have 20 different categories on your tax form; your tax bill would be fixed, but you'd check off how much would go where. You may say, "I want $1,000 to go to welfare. I want $2,000 to go to education." In all of the categories of government spending you'd get to decide how much of your tax goes to them. This would be the most direct form of democracy, and people would see a link there. I'd know where my tax dollar went. I'd know my tax dollar had gone to the arts, if I'd wanted it to go to the arts; or that it had gone to education if I'd wanted it to go to education. So that's one way to re-establish the link. But to trace things the way they are right now, it's just a tangled mess, I wouldn't know where to begin.

The point of the welfare state hasn't been completely lost. Our poverty statistics are misleading because they're relative measures. They show how well off poor people are relative to others. They don't really measure your ability to buy certain goods, like a car, food and so forth. They're not hardship measures; they're inequality measures. But it's true that poverty is still with us and that we haven't made as much progress as we should have against this problem. The reason is not that middle-class entitlements have been sucking away money. Programs for the poor have also been growing at a phenomenal rate. The problem is that these programs give very poor incentives to people who are on them.

People on welfare are in the highest tax bracket in the country. If I'm on welfare and I go out and make some money, I lose my welfare almost one for one. If I make $100, I lose, almost directly, $100 from my welfare stipend. That's a 100 percent tax. I earn some money, then lose all of it by having my welfare taken away. So I'd say the incentives built into the system are perverse. They're designed to encourage people to stay in poverty.

Meanwhile we're racking up $500 billion to $600 billion of debt, and it's going to take 15 to 20 years to pay it off, if we start putting our minds to it. And the debt also has an effect on the economy today. Foreigners see our debt and figure that in the future it's probably going to be paid for by raising taxes. So should I put my money in Canada? Should I hold on to Canadian dollars? No way! That's why foreigners, when they realize that a country has a lot of debt, will get rid of the currency of that country.

If you double taxes in the next five years, the value of the dollar, its ability to buy things, will go down by half. So people today are paying because foreigners and investors are looking to the future. The future washes back to today. It's got reverberations because investors, either domestic or foreign, say, "I'm getting rid of Canadian dollars. I'm devaluing that dollar." So the people today feel the effects as well as those in the future.

The investment climate is stunting our growth and competitiveness, and those retirees who have their money in pension funds are taking a terrible beating. People who retire say, "But hey, I paid into this thing." It was very good for the people who retired in the last 10 to 15 years. If you retired in the first years of the Canada Pension Plan, you were withdrawing 22 times as much as you put in. If you retire today, in 1995, you will be pulling out something like six times as much as you put in. But my generation, 15 or 20 years from now, will be pulling out, if things go as planned, maybe 50¢ for every dollar we've put in. The situation will reverse because the number of the elderly is going to increase and there will be fewer in the young, working generation to support the elderly.

Decisions were made that we had no say in but are going to affect our lives. The people who took on those decisions 20 or 30 years ago weren't necessarily evil people. They were building a new and better Canada. They saw the social services coming. They thought Canada was becoming compassionate. They saw the construction. It was a good time because somebody else was paying for it. The concept of debt is still very hard for a lot of people to grasp. I've been studying this for a long time, and I really have trouble understanding what this debt means, although in my mind I know that the younger generation is going to end up bearing the brunt of it.

I guess I should feel pretty horrible about taking middle-class entitlements, but I don't. I just don't see the damage that I've done to other people. It's an abstraction to me. I don't see the fact that my demands were met with money forcibly taken away from others. You might call that a degeneration of morals, I don't know, or simply the fact that morals need some information to feed on. Humans need that emotional content. An intellectual understanding of what your actions are doing is not enough. So maybe that's why I don't feel as bad as I should.

I'd give up my entitlements if I knew that everyone else gave up their entitlements. I'll give up my subsidized train rides, my subsidized arts, my unemployment insurance, if I'm on it; I'll give up all of that if everyone else gives up their entitlements because then we're all acting together. We give up all these goodies and the taxes can go down.

You might also make me do it if you force me to come face to face with the people who are paying for these entitlements, if I had to go up to them and say, "Excuse me, you are my designated taxpayer, I'm taking this amount of money from you." And I'd be somebody else's designated taxpayer. Everybody would be irritated at each other if we saw what we're really doing to each other.

We expect a lot out of our government. We have tremendous faith, and it's a shame that it's been abused. That's eroding people's confidence in the government because they see that it isn't working. We don't have the proper controls. The government is a like a supertanker. It's moving along and you need some pretty sophisticated controls to get it where you want to go. The control system we have is democracy, but our democracy is ancient. It dates from about 100 to 150 years back, and it's hardly changed. It's like steering a supertanker with a sail. We need a modern guidance system to get this thing where we want to go. And the system would mean re-establishing this link so people can see where we're going and the consequences of their actions.

We could have referenda. There are all sorts of technology, and it's all been tested: you have a voter's card, you dial in your number for some question of the week and you make up your mind. We could also have constitutional limits on how much the government can spend. The point would be to remove responsibility from the hands of representatives, our elected MPs, and give it back more directly to the people.

Interest groups also represent us now. The problem with such representation is that you make your demands, but you don't quite know what you're getting, in many cases. It's like bringing your car to the mechanic. You say, "I want this fixed." The mechanic is going to interpret what a healthy car is; you don't know whether or not you really need that main brake cylinder replaced for $600. It's the same thing when we demand things of the government. For example, we wanted the government to run Ontario Hydro, but we don't know whether or not we're getting that at a fair price. Are we getting all of these government goodies at a reasonable price? That's very hard to see when you have too much representation and no standards of comparison. We elect a government once every four years, and all we can compare it to is what we had in the previous four years. We don't have a government next door where we could look and say, "How are they doing on the same budget?"

That's what you'd have if you went to a Swiss system, where you have lots of small communities. If you bring little Johnny to his school and he isn't doing well, you can look over to the next community and see how little Bobby or Susie is doing over there. You've got a standard of comparison. You can bring your government to account.

It boils down to information and visibility. That's what psychologists tell us is the basis of responsibility: number one is a sense of ownership; number two is information. Suppose I make a demand of the government. The cost is going to be spread wide, so I don't feel like I own it; and people don't have the information, they don't know what's happening. Cut those and you cut responsibility. And what we have now is a big, irresponsible government, and responsible people acting irresponsibly.

There are so many interest groups in Canada because there's so much up for grabs. Take the example of the plains of North America; in the days of the settlers you had all these buffalo grazing. Word got around and all of a sudden you had Buffalo Bill and God knows how many other people taking potshots, bagging 20 buffalo just to have their pictures taken with them because the buffalo were there for the taking. Here government is up for the taking. Like an open plain, government doesn't really belong to anybody. And grazing there are the resources of the economy.

For interest groups the stakes are enormous. Our government spends almost 50¢ of every dollar spent in this country. Politicians don't know how to spend that money. They get pushed either one way or the other, wherever the pressure is greatest. There are a lot of talented people in these interest groups who devote their lives to milking the government. So we're removing talent from productive uses in the economy. We're moving them away from making the pie bigger and putting them in a section of the economy where they're trying to cut the pie up.

When a country crosses the threshold, when it has too much pie-cutting, the economy starts to shrink rapidly. You get a very unstable situation. This is the problem with a lot of underdeveloped countries, where the best people are in the pie-cutting business, not in the pie-baking business. The Canadian government involves too many consultants, lawyers, etc., and I even consider myself a part of this wasteful process. I worked for a think tank for many years in Canada. I write all sorts of articles that analyze and ask what the government is doing. I spend my life, in a sense, lobbying. I could be out there, bringing some sort of product to a market or producing something, but I'm caught up in this battle. I think I'm on the good side, but really I'm not making anyone wealthier. I might be making a few people wiser, although maybe I'm kidding myself there.

It's very easy to think you're on the good side when you can see an immediate result from your actions. For example, I'm thinking of these interest groups who say, "Let's give money for regional development," or the politicians who get that grant for their region. They feel good because they've done some good for some people. What they don't see directly is that this grant is being sucked away from another productive part of the economy, and the money, in taxes, is knocking people out of work somewhere else. So it's easy to feel righteous and good in this system because it's so big and complicated now that we can't understand the full consequences of our actions.

Interest groups have this privilege of taxing other people in the economy. There are all sorts of hidden taxes that have nothing to do with government spending. Let me go back to that farmer example. You need a quota to produce milk in Canada; that means that the supply, the amount of milk, is very tightly regulated. It's restricted. When there's very little of something the price goes up. So what this quota does, in a sense, is give dairy farmers the right to tax you and me, the consumers. Dairy farmers get two types of help. The price of their goods is fixed by the marketing board. It's maintained high because they produce less than they would in competition. They also get a subsidy on top of that. But they can't pass this subsidy on to the consumer in the form of lower prices because their quantity is fixed.

But suppose they could. Suppose a business got a subsidy and could pass that subsidy on to the consumer. Would that be necessarily a good thing? I'd say no. If you have to give somebody a subsidy to do something, that means it can't stand on its own. That means you're going to produce too much of it. Suppose it costs $10 to produce a bushel of wheat, and the government comes along and gives subsidies to farmers and says, "Here's money. You can produce it at a cheap cost and sell it to consumers for $5." What you have then are consumers paying less than the real cost. They're being misled. They're encouraged to buy at what looks like a good price, but what they're really doing is destroying resources. That's what subsidies do; they destroy resources because they encourage people who don't value something to consume it. And the true cost of that consumption is being hidden. Think about it: if you value something at $10 and it costs $20 to produce, the end result is $20 cost, $10 benefit. That's destruction of resources.

In the old days the Romans were at least up front about taxes. You were a tax farmer, you bought your licence to tax, and you went out and taxed the population. Here it's a lot sneakier. It's like, "Let's help the farmers," and so forth, but what we've got is them taxing us.

Hydro companies like Ontario Hydro, BC Hydro and Hydro-Quebec charge very high rates, much higher than they should be charging. Why? They're monopolies and they represent an interest group, largely the workers and their union. Most of their benefits and profits come in high salaries. The average salary at Ontario Hydro is $70,000. That includes everyone, not just engineers and so forth. That has come about because they have the monopoly. You can only buy your power from them, or it's hard to buy it from anyone else. And they are taxing us.

There's a difference between that kind of tax and a more obvious tax. The GST, for instance, is an obvious tax. It hasn't changed in the years since it was introduced; it has stayed at the same percentage rate because everybody sees it. That's why it's a good tax — because it's a tax people hate. Those are the only kinds of taxes we should have because taxes are the price we pay for government, for the services we get, and we should know what price we're paying.

THE GUARDIANS

*Government Management or
Mismanagement from Participants
Who Should Know*

PETER MEYBOOM

A career public servant discusses the antagonism between political considerations and program effectiveness and efficiency.

I came to be involved in the Nielsen task force because Mr. Nielsen asked for me. I was deputy secretary of the Treasury Board at the time, and he asked my superior, Jack Manion, if I could be assigned to this task to help him conduct his program review, to organize whatever had to be organized and to take it from there.

Erik Nielsen had the image of being determined to slash government, but contrary to what many people thought, he was really quite idealistic about this program review. He felt that the new government had a responsibility to review all of the programs that had been in place for a long time, and to see whether or not they could be streamlined and rationalized. Expenditure reduction was not a primary task of the review. His magic words were "reason" and "rationality," and on that basis we proceeded.

Our direction was to emphasize programs that served the public. That suggested a very large number of subjects, so we broke down all government programs into families: the justice system, the environment, agriculture, etc. Social programs and the Department of Defence were not included. I don't know why they weren't. I think, and I'm speculating now, that they were perceived to be too complex. Ours was an enormously complicated review, and I think the new government felt that reviewing those other families of programs was enough of a task to start with. We undertook some 19 or 20 families of programs, and for each one a study team was appointed. They were mixed study teams, 50 percent private sector and 50 percent government people.

It was my job to provide logistics to the teams and to get government people to serve on them. The private sector involvement was largely organized through Darcy McKeough, the previous president of the Treasury Board of Ontario, the Management Board of Ontario and a private sector advisory committee. So Nielsen had a dual advisory system serving him: one segment from the public service through me, and one from the private sector through Darcy McKeough. There were 19 or 20 teams, with about 10 members per study team, amounting to some 200 people. And at any one time there were three study teams working.

Each team was given a set of terms of reference, which were all quite similar, the emphasis being on, "Can this program be done better? Should this program be done at all? Is there an overlap with the provinces?" Those were the kinds of commonsense questions. The guidelines were, "Be reasonable, be rational, show common sense and see what you can do." And there was no preset agenda. There was no goal that had to be met in terms of expenditure reductions or in terms of "These programs ought to go." The lack of specific goals showed that they approached this task without much prejudice. They wanted to have a rational review, and one way of doing that was the private sector advisory committee.

There was a very large group of private sector people, representing organizations such as the Chamber of Commerce and certain union groups, who met every Monday morning and reviewed the work done by the various study teams in the previous week. They reviewed the recommendations as they went forward to Mr. Nielsen and his committee, and changed them from time to time.

The interesting thing, at least to me because I had always worked in the government, was that within a week it was impossible in the mixed study teams to determine who was a member of the private sector and who was a member of the government. They really worked as a group with common goals in mind: use common sense, be reasonable, be rational and ask, "Should this program be done by the government? And if so, could it be done better?"

Mr. Nielsen and his committee relied very much on the work of these study teams. Each team had three months to do their work, which many said was too short. All in all, they needed about 18 months to do the entire review.

One innovative aspect of this study was its attention to tax expenditures; in other words, money that had not been paid to the state. The typical phrase is "tax loopholes," which may not be a fair description because they're all put in place for presumably good and valid reasons. The program review had the task of examining whether or not those reasons were still good and valid. Tax expenditures had never been examined in this fashion, but they were included this time for each program family.

In some instances we saw programs that had gone on past their time, but not in all instances. The reason was just the enormous variety of programs. If you look at government subsidies to agriculture or industry and compare them to a program like CAP (the Canada Assistance Plan), which is the federal contribution to provincial welfare payments, the programs are so entirely different. It's not surprising that people approached our task in their own ways.

The subsidy programs were probably the easiest to work with, from the point of view of accountancy principles and all that. For instance, "Should the Government of Canada give a large amount of money to big companies?"

The subtitle of our report became "Giving with Both Hands" because that was the view of the study teams, that the government was giving with both hands, through the tax system and by means of direct expenditures.

There was very little talk about the debt and the deficit in those days. There was a general concern that perhaps government expenditures were too high, but I did not detect, when we started in 1984, the kind of systematic concern that is now prevalent in Canada with respect to the annual deficit and the national debt.

Personally I have an intuitive feeling that we've lost the meaning of money. After the Second World War there was a large conference at Breton Woods in the United States. All the countries that had recovered, or were recovering, from the war met with the Allies to discuss world finances: the International Monetary Fund, how they were going to look at debt, how currencies were going to be established. Those countries and their economies had been destroyed. They came to a new, international understanding as to how the finances of the world would be conducted.

I think we have lost track of that a little bit. All Western countries, including the United States and Canada, now have debts. And it may well be that our whole notion of how all these debts relate to each other and how currencies relate to each other is maintained right now in a very artificial way, without a true understanding of what that dollar in your pocket means. I think it would be useful to have an international conference to re-examine the meanings of debt and money.

The books that one reads these days on the subject all predict doom and gloom, and yet the sky is not falling in. We are all well dressed, well housed and driving nice cars, so there's something wrong with the "doom and gloom" theory.

But the debt situation isn't healthy either. So where is that balance and who is thinking about it? I think that's going to be one of the big questions of the future. Simply saying that we have to restrain our expenditures and increase our taxes because our debt is killing us is not enough. You cannot simply say that everything is misery without offering some hope. That's going to be the political challenge for the future: to deal with the debt, but at the same time say, "However ... "

Debt is what made countries in Western Europe survive after the Second World War. Consider the taxes in Holland, for instance, where the minister of finance, Mr. Listing, was burned in effigy I don't know how often. He was a skillful financial person. The hope that there would be prosperity in the future made people pay the taxes, work hard and do all the things that were necessary then and may be necessary now. I think he subsequently became president of the International Monetary Fund. I'm not giving you a political view, it's a personal opinion. We are all thinking about this.

Mr. Nielsen's dedication to our task force was enormous. He had a variety of functions. He was minister of national defence, acting minister of fisheries and oceans, president of the Privy Council and chairman of the review. He had many tasks early in the Mulroney government, and he gave an enormous amount of attention to the program review. He firmly believed that the new government ought to know the content of its activities. He met in person with all of the team leaders, and he reviewed each of their teams' recommendations. He took his task as chairman of the committee extraordinarily seriously.

I think what people were most impressed by was the fact that while the image of Mr. Nielsen in Opposition in the House was as a fierce warrior, politically speaking, he went about this task in a very systematic, businesslike, rational manner, with extraordinary courtesy toward the study teams, be they public servants or people from the private sector. And everybody was impressed with his enormous grasp of detail. He read what was being written, even though it was a large volume of paper, and people were inspired by that.

What I hoped to get out of the task force experience was probably the same as what Mr. Nielsen hoped for; namely, a rational review of government programs. I had been in the Treasury Board for seven years at that time, so I knew a little bit about what was happening in government programs. The program area of the Treasury Board had not been my responsibility, but nevertheless, I'd learned by osmosis and assimilation. I realized that not everything being done necessarily makes sense. Many government programs are, as somebody once said, monuments to problems of the past; and those monuments seem to exist forever. So I thought it made sense to have a good look at all of that. But I didn't have any prejudices either. I felt that the teams had to do their work with clear terms of reference and then let the chips fall as they may.

I did know about some of the less useful programs from my work in the Treasury Board. There are many programs that people in the board speak of as perhaps having outlived their usefulness. And the same is true for departments; when you work in a department, you realize that certain things may have been useful in 1947 or 1957, but they're not necessarily useful in 1984.

The political "looking inward" of our task force had not been tried in Canada before, not to my knowledge. When Erik Nielsen was appointed, it had just been done in the United States, and I believe a similar exercise had been conducted in England. So it was a little bit fashionable to do this, and of course the current government is doing it again with the Honourable Marcel Masse. But at this scale and magnitude, ours was quite a novel enterprise.

From time to time there have been royal commissions (the Glassco Commission on government efficiency, for instance) and out of those earlier examinations, which may not have been called program reviews, came ideas that seemed to have some currency at the time and were not necessarily implemented. There were always ideas around. There's a theory of loose ends, that sometimes there comes a moment when they can all be brought together into a braid. The skill is to do that. And a program review provides an opportunity to bring all these loose ends together and re-examine whether or not it is possible to make them into a braid. For instance, the proposal that is now being made by Mr. Peterson's parliamentary committee to tax gasoline was made by Mr. Crosbie in his famous budget, when he said, "Let's have some short-term pain for long-term gain." That is an idea that has been around for some time and may have new currency under the present circumstances.

Our report said too much attention in program design has concentrated on accountability and in allowing every department its place in the sun, and not enough on service quality. There was a group in the Treasury Board a few years prior to the Nielsen task force, dealing with service to the public. It was felt by that group that departments had become too inward-looking and were too concerned about how to defend their programs to the Treasury Board, how to design program structure, how to administer things internally, and were losing track of why a program was implemented in the first place. In other words, it was felt that service to the public had been suffering. And I think that text from our report was a reflection of that feeling. Every period, every three or four years, has its own theme in government, and the theme of the early 1980s was service to the public. You may find that strange, but nevertheless it was the truth.

I'm not sure the government was receptive to our task force work. But I think that no politician is receptive to this kind of review. I remember Mr. Mulroney saying, "Program review doesn't get you many votes." Political reasoning is different than accountancy reasoning or scientific reasoning; it has its own rationale. The criteria used by politicians to say whether something is good or bad are different than the criteria used by an accountant or a program analyst. So while in many instances there was agreement between the politicians and the review teams that certain programs ought to be revised or perhaps even abolished, that agreement was by no means universal. And there were some very sharp clashes, some of which have lasted until today.

An example that comes to mind is the dairy subsidy. There was an enormous debate about it and an excellent analysis on the part of the agricultural team, truly first class. But subsequently the program review board and the ministers in Cabinet did not agree with the outcome of that analysis. The analysis said that there was really no need for that kind of subsidy, and the ministers didn't agree with that conclusion. So we are still talking about the dairy subsidy today. It may be a bit naive to say that the government maintains the dairy subsidy to keep Quebec happy; I don't think things are really done that way. But it is a political reality that 70 percent of Canadian dairy products originate in the province of Quebec. So that means something, that's an economic power of some kind, and with it comes political power. But looking at it in the broader context, dairy and agricultural subsidies are a problem in Europe and the United States. They're a problem in GATT. That's why we are talking about them now, not in the Canadian context, but in the international context of the General Agreement on Tariffs and Trade.

The Chamber of Commerce, as you may know, gave a report card from time to time. It had shown a great deal of faith in this exercise, but it might have been disappointed in the results. After a while it stopped issuing report cards, which probably shows the disappointment on its part. Some of its expectations might have been a little naive.

Guessing as to the government's commitment to implement our changes is a difficult question, a question of conscience. If you approach this kind of work with the internal belief that it's not going to go any-where, then you shouldn't start. You must have some form of belief or idealism that it makes sense to do it. That was my conviction: that it made sense to do it. But at the same time, if you take it personally every time a recommendation is not accepted, you cannot break down and cry because you simply won't be able to survive. So you have to be real-istic about that. And of course, in the final analysis you have to respect the political decisions. Whether or not you personally agree with them doesn't really matter.

We suggested other major cuts besides those to the dairy subsidy. There's a host of agricultural and transportation subsidies for grain shipped to the West and to the East in order to give a fair chance to farmers in Western Canada who are far away from either coast. Those subsidies were put in place for a good reason, and people got used to them. The whole economic structure and personal planning is based on

191

those subsidies. So we are still talking about grain and transportation subsidies. I have not followed the discussions lately, but one of the grain subsidies was in the news today. I'm not surprised about that.

Certain aspects of the task force were very much a success. There was a minister appointed at one point. I think it was even Barbara McDougall's first portfolio as minister of state to deal with regulatory matters. The way that government dealt with regulatory reform as a result was very helpful, and a great deal of housekeeping improvement came out of the regulatory review. A very great deal of improvement was made to the way that government deals with real estate. Government has an enormous amount of real property, and every department was hanging on to that, so a bureau of real property was created and it was a very useful step. Then there were dozens of smaller recommendations that hopefully added up to improvements of one kind or another.

The regulatory labyrinth in government was truly horrendous. Before a department could issue a new regulation, it took more than a year in order to get through all of the ramifications of the internal bureaucracy, and sometimes that simply made no sense at all. With tremendous delays and old regulations still on the books, the whole regulatory arena was really a jungle. But if nothing else, the Nielsen task force caused that jungle to be cleaned out. Now, jungles grow over again, and I don't know what the present situation is, but in those days there was a very dedicated and competent group of people who inherited these recommendations and did a lot of excellent work.

I learned a lot about democracy: that politicians have their own rationale and that as a bureaucrat one doesn't necessarily agree or understand that rationale. It's like the old saying: "Two cheers for democracy! It doesn't deserve three cheers, but it's better than anything else."

In a letter he wrote to the Chamber of Commerce, the president of the Treasury Board, Don Mazankowski, wrote that "program review will remain an integral part of our mandate to improve efficiency, eliminate waste, cut red tape and reduce the deficit." It was written with good intentions. That was something that was not necessarily attainable; we know what happened to the deficit in the years subsequent to that letter. But I presume Mr. Mazankowski wrote that letter in his capacity as president of the Treasury Board, and to be blunt about it, he had no choice but to write what he wrote. That was his task. Every year when the Estimates are presented to Parliament, individual analysts go through departmental programs, item by item. Of course the departments always try to build up things, and the Treasury Board tries to keep them down. So it is fair and true for Mr. Mazankowski to say that program review is an ongoing government responsibility. Program review, in one form or another, has taken place ever since the Treasury Board came into existence. And from that point of view there was nothing new about our work. What was new about it was the tremendous visibility and political emphasis that were given to it. Whether or not that momentum stayed high is another matter.

I don't think it stayed very high, but nevertheless, it was the first time, I think, in the history of the Canadian government that a group of ministers had been given the explicit task to look at the entire government. And that was the novelty of it, which raised tremendous expectations. But that letter states the truth. The Treasury Board has always been doing what that letter says, and that's really its proper task. So I'm not surprised by what Mr. Mazankowski wrote.

If the task force recommendations had taken effect, well, there would no longer be a milk subsidy, but that is too easy an answer. In our day-to-day life I'm not sure there would have been much difference because things have come along that have necessitated additional government expenditures. In fact, I was of the view when the entire program review was finished that government expenditures were bound to increase for one reason or another, forever and ever. That was probably too pessimistic a view.

Look at the breakdown, prepared by the Department of Finance, between debt charges and program expenditures. The statistics and graphs that I've seen show that the program expenditures are steady, or may even have declined a little bit, but the debt charges are increasing and therefore the total expenditures are increasing and the annual deficit is increasing. The program expenditures, which are really the government programs that Mr. Nielsen was concerned about, have been brought under control. But something on top of that, over which the government has no control, has negated that.

So would the world be different if all of the Nielsen recommendations had been implemented? I don't think so because many of the influences that we live under did not even originate in Canada, let alone in our federal government. I think that having a review of this kind done from time to time is useful in any event, regardless of the implementation of all the recommendations. It's good to examine what you are doing and whether you still want to do it that way. You may even conclude that you want to continue doing it that way, for reasons that have nothing to do with accountancy, accountability and dollars and cents, but that make sense in the political terms in which the program was created in the first place.

There is often a collision of concerns in politics. I think the most prominent one was the dairy subsidy. And I hate to come back to the poor dairy subsidy, but that was the first time that I really saw the collision between what everybody thought was an outstanding piece of economic analysis and the stark political reality that ministers are not interested in cutting the subsidy for their own reasons. And that was just it, and you have to accept that. Ministers are in charge of these things, not technocrats.

Perhaps that's a good thing too. When politicians make these kinds of decisions, their masters are the electorate; not in the sense of the taxpayer, but in the sense of their constituents. Would they be re-elected or not? That question was often a very strong force. I presume that is one of the goals of every government: to stay in power, to be re-elected, to consider what could jeopardize it being re-elected and to consider whether or not it made the right decisions. History, in this case, has shown what the electorate thought. But nevertheless, that was a very strong motivating force.

The cornerstone of Canadian politics is the constituency. A member of Parliament first and foremost represents a constituency. Then that MP becomes a minister in the Cabinet and has to think at the national level, but there is always the responsibility to his constituency, which may make it very difficult for him at times to combine those two roles. In fact, he may be in conflict. On balance, I think that the constituency concerns outweigh any other concerns and concern for the constituency can definitely hamper change. It is a difficulty that stems from our whole electoral system, the way we elect parties in power on the basis of a constituency rather than on the basis of numbers of people who vote for a particular party. The problem may be even more profound and structural than the constituency concern. It may be a deeper issue in the very structure of our democracy.

When I was in the Treasury Board I attended meetings every Thursday, and over time I got to know how ministers of the board would react. The interesting aspect of the Treasury Board is that the ministers tend not to be the big program spenders. You will not see a minister of defence on the Treasury Board, or a minister of industry. It has ministers from either smaller ministries or service departments, and on the whole those ministers are able to bring a certain amount of objectivity to bear.

But in the government in general there are all these regional concerns that have to be taken into account, and whether these concerns make sense from an economic point of view really doesn't matter much. If there is a so-called regional concern, the government feels that it has to deal with it, regardless of the economic or financial aspects. I think that is probably a reality of a big country. It seems that Canada is a difficult country to govern because of the extraordinary differences between regional interests. Such interests are on a larger scale than the constituency interests, but not necessarily national. A national government can say that all regional interests are automatically national interests, and how then do you balance all of that? That is the magic trick that politicians in this country have to perform. And they are struggling with it.

Paul Dick

A former minister of supply and services talks about parliamentary scrutiny of expenditures and government accounting and procurement practices.

I was elected first in 1972. I was here for 21 years and I left after the election in October 1993. My first 12 years were in opposition. My first 14 years were as a private member, not in the Cabinet, so I was involved a lot in constituency and committee work. I was two years as parliamentary secretary and then I was seven and a half years as a Cabinet minister. I've had the opportunity of seeing government from just about every angle.

Parliament hasn't changed so much as the politics have changed. I mean politics on the outside, how the newspapers and the media would treat parliamentarians and politicians. At one time it was considered a very important and noble sort of profession, and I would say today it's not thought of too highly. I think this is unfortunate because you're not going to get good people into politics for that and a variety of other reasons. However, inside, a lot of things have evolved. They've improved in many ways. Committees are much stronger and more independent than they used to be. Members of Parliament are about the same in the way that they adhere to party discipline and follow the leads of the whip and so on. The Canadian system is slowly maturing but it hasn't matured into being as flexible a situation as, say, Parliament in London.

The most obvious way I see the Canadian system as being immature is when the government introduces a bill. The government expects the Senate is going to pass that bill, I mean, the Senate is supposed to pass the government's bills. If it ever stops a government bill, then it becomes front-page news. Whereas in England the House of Lords stops government bills from passing quite frequently. In other parliaments outside of Canada, houses frequently don't pass government bills, but here it is supposed to be rubber-stamped.

In Canada you're not supposed to be independent. You follow the party line in most cases; there are a few rare exceptions. If you don't follow the party line, then the press will start saying the party is split and so on and that puts extra pressure on you to follow the party line. So there's not very much breaking of party ranks when it comes to votes. In England and Australia and other countries, breaking party lines in voting is not an everyday occurrence, but it's not infrequent. Whereas in Canada it's quite infrequent.

The free thinkers and debaters in the Canadian parliamentary system are not necessarily muted. It depends how strong they can be. Quite frankly, the free thinker really has their opportunity in caucus on Wednesdays. Caucus can be sometimes a real free-for-all, I'm sure in all parties. That's where real, independent views are expressed and the positions are hammered out. Sometimes you can be a little bit independent on committees, but then governments control committees if there's a majority government. So you can be moved on and off a committee if the government doesn't like what you're doing. They control the majority, the committee, so all of a sudden you find you're no longer a member of that committee. Those sorts of things are the games that government plays to enforce party discipline.

The official Opposition has taken on a different role during this whole rise of party politics and I think a lot of that came out of the Diefenbaker/Pearson time when Diefenbaker and Pearson were at loggerheads. Diefenbaker had a very strong dislike for Mr. Pearson and it became so that if you're in Opposition, you're there to oppose what the government is doing. You oppose them and don't let them introduce and pass their agenda. That way you can say at the next election that they haven't done what they promised to do. I heard that when I was in the Opposition as a Conservative and I was told that's what the Liberals did when they were the Opposition to the Mulroney government. That's where you get sort of a rat-pack attitude.

When they came into government the tables turned, except they didn't have any experienced parliamentarians to oppose them because they were under the situation that we have right now. The Liberals didn't get as much resistance and the opposition parties just opposed for the sake of opposing, which is ludicrous, frankly.

The principal change took place in 1969 when they stopped doing the Estimates in the House of Commons in what was called the Committee of the Whole. It had been a way of slowing down government by tying them up in their Estimates for day after day after day; therefore the government couldn't pass their legislation. The first year of the Trudeau administration, they changed the rules of the House of Commons by invoking closure. They moved the Estimates out into committees, outside of the House and the standing committees. They put a phrase in the rules which is very interesting: they could discuss the Estimates in these committees and should vote on them, but if they did not vote on them, then they would be deemed to have passed by, I think, June 15.

As soon as you deem something to be passed, everybody loses interest in it. So people started arguing and discussing policy at the standing committees, but they never discussed the finances of a department anymore. We've lost public scrutiny of Parliament. It's from that time on that our deficits got out of control.

It was the first year of the Trudeau government when the rules were changed. It was an attempt to stop the road-blocking of Parliament, tying up Parliament by keeping the Committee of the Whole from doing the Estimates. That was done to great extent in the 1960s. It was actually started, I think, by Pickersgill and the so-called "Four Horsemen" against the Diefenbaker government in 1962, 1963. They just tied it up on procedures and especially by doing the Estimates. They were trying to give more parliamentary time to consider other things and get the Estimates out to some other form, but in actual fact they got the Estimates hidden away in a closet and everybody lost interest.

The back-bench and the committee MPs did not become insignificant because they now could discuss a lot on policy. They could figure out resolutions and other things of this nature, but nobody was taking a look at the beans anymore. Nobody was taking a look at what was happening with the dollars and cents. As a matter of fact, the Estimates today are in a form which 99.99 percent of the population in this country haven't a clue how to read. It's a third language. It's not French; it's not English. It's accounting but nobody understands it. You at least understand the statements of Bell Canada or Alcan or one of the banks, but nobody except bureaucrats understands the public accounts and the Estimates procedures.

Even accountants don't understand this accounting language. As a matter of fact, it got to be a little issue that I was trying to develop at one stage. I got the managing partners of each of the six major accounting firms in the Ottawa area to come and sit on the committee with me and help me try to develop this theme. Five out of the six said that they did not understand the government's accounting or the government books and they could not read them. The other one admitted that he did understand it, but he had worked in government for 10 years. So if they don't understand it, I don't know who does. The bureaucrats are the ones that draw them up.

I invite anybody to go and take a look at the Estimates, which is the estimate of what the government is going to spend before the year comes into play. And then we hear about the budget. We hear that there's going to be cuts but there is no other accountability that is publicly available until you get the public accounts, which is a year after. Now, it's a bit late when it's a year after. The money's already spent, but the system of doing the public accounts does not even correspond to the Estimates. Quite frankly, the government's accounting system would be considered illegal, I think, if you happened to be a corporation in the private sector: you would not be allowed to deliver statements the way the government does its accounting. You'd be out of business.

The government is allowed to because it hasn't become an issue. I tried to develop, at one stage, a talk with ordinary citizens — both the average and the very educated person — about accounting. Well, you know, as soon as you start, 50 seconds later half your crowd is going "zzzz," having a bit of a sleep. Accounting is kind of a dry subject to try and make sexy and make interesting, yet it runs every company, every organization, every volunteer group. They all have their accountants. They all have to do a little balance sheet, an income statement of where their expenditures are.

Except I've never seen an income statement for expenditures in the Government of Canada. I've never seen a balance sheet in the Government of Canada. There aren't any. The way the government reports its accounting doesn't make any sense to the average person.

I'd call it incomprehensible; fraudulent is going a bit too far. You have to have *mens rea* to be fraudulent. But it's a way of disguising it so that the journalists can't understand, so that the business schools can't understand. Think tanks that would like to look into it do not really understand what the government is spending its money on. Even the Estimates are so general in nature. Yet I wanted to get it out in a way that the public would understand. If Bell Canada has to put out an annual report every year and have statements in it, well, why doesn't the Government of Canada give its shareholders, i.e., the taxpayers, a balance sheet or an income statement every year? Let the people take a look at it in a really understandable way. And it can be done. At one stage I worked with an accountant, an assistant deputy minister in my department. We developed a way which was pretty sensible. As a matter of fact, a number of the public servants in the department, because we switched the accounting in the Department of Supply and Services over to it, came up to me and said, "Hey, this is an awful lot better. We can use this as a tool in helping us to manage our own section better." Because it's out of control, I think.

You cannot even compare the cost expenditures in one department to another. You cannot do that. If you're dealing in the private sector you have ratios and comparisons: the debt-equity ratio, the cash-flow ratios, the quick-asset ratios. You compare what one pulp and paper company is doing with another pulp and paper company and you bring them all down to these ratios. Then you can compare and have a pretty good idea. You cannot compare one department to another because they do accounting in a different way. Every department has its own accounting system. At one stage I wanted to get my hand in on this because I was getting interested and we were trying to cut government. So I asked my deputy minister, "What's the overhead cost just for running head office here in Ottawa?" We had 138 offices across the country in those days, and I said, "Just to maintain our head office, what's the cost?" He looked at me and he shook his head and said, "I don't know." I said, "Can you find out?" He says, "Yeah, I'll find out, I'd like to know that too," and he came back a couple of months later and said, "You know that question you asked me, of how much it costs to run head office here. I found out and it was shocking: 27 percent of our budget goes to run head office. I'll have that down to 20 percent by the end of this year." And he did.

So my next question was, because another department I happened to know was entirely different, I asked, "How do we compare our head office operations to something like Health and Welfare?" So he went off and came back and said, "Paul, we can't compare because they have a different accounting system. Our head office operations were 27 percent, now we're getting them down toward 20, but they only declare them at seven percent over at Health and Welfare. Out in Tunney's Pasture they have a giant of a building. I know they have a big head office but they bury their head office costs in the only two programs they have." I said, "What do you mean two programs at Health and Welfare? They have all kinds, the Aboriginal programs and Métis programs and all the various types of programs they have." He said, "No, they only have two programs — health and welfare."

So it's hard to do comparisons if they won't tell you what the programs really are. They should be divided down into their sections. They should all be in the same accounting system so you could compare the management costs of this program versus the management costs of that program. What is the percentage of people in managerial situations in this program versus the percentage of people in managerial positions over in that program? If you had comparisons like that, just like in the private sector, you could start comparing one to the other. You could make people accountable because if you had, for example, travel costs averaging seven percent in all programs and you came across a program that had travel costs of 27 percent, you could say, "Uh oh, this guy's out of line. Excuse me, Mr. Director General, can you account to me why you're 27 percent when the average is seven percent?" But they can't even do that because every program has its own accounting system. It's even worse than just every department. And that's the letter I got from the deputy minister of the Treasury Board, who was in charge. He said we shouldn't change it and I thought we should.

Estimates in the House are all passed within an hour, in one evening. You know, billions of dollars worth. You just stand up and the Estimates are passed. It's quite laughable when you think that we're supposed to be actually looking at the public purse because we don't. Nobody does. I realized that but I was interested in some other areas. I was doing my own constituency. I was working hard trying to maintain that. I was working in areas on regional development because part of my riding was under regional development in those days.

I was deputy House leader at one stage, so I was involved in other things and I didn't get back to really looking at the beans, as the accountants would call it, until I got into a ministerial position in Finance and said, "Well, this doesn't make sense." It's not like when I took accounting at university. It's not like when I was taking business courses; they had ratios to compare one company against another or one industry against another. I started trying to ask about it, but the government doesn't do that because they don't have the data in any form that is intelligently useful. It's just not in a useful form. If it was in a useful form, then we could get critiques from political science departments, from the business schools, from the Fraser Institute, the C. D. Howe Institute and a lot of other knowledgeable people, like journalists, who could make the comparisons and they could help keep the country running in a smooth and intelligent manner by doing all these comparisons.

Kenneth Dye, former auditor general, said Canada's accounting practices are based in the quill pen and ink age. He said they're so antiquated they have to be revised. We have accounting practices today that you could not get away with having in the private sector. We have an accounting system in Canada for the Canadian government today that has allowed our accounts to get out of control. People do not keep an eye on how the dollars and cents are being spent and it does not serve the purpose. They are old-fashioned types of accounting systems. They're just not modern.

There are no priorities in spending. That was the other area that I wanted to get into and that is to publicly declare the prioritization of each program within each department; but I didn't get very close with that one at all. If I couldn't get one accounting system, I couldn't get the prioritization because you can only do prioritization when you have one accounting system that all programs have to adhere to.

If there are no priorities in government, everything's a priority and that's part of the problem. This is the classic situation where you sometimes hear governments say, "No, this is a greater priority." They make a political statement, not an accounting statement, not a business statement — they make a political statement. But you'll notice that over the years governments frequently say, "We'll have a three percent across-the-board cut." That's because they haven't prioritized which are important programs and which are not important programs.

Governments or the public servants cannot, or are unwilling, to make those decisions. In fact, they are not equipped to make those intelligent decisions because they don't have an accounting system that is the same for all programs. So they can compare one program to the other to see if one is spending 40 percent on overhead versus another which is only spending 10 percent on overhead. Well, maybe the one that's spending only 10 percent on overhead is a more important program. It's part of the equation but if you don't have that material with you, then you cannot prioritize.

Therefore we never prioritized in government. They do the old three percent across the board, two percent across the board, five percent across the board, and it stops everybody from being accountable. It just means we whittle down all the programs a little bit. The trouble is, the good, well-run programs are whittled down and the fat programs, which have all kinds of extra fat in them, are only whittled down by the thinnest amount. You're penalizing the good programs as well as letting the fat programs off.

The term "prioritization" is, I think, important. Everybody prioritizes things in their life. What is the most important thing? Is it buying the house or a car or a cottage? You make a decision on what is your most important. In government, what's your most important program? It probably is health or old age pensions. What's of a lesser priority? Maybe it's the New Horizons program or maybe it's some other type of a program that is not nearly as important as health or senior citizens' pensions. Those are probably the two highest priorities and probably everything else is of less priority. I think to prioritize all the programs would take some political will and courage, there's no doubt about it. But if you could prioritize them, then you could say, "Well, we've got enough money to pay for the first 55 programs but these last 13 programs, we've run out of money. Do we have to have these programs? If we do, we're going to run a deficit and it'll be this amount." It forces you to make that decision of going into deficit based on which programs are of a lower priority but still important enough that you have to run a deficit. We don't do that today. This country has not done that for decades and decades and decades. We have been running fiscally out of control. We just have not had the accounting systems to handle what we're doing — or the will.

The politicians have to take some blame. I think the public servants have to take some too. They're the ones that love the system and they keep enforcing it. I think the press, well, everybody takes a share of the blame because nobody's demanding the accountability. They aren't demanding the politicians to be accountable to the public for spending the money in this way, that way and so on. And the politicians aren't demanding that the public servants be accountable to them for putting the Estimates together.

Remember, the public servants put the Estimates together. They're planting intentions for the next year and that's where we get some real lulus now and again. Under CIDA (the Canadian International Development Agency) we financed the victory arch in Algeria. Public Works, about six or eight years ago, was building a nuclear bomb shelter in Fredericton when we were past the nuclear-bomb-shelter stage. That was back in the 1960s, so there are a few lulus that creep in now and again, and nobody ever picks them out.

The bureaucrats get away with this because nobody has insisted on a better program. The politicians haven't, the people of Canada haven't and the press hasn't. Some people have tried to get a better accounting system into government and I know of people that the bureaucrats have pushed out, fired. Retired them because they don't want the system changed either. If the system stays cloudy and murky and in a great big sort of fog, then they have no accountability. They're accountable to nobody and they can just carry on and they like it that way. Some of them do. Not all of them. Because I know some public servants who really are frustrated and would like to have more accountability. They're seriously dedicated, but their voices get lost.

Bureaucrats don't want to have a serious oversight of accounting books. That's the biggest trick. If you sit down with the government books and they're put together by public servants, you will not understand how much is paid in salaries in that department or what programs that department has. You cannot tell how much is being paid in travel expenses. You won't find that out. None of those figures are available by looking at the government books that the public gets.

Now, that information is available in data behind the scenes, which the auditor general might get. I talked to the present auditor general and he said, "Well, it's not the best system, but for seven years we've been trying to say that they should have a better accounting system and our message doesn't get carried by the media." That's because the auditor general is a 24-hour wonder. He comes down with a 400- or 600-page book, which he's got 500 people putting together, and it's tabled. For 24 hours all hell breaks loose. And after that nothing happens. So the press goes after the six big headlines, the juiciest stories. They don't get into the fundamentals.

There are two auditors general in this case. The present one and the previous one were both talking about the accounting system and how there should be a better accounting system. But that gets missed in the shuffle because it becomes academic, not very sexy and not very interesting. It's much more interesting to say, "Hey, we found that they had 200,000 square feet of unused office space which cost us $14 million." People can sell that and buy it, and they can see it and they can feel it and they can chew it. You can't do that when talking about accounting.

Over my 21 years in government the term "policy" has come to mean "to expense." What we have to do is get rid of policy people. Every time you have policy people in government, they are dreaming up new policy, which means more expenditure of money. We do not have cost accountants. We do not have control on the budgetary system and I know how it has been built up over the years. I've talked to people who were in the Trudeau government, the Cabinet ministers, about how figures meant nothing. They were just told, "I don't care if there's money there, go out and develop some policy for this." In developing policy, if you come up with a new program, you have got to fund it and throw some money at the problems.

I don't know if there are any whiz kids in the Government of Canada. I think they're absent. I don't think we have any. I guess the policy people were the whiz kids in that sense. They took real control in the 1970s. The public service of Canada was growing at five percent a year under the Trudeau/Pitfield era. Pitfield was the clerk of the Privy Council at that time and they lost all control. I still think the public service is really trying to get back to the high-calibre public service that Canada had prior to that. They don't know how to get back to it because all the people who were senior bureaucrats came in and grew up in the 1970s when things were out of control. I think that the country needs a good dose of outside cost accountants and serious private sector managers sprinkled in.

I found that the senior bureaucrats didn't deliver nearly as much as they should have. Some of them are excellent, but a lot of them did not deliver nearly as much as they should be able to deliver. A lot of them got tied up into policy and they forgot to look at the dollars and cents. We've got the deficit and we've now got the debts to prove it, and young people are going to pay it off.

I think it's a moral issue. That's one of the things I failed at — I wasn't able to bring the principle of cost accounting for policies and programs to fruition, in a sense, although I tried in the last five years. I talked to Wilson about it. I talked to Mulroney about it. I talked to Don Mazankowski and he recommended it to the new prime minister, Kim Campbell, and she actually announced that she was going to introduce that during a Calgary speech in the election campaign. But of course history shows that she was defeated. Again, the bureaucrats took over a new government and that sort of agenda has disappeared. We have to get back to it eventually if we're going to have sound good government in this country.

The elected representatives are there to represent the people. It's become very much an ombudsman sort of a role. They don't have that much of a say in government policy and expenditures because they don't know what they're spending the money on. They don't know how the money is being spent. We have to get the accounting in a way that people will understand. We have to let the parliamentarians go back to counting the beans, that's the dollars and cents, and force the public servants to be accountable for how they're spending the money and on which programs.

In my 30s, when I first came here and I was busy doing some other things, I really wouldn't have got into the crunch on dollars and cents and cutting budgets and so on. During the Mulroney government I started to appreciate this more. Perhaps I should tell you that just before Mulroney was stepping down and just before Kim Campbell took over, I made a couple of speeches on getting one accounting system right across government. This was one of the ways that the central hierarchy of the public service can try and control things: I have a four-page letter from the senior bureaucrat in charge of government accounting systems, who said mine was a very foolish idea. He said each manager of each program should be allowed to create his own accounting system as they do at the present time. I would be interfering with their managerial responsibilities if I tried to impose one accounting system on all of them. I just had to laugh and think of some large newspaper chain like Ken Thomson's newspaper. Do you think each newspaper runs its own accounting system? I think all 170 newspapers have the very same accounting system, and if a guy gets out of line, the editor or publisher, they can see it in the figures. The figures show up and that's how they maintain profitability and control.

Also, during the time I made these speeches some other people inside told me they thought it was kind of laughable. It was suggested by some senior bureaucrats that maybe I should be dismissed from the government because I was speaking out on an accounting process which the government had adopted. Since I was speaking against the government as a Cabinet minister, I should be dismissed from the Cabinet. But a wiser head said, "Look, there's going to be a new prime minister in two or three weeks, let's not rock the boat." So the fact that it was even mentioned shows how the public servants will go to some lengths to try and maintain the control in a mysterious system, a mythical system that has no meaning to it. But it also allows them to avoid accountability.

I know of examples where they have fired and let go and forced out of the public service other accountants who wanted to have a good accounting system. They've sort of edged them out and pushed them out because they didn't want those people left in government since that would force the public servants to be accountable. So that's where I think some of senior management in the government is a lot weaker than it should be.

The tendering process was that anybody who wanted to sell to the Government of Canada had to apply to the Department of Supply and Services to get on a source list. If you then were able to get on a source list, you may receive a tender. I said, "This is ridiculous. Why can't everybody in Canada put in a bid?" Well, there are reasons you can't do this and they gave me 15 reasons. I said, "Look, why don't we change it all." I had in mind changing to a system like they have in the United States with the Business Commerce Daily, where all tenders are published. I said, "Why don't we do that, Mr. Minister?" It would take at least eight years to do that and they didn't want to do it. The public servants didn't want to do it. I was talking to the deputy minister. I said, "Well, I think we could." Then somebody suggested we go electronic, since this is the modern age. So we started with a small section called the scientific procurement because they all used computers anyhow. So we put that on the computer and then we started to expand it.

Actually, within three years we got most of the government bidding on a computer system that we called open bidding. We got great compliments from industries across the country that said they never knew we were bidding for things like that before and now they have a free opportunity to put in a bid. It made it a much fairer system. The other way, it was being kept in somebody's drawer somewhere and you never knew if it was secret and out of sight or a free and open bidding system.

As a matter of fact, if you got on the source list — and you had to make sure you got on the national list and the regional list because they had two source lists — you were still not guaranteed. This is because if there were 100 people on the list, they would only send bids out to 20 people. I was told that we rotate the 20 all the time, but I don't think that they did because I know people who are on source lists and they say, "But I never get an opportunity to put in a bid."

So I said, "Why don't we just let everybody bid. That's free and open. That's fair. That's democratic. We'll take the one that is the most excellent one within the budget that we have on the evaluation side and try to push all the emphasis on the evaluation." So I got the front end opened but then I was hoping to introduce the evaluations at the procurement review board; but the public servants didn't want it because the decisions — and talking about the Department of Supply and Services, we do over 1,000 contracts every business day of the year — are made by public servants. I didn't know what was going on in 1,000 contracts every day. Unless it was a really monstrous contract or an irritating contract and somebody had petitioned me that there was something stinky about it, I wouldn't really get to know about it.

But the vast majority are going through and the public servants are making the decision. If we had a procurement review board, if somebody didn't like that procurement and didn't feel it was done in an ethical manner, they could appeal to this tribunal, which I thought was fair and reasonable. But the public servants didn't want it because that meant that their decisions would be open to public scrutiny. If they had done something, wink-wink nod-nod, to some friend of someone, it would come out.

Under the free trade agreement Canada was forced to have a procurement review board set up and we set one up in 1989 to coincide with the free trade agreement. Of the first 50 cases which went to the procurement board, nearly one-third of them decided that the public servants had not done the award of the contract in accordance with their own rules. If it's that high a failure rate, then I think all of government procurement should be allowed to go to a procurement review board to make sure the public servants follow the rules explicitly and it's not just done behind the scenes.

If you wanted to sell staplers to the Government of Canada, you would apply to the Government of Canada to get on the source list, which is a list of all the people who would sell staplers. If a contract comes out for wanting staplers, if you're on the source list you may or may not be allowed to bid. If you're not on the source list, you don't have a hope of bidding. There are so many ways that you can control a source list. You can control a source list by saying, as they did, "I'm sorry, we reviewed all the factories manufacturing goods for the government and we only do that once a year, and we did that one month ago, so you'll have to wait for another 11 months." That's one off-ramp. Then you can say, "I'm sorry, you have not been able to prove to us that you have enough financial capacity to get us through this contract and the government doesn't want to bail you out." That's the second off-ramp that can keep a person out. There are all kinds of them, if you're controlling a secret source list.

So it's not an equal playing field when you're trying to get on the source list. You have to struggle to get on and sometimes I've found the public servants did not want a lot of people on the source list because then they have to manage a lot of people on it. They have to send more bids out. They were quite comfortable having six, eight, 20 or 30 people on the source list and they could manage, maybe send out bids to 10 or 15 of them; that's a manageable number. Where if you opened it up to the whole world, they might have 150 people putting in submissions and they'd have to evaluate 150 rather than 10 or 15. We've been able to change that, so source lists have by and large disappeared. We have moved on to the computer stage, we have opened up the system.

But there are still ways in which they control it, by making a person qualify. Once you say, "We're going to build a certain atmospheric tank of some nature or other, all those that would be interested in bidding on that, would they please meet the following qualifications," if you don't meet certain qualifications, then you're forced out. It's halfway; it's not as bad. At least it was opened so that everybody could have a shot at it at one stage.

There is definitely patronage involved in giving out government contracts, more so by the public servants than by politicians. Politicians are too busy. Public servants are not, as it happens. It's not because they're getting paid off or anything like that. Maybe it's a sense of power. Maybe it makes their job easier because they give it to Fred, the same Fred who supplied them for the last 15 years and always did a good job. But without an open system there are abuses. I know of a couple of cases with the procurement review board that were pure hanky-panky. It was giving contracts to friends.

I didn't go through the thousands of cases. I know enough cases that I know that it wasn't an open, fair or honest procurement, that it was to friends or for whatever reason, and it wasn't right. If we opened up the system at the front end, we'd make a fair system. I wanted to see an open review of the judging of the bids submitted at the back end. They got the front end opened up when I was there but I did not get the back end opened up. They stalled me for 18 months. I read 14 Cabinet submissions on setting up a procurement review board. I've got copies of letters where they said that it was a foolish idea that shouldn't be done, and some of the suggestions in it were actually illegal according to legislation in this country.

But they stalled it long enough that it finally was thrown in with an omnibus bill. It was killed in one of the rare occasions when the Senate was filled by Tory senators, who killed the tail end of a good review board because they had some concerns over the Canada Council for the Arts funding, which was also included in the bill. The bill died in May or June of 1993. I just hope that somebody will put together an open procurement review system. It's going to be forced on Canada anyhow through GATT, the World Trade Organization, NAFTA, so why don't we go there voluntarily? Get there ahead of the rest of the people and have a good, clean system. I don't understand why they refuse to do it.

Lobbying, as a profession, was called "government relations" up until about 1985, when it became the lobbying profession. I'm not sure who decided to change the name. They spend most of their time going to see public servants. In most cases I think lobbying is very fair. I think it's legitimate. I saw lots of people who were lobbyists and they wanted to bring the president of a company in to see me on some contract or other, and that's fine. I told them, "Sure, you can come out and see me, all your competitors are entitled to come and see me as well." I don't think it ever changed my opinion because, quite frankly, the public servants are the ones that made the decision. It wasn't me making the decision. I didn't jettison public servants' decisions on who's going to get a contract because I'm not knowledgeable in boat-building or helicopters or ship design or in all the various contracts that we're involved in.

It's important, perhaps at a lower level when they're leading up to putting out bids, to make sure that somebody is knowledgeable. One of the ways you can rig a bidding situation is by making the specifications such that only a certain type of instrument could be used. If somebody else was bidding, he might have a lobbyist or somebody from his own company if they know where to go, but most of them don't know where to go. That's why they hire somebody in Ottawa to go and find out where to go. They don't know where to go because they're in Vancouver, they're in Edmonton, they're not in Ottawa. They're in Toronto. With a maze of government of 210,000 public servants, they don't know who to go and see. Moreover, they don't even want to know half of them. So they say, "Well, I'll hire a person in Ottawa."

Some of them hire a person on their own staff to be in Ottawa, to be their sort of lobbyist or government relations person. Some of them go and hire somebody else to do the job on a contract. Hopefully they'll get to the right people and say, "Hey, don't just put the terminology and the specifications that way, make sure they're broad enough that we can also bid." If they do that then they're doing a good service to the country and to everybody else. By and far the majority of the so-called lobbying or government relations is done in that type of a way.

There are examples, I'm sure, that show that some lobbying is done in the other way. That a little bit of favouritism or government relations leading to favouritism has taken place. That's not proof that shows that lobbying and government relations is such a terrible business, because sometimes there have been these scenarios. The majority of it is legitimate. But there is some of it that has not been legitimate and has coloured things, which I think is regrettable.

If your department alone is giving out 1,000 contracts a day, you do need somebody to help. Let's say one of the procurements I put out is an atmospheric tank, but the atmospheric tank is being used by the Department of the Environment, by the Department of National Defence and maybe another. And they're all putting in money and they all put in specifications. You want to go to the people in all those departments, as well as the person in the Department of Supply and Services, and make sure that your module fits within the specifications they're all recommending to Supply and Services, which finalizes them. So, yes, that's why they hire people in Ottawa to lead them around to the right doors. To sort of say, "Hey, help us to make sure that it's reasonable and fair." When a business doesn't win a contract, they usually wimp out. I've had businesspeople come to me before I was in the Cabinet and afterwards say, "Oh, why didn't I win. I should have won." I said, "Well, complain, yell, scream, take the government to court." They'd say, "Oh no, I'd better not do that, they may not invite us to bid on the next contract."

I look at that in comparison to what our cousins down in the States do. Their businessmen fight like cats and dogs to get a contract. If a businessman doesn't get it and he thinks he's been robbed, he screams, he yells, he takes on the government. Plus, he lines up next week to bid on the next contract and expects it's going to be fairer — and give him a fair shot or else he'll take the government and beat 'em up again. But here, our business leaders, they're so spineless. If they think that something is wrong, they should stand up and squawk. But here, no, no, don't ruffle the feathers. They might not treat us nicely the next time. I just think that business should stand up and shout a little bit more.

The private sector is concerned with what government thinks because in Canada the government sector is so pervasive, is so big, is a greater percentage of the gross domestic product than it is, say, in the United States or in some other countries. They're by far the biggest buyers of goods and services, and maybe the private sector feels they've got to be nice to the government because they sell one-third of their product to governments, provincial, municipal, regional and federal. They don't want to be known as the bad guys who rock the boat if the government is nasty to them and get all the public servants mad at them.

However, if a series of businesspeople would shake it up all in a row, then I think it would help to make sure that procurement was done in a completely hands-off, open, honest manner and they'd all get a better shake. But until business wants to stand up and do that, then they're going to be treated as they are, which isn't necessarily best for business and it's not necessarily best for Canada.

There are people who make a business decision not to sell to governments because of the red tape and because of the all the loops and the difficulties. That's a legitimate business decision to make: to say, "I'm only going to sell my rubber mats in the private sector. I refuse to talk to governments." And there are people who do that, but since government is so big and there are so many levels of government in Canada, the majority of businesses do want to sell to the government at some level or other. A lot of those are not willing to stand up for the principles of making sure they get a fair deal. They're always worried that they might not be treated nicely the next time. I think they'd be treated nicely the next time if a whole bunch of them would stand up and scream at the government and make sure they're treated nicely now.

I have been to the Public Policy Forum. I've spoken in front of it before and I found a lot of the people who go there are there to do a schmoozing with senior bureaucrats, trying to find out how things are. They might want to know what big contracts they'll be looking for in a year or two. You know, large $300-million contracts; they're planned months or years in advance. Maybe they're taking the opportunity to do a little lobbying on their own. Finding out what's on the government's agenda, rather than trying to force the government to do something that is on their agenda, like making sure there's good accounting or making sure that it has a proper procurement system or an open and honest procurement review tribunal. Those are tough, nasty questions and they shy away from those.

I think there is a dependency loop with business and government, more so in this country than in the United States, which is our closest neighbour, and more than in perhaps some other countries. But businesses are dependent. They could have their cake and eat it too if they'd just stand up. They got so badly beaten up in the 1970s that I think they're so willing to just take the crumbs off the table and run home.

They've lost all their spine. I don't see a lot of businesspeople insisting on having the fairness and the openness and the accountability that should be in government.

MAXWELL HENDERSON

*The well-known former auditor general offers outspoken
views on government mismanagement.*

The reason I was unpopular in government circles was because I exposed so much of their waste and extravagance over the years. I got such tremendous press doing it that in no time at all I became a folk hero and that put me in competition with the politicians who liked the media. Mr. Pearson put up with it. Mr. Diefenbaker and Mr. Pearson accepted it for what it was. But Mr. Trudeau decided he had to do something about it because I was giving him and his ministers severe competition. So they decided that they would make my life difficult and they proceeded with a series of events which did just that, namely, downsizing the salaries of my men, freezing my staff and trying to prevent me from disclosing so much in my reports.

I suppose that I took a risk but I didn't give a damn. I had come from business. I was a professional man. There was a job to be done and I went to work and did it. Trudeau introduced the bill in the House of Commons to cut me down to size and there was such an uproar across Canada, so many letters, telegrams, media attention, that he withdrew it on December 3, 1970. And the cartoons all burst forth: "Max flies again." I went right after him for the rest of my time in office. I remember a cartoon appeared in the Victoria paper; he's having tea with his new wife and they drink a little toast to Maxwell Henderson, retiring next month. Now, they've since changed the act and they've curtailed the auditor general so that he behaves himself. That's the tragedy.

The government definitely tried to keep me quiet — they even said so. Mr. Bud Drury, the president of the Treasury Board, and not a very attractive man, said, "Why give him more money to have more staff to find more mistakes?" But I went right after him, and he and Simon Reisman, his deputy, and later the man on the free trade negotiations, tried everything in the book. For example, I had taken on the audit of the United Nations as well as Canada. They paid their own freight, and I told the prime minister one day, "Damn it, you're getting two jobs for the price of one because they pay for everything." Well, Mr. Drury and Mr. Reisman accused me of auditing the United Nations books illegally. I said, "What am I supposed to do when the prime minister comes and asks me to let my name go forward to the General Assembly of the United Nations in New York, and I get elected as chairman of the Board of Auditors, what am I supposed to do? Why is it illegal?" Well, Drury said it was because I didn't sign a certain piece of paper. I said, "Go to Hell!"

Mr. Diefenbaker never interfered. Mr. Pearson was a charming man and he tolerated everything I was reporting. Mr. Pearson and his ministers were very good. When Mr. Trudeau became prime minister and moved in with his Liberal administration I saw a change. The Liberal people around Mr. Trudeau ganged up. A lot of new boys, like Warren Almond of Montreal, sat down at the table at the first Public Accounts Committee meeting and said, "Oh, so that's what you look like. I had a hell of a job getting here because they threw the book at me for what you were doing." So of course they backed Mr. Drury and I had a sort of a gang in that Public Accounts Committee. It became all political. I never understood the difference between the parties anyway. They all looked the same to me. But this is the way they behaved. So if I became unpopular with the government, that's the reason. And I knew that by being unpopular with the government I was doing the job the way it should be done. Because that's the only way the auditor general can succeed. If he's popular with the government, he's no good.

But the moment Trudeau came in (and Trudeau was a shrewd man, I don't underestimate him at all) he felt the auditor general reporting was a loose end he had to get into and he waited some years before he opened up. That's the story — I don't care. What the hell, I wrote a book about it and that's the end of it. The job has to be done.

I hate to brag, but in all the speeches I made since I retired, I prophesied what was going to happen. The depreciated dollar, the incredible size of the national debt, the terrifically high taxes that would sap the incentive of our people; they were building up. I warned them. I showed them the staffs were multiplying, mushrooming, blossoming out. Expenditure went up 500 percent in the 10 years from the time that I started. And there's a long story as to how they did it. I've got Mr. Chrétien's picture here. You might like to know that in 1977 he was saying we were spending too much money. We'll have to cut our spending; we'll have to cut our staffs. Well, he's saying the same thing in 1995.

I saw spending starting to go out of control about 1963 with the implementation of the Glassco Royal Commission on Government Organization. That was the point when all the departments made thousands of recommendations, and very good ones. Management consultants got in there. It became the hottest place in Canada for management consultants. They came in and they examined all the departments, you see, and they made reports. But the reports generally were designed and written the way that the head of the department wanted it so he could then go out and hire more staff, increase the size of his office, get himself in line for better promotion and, of course, send the bill to the Treasury to pay because they encouraged them to do this.

All over Ottawa these things happened, but then they interfered with the internal management control of money. And that's where I, as the auditor, had to watch it and move in. Where they once had had a treasury officer assigned to check all the expenditures, he was no longer there. He was now called assistant to the chairman or some fancy title, you see, getting more money. So it was empire building at its best and that was when the explosion really occurred. Trudeau with his gang moved in and then when Mulroney came along the whole damn thing compounded again — until we've got to the figures we've got today.

Before the 1960s and 1970s government spending was quite modest. One of the essences of spending money is that Canada has a Consolidated Revenue Fund into which all money must go and no money must be taken out unless Parliament votes it. Each vote becomes law. But they began picking away at this. They began cutting down the number of votes. We used to have about 500 votes and each vote would have language which became the law of the country. My job was to see that the money was spent in that manner. The government managed to chop the number down to about 236, I think it was, and when I was in office Mr. Drury, as president of the Treasury Board, came to the committee and proposed to cut it down to 100, which was terrible. So I had to point out, on behalf of the Public Accounts Committee, that they were losing 100 opportunities to vote. The votes became huge because the expenditure was going up and each vote was for an enormous figure. Drury didn't like that and I thought, well, the committee backed me 100 percent, but the Liberals had the power in the House of Commons and they got it through. So today you've only got 100 votes with all that money being spent — $120 billion of government spending this year reduced to 100 votes. You can imagine the size of each vote. It's enormous.

These MPs don't understand; they're all new boys having great difficulty understanding it. Look at those reports. How do they get to grips with that? Up until the early 1960s budgets were presented in a much fairer manner — in a much simpler manner. They were very concerned about public waste. When I took office my predecessor's report was only about 80 pages, in which he detailed the waste and stuff like that: it was quite simple. Now it's over 1,000 pages. And as I say, there were about 500 votes. They were all discussed. Everything was set out for them and if they didn't understand it, it was explained. They were much more conscientious then. And of course, if we go back to when we were in World War II, that was when things were really watched very carefully. I can tell you many stories about that. That was when the proper thing to do was to handle public money as it should be handled. It was trust money. It's the money of the people. And when you're handling other people's money you should be pretty careful what you do.

I was asked once who I thought was the finest Cabinet minister Canada ever had. I thought for a minute and said it must be the Honourable J. L. Elsley, who was minister of finance under Mackenzie King at the outbreak of war. Mr. Elsley was so thrifty that he took the streetcar to his office in the East Block. I was with Donald Gordon in the Wartime Prices and Trade Board and we set up the ration administration. We had to ration a lot of things in those days. The staff worked every night and the question came up about their having supper money.

We had to go to Mr. Elsley to get an order-in-council; we couldn't pad it. So we went to Mr. Elsley and we thought 75¢ was a fair price for supper money, but Mr. Elsley thought 50¢ was enough. The matter was debated and he actually took it to Cabinet before they paid supper money to the public service. I knew Mr. Elsley, and one night he phoned me at home. He said, "Max, the Cabinet has agreed to 75¢ but you'll have to have a special receipt signed by every employee. It will have to be countersigned by my parliamentary secretary, Mr. Doug Abbott" — who later became chief justice of Canada — "and you pay the money and give us a complete accounting. I think I can support that in Parliament." And that's the way we ran it.

Now, if you wanted a telephone in those days, if you were an administrator who was paid $1 a year, and we had several hundred of them from industry at $1 a year to help in the war effort, then you were entitled to a cradle telephone. But if you were just an ordinary Joe who'd come to work for the government in the war, then you had to have an old-fashioned kind, a stand-up telephone, you see — providing you qualified before the Treasury Board telephone inspector.

If you were an administrator at $1 a year, you were expected to pay for your own lunches because that connoted that you were a wealthy man, and therefore you could afford to pay lunches and take friends, take guests. The administrators could also have a lower berth on the train whereas the likes of me had to take the upper berth, and I got $5 a day to eat on. That was the way the Treasury Board looked after us in those days. So if that wasn't being thrifty, I don't know what was. A lot of the administrators didn't like it. They thought the government was an old meanie but they did their job notwithstanding, and they framed their dollar at the end of the year when they got it — those were the kind of people.

We had some tremendous men handling Canada's war effort and some of our budgets were in surplus. And the men included Clarence (C. D.) Howe, the minister of munitions, who knew his area like the back of his hand. We had to conserve American dollars because we had to buy all our supplies, a lot of our supplies, from the States. And there was Donald Gordon, who ran the home or domestic front. We kept the inflation rate quite level at the end of the war. It was a remarkable achievement. Not a great deal has been written about it but if you read my book, you'll read about that. It was a tremendous thing.

Well, that atmosphere carried on into the 1950s. The government sometimes would have a surplus; not a deficit but a surplus, though sometimes we'd have a modest deficit. Nobody took a very dim view of it until this balloon took off come 1960. So that's the way it was. These were all very prudent people. And after all, I say to you again that other people's money is a trust fund. You owe it to yourself and to your country to look after it. That's the way I approached it.

And I myself never sought the job of auditor general. When I was appointed in 1960 I had had this experience in the war. I had been in business in big executive positions, I'd had to meet a payroll. So I knew what it meant to meet a payroll because if we didn't have the income coming in, we couldn't pay the help. I became comptroller of the CBC before I became auditor general and there, in the CBC, I set up a new accounting system and tried to rein in their costs. I'll tell you about the CBC a little later because they had an extraordinary way of getting their money from the government. The government would dress up its books in such a way and I undressed them. They didn't like that. I mean, the government didn't like it. I opened up a lot of cans of worms, you see, but that was my job — that's the way I saw it.

If there isn't trust in any relationship, as the great American president Harry Truman said, and particularly trust in the governments, if you can't trust the people that are in government, then the whole works falls apart. That's why we've got to have people there that we trust and that's why, with all due respect, I think if you're interesting yourself in these problems that you should do your damnedest to join parties or join groups and search out the best people to run for office that you can find. The people you can trust. Because without trust you've got nothing. And I'm afraid today there's so much disillusionment and this is the root cause of a lot of the unhappiness that prevails. We're in debt very heavily, for the reasons we're discussing here. In a sense the people running the system have betrayed you. They've let politics move in and they've practised so many slick and smart deals all down the line that have been exposed. Great exposés such as you read in the book *On the Take*, stuff like that. The public have caught on.

And the letters that I've got — thousands of letters from people applauding what I was doing and saying, well, we never realized there was so much waste going on. For instance, I just read a case about the minister of transport, who's spent $750,000 getting private aircraft for himself and his family because he didn't like to use Air Canada. He didn't trust Air Canada so he hired private planes and he had the nerve to get up in the House of Commons and defend that.

I've said in my book that the Treasury Board spent more time circumventing parliamentary control than improving efficiency in government. As I explained, Parliament has to vote the money. Parliamentary control is basic. The money is put into votes and the votes become law. They very soon found a way of circumventing that. For example, I think I've got one case of $281 million which was worded in such a way in the vote that it could be spent at the pleasure of the government in future years, without having to go back to Parliament. And in another case before the Public Accounts Committee, we had some votes that were being circumvented. They were getting around it in the wording. The wording is very important because it's law. And as I said earlier, we are down to 100 votes, that's all. Bob Bryce, the secretary of the Cabinet, was summoned before the Public Accounts Committee, for which the auditor general is the advisor, to explain how come these things were paid when the vote expressly said they couldn't be paid. They gave him a thorough dressing down. He was wrong. I'd caught him out and he was a friend of mine, but I'd caught him out and I just had to trot him in. He was a neighbour and we would walk to the office every day. Bob and I walked down Parliament Hill and he was furious. You know, secretary of the Cabinet — you don't talk to him that way. He came down and he said, "Who do those bums think we are? Who's running this country? We're running it, not them. We're running the country, we don't need those bums on the Hill." That's the contempt that they had for the government, so they'd practise everything in the book, and all the time these transactions were going through.

Now, secondly, Canada sold a lot of airplanes to Venezuela, $35 million of them and the money came from Venezuela. It should have gone into the Consolidated Revenue Fund, in order to come out as an appropriation. But instead of that, they circumvented it and put it into private bank accounts so they could spend it at their pleasure. I aired that one and that brought in External Affairs and the government of Venezuela. There was a terrible brouhaha over that but I was right. When Canada receives a big payment like that of any money, even your income tax, it has to go into the Consolidated Revenue Fund of Canada, by law. It only comes out by Parliament passing a vote, the government and the auditor general checking it.

It was doing things like that that didn't exactly make me a pal of Trudeau and his ministers. I didn't care, that's the way it is. That's the way Mr. Elsley ran it, and that's the way Mackenzie King ran it, and that's the way I was brought up to run it.

In respect to the debt and spending going out of control, you can blame Mr. Trudeau and his ministers for inaugurating it. They started it. Mr. Chrétien was one of the people that built it up, for God's sake. He was a junior minister only at that time, but nevertheless included. Also, ministers like Mr. MacEachen, today Senator MacEachen, that's another long story, are the people that built it up. People like that.

Mr. MacEachen was up to a lot of tricks. He made a very pungent reference about me. He never liked me very much and I didn't have much to do with him, but I had criticized CIDA, the Canadian International Development Agency, for blowing $1 million in Vietnam on a hospital. The Public Accounts Committee never referred the CIDA report. You see, the government has to refer my report and the report of the Crown corporations to the Public Accounts Committee, but they left CIDA out of it. So Mr. MacEachen came out publicly and said, "I don't know why I'm being criticized for wasting money in Vietnam. The Public Accounts Committee has never examined the CIDA report," and he said the auditor general hadn't even mentioned it in his report. I came right back and I said, "Mr. MacEachen is not telling the House the truth. If he'll look at paragraph so and so in my report, he will see exactly what took place." And then I gave him chapter and verse and he shut up. He's a very devious gentleman, that chap, although he's a Nova Scotian — I'm a Nova Scotian chartered accountant.

Right now you don't have much cause to trust Parliament, as you look and see the debt that's hanging over your head and what they're going to do with it. I would hope very much that they will restore our trust. Mr. Paul Martin's budget promises a lot of things. We haven't seen the performance yet. Remember, the civil service at the time of World War II was only about 45,000 people. Today it's nearly half a million. With 45,000 we ran the World War II economy. Today we are over 500,000. Mr. Trudeau went on the air back in 1978 and 1979 and he said that we've got to trim our spending, we've got to live within our means. Well, nothing new about that. We're still trying to live within our means. But the government doesn't live within its means. That's the point. I would hope that you would come to trust government and that you would pay your taxes but, as I mentioned, President Truman said that without trust, the whole works falls apart. And I think that's true.

It's a very serious situation because there are a lot of imponderables that we don't know the answers to at the moment. You have the Quebec situation. And I've just gone through the Mexican bankruptcy over the peso and I must say Canada looks very much the same. Our dollar is down to 70¢, which I think is disgraceful. Maybe good for exporters but nobody else. I'm ashamed that it's down to 70¢ American. I'm downright ashamed, but I told them, in my speeches to the Canadian Clubs across Canada, that your money's going to be devalued if we keep on going this way.

But Canadians are not given to rallying very much, you know. Maybe we have the makings of a tax revolt now, but we're an apathetic lot. In fact, I'll give you Jeanne Kirkpatrick's great remark at the United Nations about Canada. She was the American ambassador and I asked her one day, apropos of what we were discussing, "Miss Kirkpatrick, what do you think of Canada? What's your opinion of Canadians?" She said, "My dear friend, they're like vichyssoise, stiff and hard to stir." And I think that pretty well puts your finger on it.

Well, of course you can say that Canadians have got the governments they've deserved. I suppose we have. In 1988 we certainly got what we deserved with Mulroney, didn't we? I would have backed Turner. I didn't think Turner was so good but he would have been a lot more honest, I think, and I would have trusted him more than Mulroney. But Canadians went for Mulroney and look what happened. Everything got compounded. So there you are.

Things were on a smaller scale before the 1960s — a pretty level sort of a scale. We had been accustomed to the government of Mackenzie King, St. Laurent and then Mr. Diefenbaker. And Mr. Diefenbaker's demands on the treasury were very mild. He didn't start any big stuff. He did start the Glassco Commission, and then he left office; but he was the one that introduced that. It was a good thing, only it went off the rails. But I don't think Canadians were simply led in their voting by the media or the parties. They were pretty angry with the government under Mackenzie King and St. Laurent, as you may know from the history books, over Mr. Howe's famous remark, "What's a million?" or "So what's a million?" They threw the Liberals out and in came Mr. Diefenbaker. That was a very traumatic change for Canada's pipeline debate, the pipeline debate of the 1950s and building the Trans Canada Pipeline, with the American influence and all that stuff. So they changed the government then.

I think they were influenced largely by the media on their votes, as they are today. I think the media's responsible for a great deal of this. I don't know what you do in its place, but advertising is a very potent force and I suppose that politicians are free to be influenced. Anyhow, we make it easier for them by giving them tax relief if you contribute to their parties, so there you are.

A lot of things have contributed to this disregard for spending. A lot of people don't think too much about this unless they're woken up. I worked on the basis that I had a job to do. I didn't give a damn what the outcome was. I knew I was there till age 65. They couldn't get rid of me. That's one of the advantages of that job, you see. And as I told Ken Dye, and as I told the present auditor general, "You've got to get in there, don't pussyfoot it. Hit them with a two-by-four." That's the only thing they understand, and I got in there and did that. And that's the only way you'll get it into their thick heads, these politicians.

If the auditor general is disliked or controversial — good for him. That's what he should be. Then he's doing his job. Canada had a few of them in the beginning. The first two were very difficult. The first fellow raised hell back in 1878. He was so distrustful of the government in those days that he kept the cash, the spare cash, in a cash box, and if they wanted to travel they had to go and ask him for it. He was both the treasurer and the auditor general.

I think it's true that business has become part of the establishment and involved in a change in the way our country's been run. I think this is one of the influences at work, more so today than ever before. You see, Canada is a small country business wise. Everybody knows everybody and most everybody knows the government officials. You have to know them because government is the biggest business of the country and one way or another the success of your business depends on getting government contracts. Therefore you are very loath to speak out and criticize the people that are feeding you; because if you speak out and they take note of it, you won't be asked back. You won't be given a chance to bid on this contract or that, and it's a very unhappy state of affairs. Mind you, the same is true in Washington, except that in the United States it's a much, much bigger situation. You can get away with a lot more than you can in Canada, and some of these people wield so much influence with the government that they can almost dictate what the government is going to do.

I know this because I was in business for a great many years. I was the treasurer of a very big company and we had to get a certain piece of legislation changed that we didn't like. It was hurting us and so I went to work in Ottawa, lobbying, and I got it for my boss. I thought to myself, it's a disgraceful way to have do business but that's the way it is. Now you're seeing another case today with some of these bankruptcies that have gone off, and I speak particularly of the Royal Trust Company, which was the Gibraltar of Canadian trust companies. It was the Rock of Gibraltar. It was brought to its knees and people, between 4,000 and 5,000 stockholders, have lost their savings in the Royal Trust Company. They are going to sue the directors but the directors are a very close corporation; they're the biggest names in Canada and yet they never told the stockholders, a year or two before the event, that they were going to go belly-up. Had they said one word, two or three words, the people would have had a chance to get out, but they didn't know. And I have accused the chairman of that board in the strongest terms because I think it's the most disgraceful state of affairs.

But what is more disgraceful is that the regulatory authorities, Queen's Park in Toronto and the superintendent, the financial institutions in Ottawa, aren't even answering the letters that we write. Now there's a lawsuit going to be launched very shortly and they have got a very competent firm of lawyers. They couldn't get Toronto lawyers because the Toronto lawyers are all tied to the establishment, you see. So they had to go to Windsor to get a law firm. But they're a very capable litigation committee and they're going to be launching a lawsuit and I hope they succeed. I think it's a reprehensible way to behave, and I would look for some leadership from the federal government and from the Ontario government in a case like that. But nobody wants to throw the first stone because he might muddy the waters for his future relationships with that particular government. And that is a very sad commentary that I have to make, but it's true.

That's one of the reasons that business stands back. Business is concerned with making money, not improving government. It should be concerned with both, in my view, because some of our best brains in Canada are in business, they're in the big legal firms. They don't want to touch government because they're afraid that if they do they will be tarnished with some scandal or something like that, so they don't want to get into it. They're making far too much money in their line of work, and I think the result is we end up in government getting people that are not experienced. They get into very important positions and are not experienced and that's very serious. That's why I would urge people, if you're interested in this, to join any political party of your choice, but get in and try to influence the selection of competent people you trust. That's the only hope we've got and I think business will improve its image because it's very quick to turn around. But right now it's everybody for himself.

It may be joining the establishment, but as you get going in that establishment, you and your friends, you can wield a great influence causing that to be changed, to bring it round. If you go in alone, you're crying in the wilderness. If you join a party like the Liberals or the Conservatives, you can at least make your presence felt over the years; if not, don't belong anymore, but if you can do it, stay with it. It's hard work, I know that, but you and your friends could go a long way to influence them. I should think the young Conservatives in Canada today have got a brilliant chance to resurrect the party if they want to, after their terrible history with Mulroney and Kim Campbell and all the rest of it. Preston Manning is a young man, a nice young man, and I'm sure everybody wishes him well, but give him time. He may not be the one to ultimately hit it, but it may result in a top-flight man coming in. That's what this very influential commentator that I met in Mexico said to me. He said Preston Manning is the catalyst that started the Reform Party but he said there'll be somebody come forward that will be charismatic and will pick it up and go to town with it. And that's usually what happens. Whether it could be Preston Manning, I don't know.

Beginning in the 1960s changes in morality or moral values have changed government. Money was at stake, and the moment that the money was flowing the empire building was taking place. People were reaching up for higher positions. Ottawa was buzzing; it was the hottest place on the continent for all these experts. Then greed took over. Greed moved in and they saw a chance to propel themselves forward like nothing had ever been before, and all kinds of things sprung up. All kinds of new departments, new programs, new everything. If you'd got a new idea and your minister liked it, bingo, you took off on cloud nine right away and you got all the money you wanted. It was, in other words, self-aggrandizement or whatever you want to call it, but I just call it plain old-fashioned greed and everybody for himself. That's what took over, the morality of the thing was missing. And you didn't have any people that you respected very much, upstairs. The prime minister, like Trudeau, was jetting around the world and spending money and just all over the place, building this up. Mr. Mulroney comes along, he doesn't set any example to the people underneath. Now, remember, in any organization, if the head man sets an example, the rest will follow, but if the head man is playing fast and loose with things, they'll play fast and loose all down the line. That's where morality comes in and I'm sorry to have to say it, but that's what's happened with us or we wouldn't be in this mess.

The auditor general is somebody that they always figure should be seen, just seen and heard from once a year, a nine-day wonder, and as long as he was restricted to that, fine. And when I came along I changed that by speaking out as nobody ever spoke out before. He is the guardian of the public purse. Anything that in his opinion Parliament should know, he should put in his reports, which is exactly what I did, but I put too much in for Mr. Trudeau. Now the auditor general's writing a lot of pieces. They've changed the complexion of the job, they've given the auditor general a 10-year term and he's very much a tame watchdog. He's busy in those reports; he's complimenting the government. It's not his job to compliment them. You don't go around saying how good they are. Your job is to report to Parliament anything you think Parliament should know, and Ken Dye was coming out patting them on the back, trying to avoid being disliked the way I was. Whereas he should have gone right to town and hit them with the two-by-fours. That's the only language they understand, and there's no other check. The auditor general is the only check you have on them.

Desautels, the present auditor, is getting into the business of passing judgment on the way in which the customs officers do their work, and the way they dress and the decorum in the jails. That's not his job. His job is to see where the hell the money's going and what we're getting for it. But they've enlarged it so they have now on the staffs a lot of psychiatrists and fancy-pant people. We don't need that. I just went to work and I did the UN as well.

The example of unemployment insurance is a classic. That's had a very checkered career. It started out on the basis that the contributions to unemployment insurance, properly invested, should yield sufficient return to pay for unemployment insurance. Pretty soon, in 1971, for political reasons, they came along and they cut the waiting period down from 30 days to eight days so you could get it quicker. They also provided unemployment insurance to anybody who, after age 65, no longer had gainful employment; he'd retired from the labour force, I think was the wording to that end. So I actually saw for myself several deputy minister friends in Ottawa who reached 65 and collected unemployment insurance because they were not gainfully employed. They were getting a federal pension, you know, but they were not gainfully employed. They said to me, "Well, you go," as I could have gone when I got to be 65. This program change was so devastating that they then found they had to have more money, so they doubled the premiums. Then the unemployment insurance fell into the hands, in the early 1970s, of a gentleman who was the minister of labour, Mr. Bryce Mackasey from St. Henri in Montreal. Mr. Bryce Mackasey was a very aggressive Irishman, and I said to him one day, "Well, Bryce, you've inherited the Unemployment Insurance Commission." He said, "Yes, we don't do much insurance now, Max, but it's a wonderful thing to get me re-elected in St. Henri because we're just doling it out, no insurance principles."

So they put in the president of Canada Life to examine this unemployment insurance thing and he pointed out how far they'd departed from insurance principles. It had become a number-two welfare plan, and this is what it is today. Mr. Gill, the president of Canada Life, a very able actuary, spent the last five years of his life examining this thing and it killed him. He was so upset because the government would never adopt his recommendations to put it back on base.

Earlier on I mentioned the CBC. Well, I was its comptroller for a couple of years before I was auditor general, and I put in their now current accounting system. I liked a lot of things about it very much, but it was when I became auditor general that I found myself auditing the CBC and I had to turn around and get off a lot of things. And one of the things that always struck me as very funny was that the government gives them a grant every year; you probably know that. They bellyache because they don't get enough. It gives them a grant every year but it gives them a grant in the form of loans, and the CBC would show them as a liability on its balance sheet. And it owes the government quite a bit, a fantastic amount of money. But the CBC never had any money to pay the loans off, and we had to sign all these interest-bearing notes. So when the interest had to be paid the government would give us more money to pay the interest and then the government would not put these loans into its budget as expenses. It would put them in as loans to a Crown corporation, and it would show them as an asset. Even though the poor CBC could never pay them back, it called them an asset. So I debunked that, and I made a lot of people very angry when I said I've never seen anything so ridiculous. I often wondered how the government handled it and now I know. "Well, we give them the money every year," said Mr. Bryce, "and we later send it to their loans." I said, "Yes, and you add it to yours." We aired this before the Public Accounts Committee in a historic session, and I explained to them, as I'm explaining to you, what was taking place. I said the poor old CBC could never pay it back, so they give them more money. I said it's just like giving money to your wife. You have to give her more money so she can pay you back. The whole committee got terribly excited and Bryce got red in the face and said, "I've never heard anything so ridiculous." And I said, "That's all it is. If I lent money to my wife that I've got to give her and I want it paid back, I've got to give her more money so she can pay me back. That's all you're doing here and you're cooking the books. You're not showing your proper expenses and your statements are wrong." So I made the government change the statements.

Now they're up to all those tricks all the time. Ken Dye got a lot of stuff cleaned up like that. There's a lot more besides. They did the same damn thing to Air Canada, except Air Canada had a little bit of revenue. But it's to keep the grants that they're giving to these Crown corporations out of their budgetary expenditures. They're leaving it to a corporation, same thing with the post office. Well, I thought this accounting practice was fraud so I said that. I wouldn't sign the financial report, but then, after they corrected it I signed it. My deputy, Guy, wouldn't sign it. I gave him full marks for that. He said, "I can't sign it, it's an incorrect statement." Well, they cover that up in Parliament, you know. They just don't mention it. You'd go to jail for doing that in private business; I recognize that.

But the Government of Canada has an extraordinary balance sheet. It leaves a hell of a lot of things off; it has for years. Particularly in the Canada Pension Plan, which is another cookie that they introduced in those lush years — the Canada Pension Plan. Let me tell you about that because it's going to be bankrupt in 2010; the government came out last week and said it. So they're having to double your contributions to the Canada Pension Plan. But the reason the Canada Pension Plan is in such dire trouble I discovered when I did a job for Premier Davis at Queen's Park. I wondered where Queen's Park was getting the money to pay its deficit because it too was not living within its means, and yet it always was getting money from Ottawa. It was Darcy McKeough, the provincial treasurer, who said to me, "Max, don't tell anybody but I've got a straight pipeline to Ottawa on this, I get Canada Pension Plan money. They lend it to me at four percent." Four percent interest. And he said, "Quebec's getting it too, so I thought I better get it for Ontario." So the poor old Canada Pension Plan never had any money to earn any interest to pay you and me the pension. That's why it's going bust. Nice bookkeeping, eh? I don't think that's very honest and, as you would say, if you did anything like that in business, you'd be cooked. At least I would, I reckon I would be. But the governments can get away with all this stuff, you know.

You may ask whether there is some way, some mechanism, whereby citizens can bring a lawsuit for accounting procedures that hide or distort. I think the short answer to that question is, there are no ways the citizen can do it, unless the citizen wants to say to the government, "Now, look here, we've had enough. We're not going to pay any more taxes until you get this thing put right." Now, enough people would have to get together to do that, and I can only tell you the government was scared to death over one of the criticisms that I made of the famous auto pact between Canada and the States, where they refunded or they forgave a debt of the Ford Motor Company, which owed $80 million. It wouldn't pay and so the government forgave the Ford Motor Company the $80 million which they should have paid. I opened it up in my report and they soon discovered who it was, and the Ford Motor Company was speechless with anger at me. The president, in Oakville, just blew his fuse, which didn't bother me. But the ministers, several ministers from Mr. Trudeau's Cabinet telephoned me and they said, "We've had hundreds of letters. People said, 'If you can give the Ford Motor Company $80 million, you don't need my taxes, so I'm not filing my return.'" And a minister said, "Max, we've got between 200 and 300 letters, they were brought to the Cabinet. We can't take that. If a thing like that spreads, we're finished."

So if you decided not to file your tax returns at the end of this month, you'd bring them to book fast. But you wouldn't want to be alone; you'd want a couple of hundred with you. Put the money in trust somewhere and just don't pay it. You take a little action like that, if Canadians have got the stomach to do that, why, you'll bring them to book. They'll come to book fast because money talks. Don't ever forget it, money talks. It talks in business and it talks in government. It takes a little intestinal fortitude to do a thing like that, but these fellows were writing in and they wrote in to the Cabinet ministers, not to me. They wrote in and Cabinet was scared stiff. I never saw such excitement. They said, "Listen, you can start something, we couldn't stop it." And I said, "Well, you shouldn't go around giving $80 million to a big, wealthy company like that, that's all."

But that's what it will take. Now, we may wonder whether the only sign we've seen of a tax revolt is in the recent budget. I read about it. Stop Mr. Martin increasing the income taxes, which are already so high that they sap your and my incentive to do anything. If I were a young person, I couldn't take those taxes, but at my stage in life, that's fine. I don't care. I like the country, it's been pretty good to me and I'm quite happy to pay it. But it's a shocking thing and it's killing the incentive for young people. You don't pay taxes like this anyplace else. You don't pay it in the States; you don't pay any taxes in Mexico to speak of: that's probably why they're in a mess. But I think that's very serious because in Canada the young people deserve to be self-reliant. We've had to build. It's a hard country, a hard climate and in many respects a hard life. I think they should be given much more incentive than this. They don't want these fancy Canada welfare schemes or anything. They just want a job with decent pay, so whatever you can do to help put the right people in the right place, the better. That's all I can offer you.

KENNETH DYE

Another former auditor general discusses the role and history of this important office.

The role of the auditor general begins with an audit act, which sets out the specific requirements. To put it in everyday language instead of legalese, the responsibility is to audit the public accounts of Canada. To look at the compliance of the various government departments and Crown corporations with the law and to do what we call "value for money" auditing, looking at the performance of government in the departments and in the Crown corporations. Basically it's an after-the-fact kind of look at what the government's done. Then there's a requirement to report to Parliament, and when I was an auditor general we reported annually.

The auditor general plays a major role in terms of policing the public purse. That's probably the job in terms of reporting to Parliament. Actually, it's the parliamentarians who have the policing work to do in terms of the courts and the jury, but the auditor general presents the evidence, if you will, to the parliamentarians. I think this policing work is very effective. There's a tremendous amount of follow-up on audit projects. We had a tradition that if we did a project in one year, we'd follow up two years later. Bureaucrats don't like to be caught out or be embarrassed. A political embarrassment is sometimes career threatening, so being caught at it once is horrible; but being caught at it twice can be quite traumatic for a bureaucrat. So they tended to take action on our recommendations.

I always thought the Canadian audit act was pretty good. In fact, I thought it was the best in the world. You saw other countries model theirs after the Canadian act, such as the British, the Australians — the Australians are just doing it now — the New Zealanders, they followed the Canadian pattern, so my view is that it's a very good piece of legislation. It gives the auditor general all the authority that he or she requires to do the job and the words are very plain. The only problem that I had with respect to the act was access to information.

For instance, I sought information for a specific case, the acquisition of Petrofina by Petro-Canada. The way I read that section in the act, I've forgotten which one it is now, but clearly the auditor general is entitled to that information. The government took a different point of view and I wound up suing the government because they were refusing to give me the information that I thought I was entitled to have. And we won in the first court we went to. We lost in the appeal, in the third level of the Supreme Court, where they took the position that the issue was non-judicable. In other words it shouldn't have been in front of the courts. Then they sent me right back to Parliament where I started. So I had some difficult times with Prime Minister Trudeau and Prime Minister Mulroney on getting access because they just simply didn't want me to do that job.

I'd say they were obstructing me on advice from lawyers and senior bureaucrats. I think it was an embarrassment. They knew the story would be embarrassing. We got into it in some depth and the country paid $1.7 billion to acquire Petrofina and an evaluation was done. Independent assessors determined that the thing was worth $1.2 billion. So that's a half-a-billion difference. In addition to that, there are all kinds of tax factors involved, so really the $1.7 billion could be said to be $2.4 billion, for which we bought something that was worth $1.2 billion. Well, the difference was written off later. This kind of behaviour didn't happen very often. There was only the one specific case. Generally I got all the information I wanted and there was not too much problem. The people providing the information weren't the politicians, it was the bureaucrats, and there were times when they were cautious when they said things.

There was another set of data that we sought and that was to do with the cost of travel by ministers, and we knew that that would be a very sensitive item. We set out a little plan, a little pilot project, which went pretty well, and we thought we were going to carry on and do a full-blown study of ministerial travel, but that got stopped by politicians. They felt that would be too much exposure. But they allowed, for the first time, the audit of the House of Commons. That had never been done in the world before. No auditor general had ever audited the parliamentarians' own house. And then we audited the Senate — now, there was more resistance to auditing the Senate than there was to auditing the House of Commons.

The ministers stopped our investigation, though it was eventually done by my successor. I guess it's Chinese water torture, but four years later the results became public. Trying to stop an auditor from investigation isn't considered fraud. Your auditor probably would get access anyway; it just would not be in the newspaper. But anything the auditor general did in terms of reporting became public property and could be far more public exposure to those involved than, say, a private sector transaction.

Politicians get mud thrown in their faces if something negative is revealed about them, I mean, newspapers do that. They take a lot of time to analyze anything that looks to be scandalous or something that people would understand. The average reader of a newspaper understands what it costs to take an airplane ride and he understands that he can't go along and take his wife for free. But ministers of the Crown would take wives just as presidents of corporations take their wives and I'm not saying that's wrong. The president of a corporation takes his wife to a business meeting and nothing is ever said but a minister of the Crown takes his wife and there are people taking pictures. The TV cameras are there. The newsprint guys are all recording this for posterity.

We knew that when we asked about travel costs, the costing system was so bad that if you asked how much it cost to take the prime minister down to Florida for his vacation, they'd say it costs so much for fuel. Not taking into consideration the depreciation on the aircraft, the cost of the crew, the cost of supplying everything that goes on in an airplane, that type of thing. So we'd be getting costs of $700 or $800 an hour when the real cost of flying an aircraft could have been $5,000 an hour. The costing system was poor and we were trying to get at what were the real costs of travel on the fleet of a Canadian aircraft. You know, we have a lot of jets that people fly around in.

I think the information provided to the public is probably pretty good but the average citizen doesn't read it; in fact, they probably don't even know that the information exists. I mean, there's a tremendous amount of data around to describe what goes on in government. You've got Part Two of the Estimates, which is a discussion paper for every department outlining everything that goes on in quite considerable detail. Then you've got the public accounts, three volumes in four books; at least it was, it might have changed. These have tremendous detail. You could find out what parking fines an RCMP constable paid in Regina. I mean, it's down to that level of detail but nobody reads it. It's in your public library but the average Canadian simply doesn't take the time to read. They wait for interpretation, usually through the newspapers, and newspapers are there to sell newspapers and so they pick out the sexy things that they think the readers want to read and they really don't give a lot of thoughtful analysis. The information is out there yet we're facing a fiscal crisis. I guess because those that were making the decisions at the time didn't have the courage to say no to the programs put in front of them for approval. But I don't think there's any one person who's to blame. The public has a role. For example, the politicians of the early 1980s, when the deficit and debt were increasing, would have reacted more vigorously if the public back in their constituencies were riled up a bit about deficits and debt.

We produced documents for Parliament that explained carefully what a deficit was. People used to mix up deficit and debt. Those are technical terms and you have to understand what they mean. They wouldn't know the difference between an annual deficit and an accumulated deficit and, again, you know, these are techy accounting terms. Start using bean-counter terms and people don't understand. So there's a matter of perhaps a lack of education in the numbers. Certainly the numbers are out there and I wanted to make sure parliamentarians understood the numbers; I even drew pictures for them so they would begin to understand.

Today, in 1995, I find people do understand the difference between deficit and debt. They've heard about expenditures. They know these terms that were sort of Greek language to them a decade ago. Why? Because the journalists are putting it out in front of them and it's a constant diet, people are getting used to those words.

In 1981 we had significant deficits and a huge debt. And $1 billion was a lot of money back then. But it still is. The average person hasn't got a clue what $1 billion is. I mean, if I stacked $100 bills from here up to the ceiling, would it amount to $1 billion? I think you'd have to have several stacks. It's a big ton of money. It really is too big a number to understand. People can understand $1 million, I mean, you can win $1 million in a lotto. That will buy you three or four or five nice houses — except in Vancouver it'll buy you one. But $1 billion — that's 1,000 nice houses in Vancouver. That's about the right speed. It's certainly more than the average human can spend in a lifetime, and then some.

I wouldn't want to suggest that there was some plan that because $1 billion is hard to identify and relate to, the parliamentarians went ahead and used it. I don't think the parliamentarians understood as well as they might have. We're very aware that the accounts of the country didn't reflect the realities of the economic activities of government. So in 1984 we started a study called Figures, the federal government reporting study. It was an exercise to set out for the public, the lenders, the parliamentarians, unions and the media a simple set of accounts so the average person could open up a book and it would look something like a financial statement from a public corporation. It would say this is what we own, this is what we owe, this is where the money came from, this is where the money went, and this is how much we're in the hole.

It was very informative and I'm very pleased to know that after we did this study in 1984, 1985 — we did it jointly with the Americans because they didn't have a set of financials; we had a reasonable set but not a complete set — I'm very pleased that the government responded and the public accounts improved over the years. Just last November the government produced its summarized set of consolidated financial statements, so the average person now can see in a nutshell how Canada stands financially. That's a very big step forward. It's a first in the world.

I promoted it 10 years ago. It took 10 years for it to happen. Things move slowly in government. In that case I think the government was trying to get its accounting policy sorted out. There were certain things, like unemployment insurance, for example, that were not on the books of Canada. We got that in the books at that time and there was an

$11-billion deficit. I think it was more like $19 billion last year. No, sorry, I've got that wrong, the deficit wasn't that big, that was the operation. There were expenditures of about $19 billion last year. That's bigtime money, not to have $19 billion on your books.

The Canada Pension Plan has always been on the books of Canada. You may not realize that Canada doesn't hold the money; it's held by the provinces. The money comes in from payroll deduction and taxation and it's immediately transferred out to the provinces. The provinces borrow it from the Canada Pension Plan. The problem there is they don't have the money to pay it back. So in order to make that fund viable over time, and you've seen two adjustments over the last decade — I may be wrong on that point — you see increases in the rates in order to have enough money to pay the pensions that have to be paid out.

All that information is sitting there in the public accounts, on the balance sheet. But do you think the average citizen would be able to determine if they're getting the value for their money? How many average citizens can read a set of financial statements? I'd say 25 percent is maybe a fair estimate. If a former minister told you that five out of six senior accountants couldn't understand the figures in the ministerial books, well, I think they could today. Things are set out quite clearly. There was a time when it was very difficult to figure out. The numbers were there but they were incomprehensible because you had to be very talented. Today the formats are much better, much more readable.

It is tremendously important for governments to present more performance measurement and value for money to the public. If you had programs that started out saying, this is what we intend to do; that said, this is how we're going to measure our performance; this is what we expect to happen, this will be the impact and this'll be the cost, then you go back and look at it and say, what did happen? What did it really cost? Did they achieve what they said they were going to do? If you do that for every program and it works well, you're achieving value for money.

If you go back a decade, assessment was just one-year chunks. If you wanted to start off a new program, you might put in your first $400,000 but the darn thing had a tail on it of $40 million. But parliamentarians making the decision at the time would be told maybe $400,000 was what the program was going to cost. The proper things we did in defence were we got the defence people to acknowledge full program costing. So if you bought yourself a fleet of CF-18s, you're really buying a bunch of spares. You're committing yourself to a ton of training. They take all kinds of armament and it's not just buying a fuselage, you have got to put an engine in it. You have got to put the aeronautic stuff in it and all the armament stuff. And that is a huge, huge cost.

So to buy an airplane, I can't remember what they cost, but let's say they are $20 million, it was probably another $5 million or $10 million worth of costs that were real in terms of that purchase. So if you got the full costing of a program, then the parliamentarian had a much better chance to make a decent decision of, do we want this kind of aircraft? Is it appropriate for the job it's supposed to do? Can Canada afford it? What will the fleet look like 25 years from now? (Because these things last a long time.) Will there be re-fits after 14 years? These ships and airplanes don't last all that time, they have to rebuild them.

The Office of the Auditor General has played a very significant role in getting good information in front of Parliament so they could make decent decisions, but there have been lost opportunities, which means there is an opportunity cost for failing to take a decision. A very big cost. Look at the pain we're enduring today with respect to the annual deficit, which was probably avoidable had somebody done something about it a decade ago when it was apparent. And people were concerned then. But action wasn't taken. Now, you know, is that a big scandal or is it just bad management? Is it good politics? I don't have the answer to that, but we could have avoided all this and had some other issue to be the news of the day.

I haven't a clue what it would cost to deliver the same level of programs today if the best cost-performance measurements and value-for-money reporting had been in place in the past 20 years. Remember, the government doesn't cost its programs in the way a company costs. It doesn't have a costing system. It really is just a cash-receipts and cash-disbursement system dressed up to look almost like a full accrual system. Now these are techy terms again, but just from operating a bank account you recognize that you may have bought something but you haven't paid for it, you've got liabilities or you've got inventories around, or you've got someone who owes you money. So it hasn't hit the bank yet. So we've gone from an accounting system that just records bank transactions to one which reflects the full economic reality of what's going on.

If the government had always been required to provide the same level of reporting activity that a business did, we still might be sitting here today. The political choices could well have been to mortgage Canada to buy the groceries for tomorrow. I mean, that's the decision we've been taking for a long time now: mortgaging the country to buy the groceries. And I used words like that in the 1984 report; you'd have thought somebody would have listened then.

But the auditor general obviously can't control spending. The auditor general's job is not to do that, that's Parliament's job. That's why you elect members of Parliament. They need information and they get that information from the government and they get it from the auditor general. Yet I was clearly warning Parliament about some of the perils of this debt and deficit. I gave them all kinds of evidence. I even drew pictures for them, graphs that showed the revenues and the expenditures, the debt curve going up and the next financial curve upward; I mean, these things were all laid out so plainly that you couldn't miss it.

Why do they ignore them is the question. They're aware of them but it wasn't a political issue. Had the newspapers maybe printed those graphs that showed curves going skywards maybe the public might have said, "Hey, this is getting out of hand." The role of politicians isn't necessarily to lay out the options and the future consequences of current actions. You have to go back a couple of steps because the bureaucrats have to lay out the options for the politicians for their consideration. They have to explain what it's going to cost to run the army. And do you get a big army or a small army? And this costs this and for less you can do fewer things. So those options are laid out for the politicians. I see no problem with politicians doing that. They tend not to. If you look at how it's done, they tell you what they're going to do. Having made those option decisions privately, perhaps within the caucus, within the Cabinet, maybe with some discussion in Parliament, but generally the discussion of the budget is, here's what we're going to do, not, would you like this or that?

I think there's some truth to this idea of the auditor general as a 24-hour media wonder. The media aspect of it started with Maxwell Henderson and continued through Mr. Macdonell's time and my time and today, with Denis Desautels, there's a lockup, it's quite a fanfare. It dominates the paper for one day. The truth of it is, it goes on in the paper for probably another week, but if you issue a report on a Tuesday, it's big news Wednesday and you get some thoughtful articles on the weekend where the people do more research. They'll write some, but then it's gone because something else overtakes it, be it a fire in a local community or some scandal. News is news.

I wanted to change the system so the public could be exposed to this more. I wanted to report more frequently because the audit reports were getting stale. We tried a number of times to persuade Parliament to change the act. The governments of the day were not interested in more audit reports coming out publicly. But the members in opposition were. One member on the NDP side took it three times to Parliament on a private bill and it got talked out. Just last year the former chairman of the Public Accounts Committee, Jean Robert Gauthier, was able to persuade his colleagues that they should vote in favour of periodic reporting. So they've got that now and I think their first one is coming in May of 1995 and that'll be the first time there'll be a more up-to-date kind of report and it'll be a partial report.

I'm not so sure the exposure would be a motivation behind these reports. Other countries have been doing it for years. The British have 50-plus a year, the Americans between 700 and 900 a year, New Zealanders have periodic reporting and the Australians are going for it. Canada was behind the times. It was time to change a long time ago, but we finally did it.

We had a comptroller of the treasury up until the 1960s sometime, and the last one was a chap named Herb Balls. He was very involved in the detailed approvals of expenditure. At one time there might have even been a pre-approval process and then that office was abolished as a result of a government report. They went to saying, "Let the managers manage," and they did. That went on until my predecessor, James Macdonell, decided there should be a chief accountant for Canada. That resulted in the creation of the comptroller general of Canada and that was 1979, I think, though it might have been 1978. That person became very involved in the design of the accounts of Canada and the internal auditing in government departments.

I think Macdonell was right when he made his very quotable phrase, "We are losing control." It was said a little more poignantly than that and the government did respond to it by appointing or creating the post of comptroller general. Now that whole exercise has been downplayed in the last few years. The comptroller general's office has been merged into the Treasury Board and the secretary of the Treasury Board is also the comptroller general, so the role has diminished considerably from what Macdonell envisioned. He saw a chief accountant of Canada who would get the books together and make sure the information was complete and timely.

That never really happened, although a series of comptrollers general did their best. It's sort of an uphill fight for them to try and improve the accounts of Canada. And a lot of improvements were made with the joint efforts of the auditor general and the comptroller general. Some very interesting things happened. But it was a fight against tradition. It's always been this way, so why fix it, is it that broke? Yet auditors were very concerned because things did need fixing in their view.

I don't know if it's quite as devious as the bureaucrats wanting to maintain their spending ways, it's just that there are only so many things a government can do. They can only undertake so many initiatives at any given time. This was just one more initiative and where does it rank in the priorities? Well, compared to winning wars or defeating poverty and keeping Canada healthy, it was not a high priority.

I think if the public started to take a look at this summary — you may not have ever heard of that summary, I don't think it was widely distributed — but that's a terrific piece of information. Now, who's going to sit down and read a set of accounts, even if it's simplified and modernized and in a language that one would understand. Chances are the general public would probably want it put in a consumable form by the media somehow or have somebody talk about it. Have a TV program on it. Have a series of articles in the newspaper. I can't imagine a huge appetite in Canada for people to say, "Hey, the government's published its accounts, I've got to go down and buy them and read them." That's just not on.

We proposed 10 key indicators that would give you a ballpark picture of how the country's doing. This last report started to produce that kind of information, so it's coming. It's coming now because there's been a lot of pressure from the Office of the Auditor General. It takes time for these ideas to gain popularity and people are better educated today about public accounts than they used to be. If there was greater visibility of the costs of programs 20 years ago, the effect on the public's perceptions and demands for fiscal responsibility would simply depend on the individuals.

For example, you don't know what it costs to go to the doctor. You don't get a bill. You go and have a wart removed, you don't get a bill. It's almost treated like a free good. The public has an absence of knowledge.

My guess would be that if people knew how much it cost to do things, there might be more concern about the kind of services they're demanding or the services they're using. Some of these things are discretionary. You don't get a bill. You don't know what it costs to educate your children. If people are going to be given information, it has to be information that relates to the way they live their lives. It's got to be put in terms they can understand. You tell somebody that the budget's gone up or down $357.3 million in defence this year but you just don't know what it means. It doesn't mean anything to you.

The information is available. People don't read it. There are suitcases full of that stuff but people don't read it. I think the municipalities do a much better job of making it available. If you pay city property taxes, you get a nice little folder every year with pie charts on it saying, this is where your money came from and this is where it went. It says so much came in from dog tags, and so much came in from park fees, and so much came in from property taxes. So much went out to schools. So much went out to parks and to the police department, and you get some feel for it. But again, does everybody read those folders? No, but it's simple.

The debt is a very real IOU to a young person. I'm down at the other end of my career and I've had the advantage of the government spending money on things I didn't ask them to spend money on. But they sure spent it and you're going to have to pay for it. I've paid huge taxes throughout my career, tons and tons of taxes. But my little share simply hasn't been enough to make any difference. Those taxes are still going to be there, big time. High taxes have come way down the weight scale. It used to be that only the high earners paid big-time taxes. Today the average earner pays big-time taxes. And that's going to be there and I think if the public demands to know more, they'll get more.

The information is there. It's a matter of packaging the information — if the media spent more time on making some of this mumbo jumbo simpler. The government has certainly taken big steps to make it simpler. For example, the annual report on Canada didn't go in the news. It just didn't hit the news at all. For a professional accountant like myself, I see Canada producing the first and best product in the whole world; and not a peep to tell the average person what's going on. If somebody like me, and there's a lot of other people like me, could sit down explain that to somebody, then maybe people would get the message.

The implications of the debt are huge because there's a deficit. A small businessman's paying far more interest than he would otherwise pay if the government looked at the balance. International lenders are saying there's more risk in Canada because they have all this debt. That debt was created because we had deficits. We spent more than we took in. So the average young businessman is paying far more for the money he's borrowing than that person would in a country where the financial situation was better tended over the years.

The political process is to dole out more good news than bad news. You don't get the bad news unless there's a political agenda which says we've got to give people some bad news to cause a different behaviour, which is what you're getting right now. We're getting a lot of concerning news about accumulated deficits causing huge debts that are now important messages for politicians to get out; so they get a different behaviour and so budgets get accepted because people are now concerned.

In the next 10 years, if we stay on the same spending course, the kind of services available will be far less than in my generation. I don't know which services but there are going to be old fogies like me who will want the services we've paid for. If you pay over $100,000 worth of income tax in a year, you feel as if the country's going to look after you when you're an old person. So I'm looking forward to my Canada Pension Plan, which I've paid for. I'm looking forward to hospitalization if I need it because I've sure as hell paid for a lot of hospital costs over time. When those days come, those systems will be there. You as a younger person are going to say, "Hey, that's OK for those old folks but I'm paying taxes too and I want my share." We're going to have a political squabble over who gets what.

The younger generation will probably pay higher taxes because in the foreseeable future I can't see taxes going down. The only way that I could see taxes really coming down would be if the deficit became a surplus. The revenues of the country would have to be sufficient to pay for the programs of the day, and if we had a strong economy sustained over time, you wouldn't have money going out on welfare as much. You wouldn't have unemployment. You wouldn't have payments to fishermen because there is no cod; there'd be other kinds of jobs. You're seeing those things go away now. The Crow Rate — it was plain as the nose on anybody's face that that was something that was out of date.[1] It had been around for a century and yet that subsidy was only turned off this year. It's very interesting to see the political reaction, which would have been violent a decade ago. People are now accepting these things because they know there's no money left.

The government used to run a surplus. It would bobble around near breakeven, but what's wrong with a surplus, especially when you've got some debt to pay down? You can use surplus moneys to get that debt down, which reduces your debt service. As debt service gets smaller, there's either more surpluses or more money to provide programs that are judged to be needed. If you look at contemporary Canada, there are four provinces now predicting breakeven or a little surplus. That's a very big turnaround from the directions in which they were going. It just gets to the point where there's no money left to run the programs and pay the debt service of the debt that's been piled up. It probably takes a crisis. You get a new stop sign after somebody's been run down. They don't put it up before.

If you want to talk to somebody else about how we got to where we are today and where it all came from, you might want to talk to some former finance ministers who really fought the battles in Cabinet. Former auditor general Maxwell Henderson comes to mind. He's still alive, in good health, and he's a very interesting man who can speak very knowledgeably about the 1960s and 1970s. You might want to talk to Harry Rogers, who was the first comptroller general of Canada, to perhaps Mike Rayner, who was the second comptroller general of Canada. They'll give you some insights.

Talk to some presidents of the Treasury Board. You've got Don Johnson, Bob de Cotret, among others, who could perhaps give you some insights into why more money was spent than was taken in. Former ministers of finance, Mr. Wilson was certainly there — he was trying to be a saviour in a Cabinet full of spenders. Talk to his predecessors on the Liberal side. Marc Lalonde's still around. Speak to Mr. Trudeau and Mr. Mulroney, the key people who headed up governments to spend more than they took in.

The closer you get the government to the people the better. If you're in a small town and you have a mayor, you meet the mayor at the hairdresser's and get a chance to talk to him, whereas you may not know your member of Parliament. That person's far more remote. They've got 90,000 to 100,000 people they have to meet and they're not even in the same town, they're over in Ottawa doing their thing in Parliament. They're a long way away from the people they're representing.

In terms of federal and provincial differences in reporting, they're mixed. The provinces are catching up with the federal level. I always thought one of the best reporting practices was in the Northwest Territories, although it's not a province. It really had a marvellous accounting system and quite good accounts. It is a small, little government, but in terms of meeting good accountability requirements, I thought they were excellent. Canada is a good model to the world. I mean, Americans don't have a set of accounts — which would astonish the average American. They don't know where they stand. In fact, the Figure study I was talking about earlier, the government reports study, determined that the debt of the United States of America at that time was $5 trillion. There was a bill going through their Congress, increasing the borrowing levels from $2.5 trillion to $3 trillion, yet they already owed $5 trillion and Americans hadn't been told.

NOTES

1. The Crow Rate was a federal government subsidy given to Western farmers in order to reduce the costs of shipping their grain. It was determined by the size of the farm and its location.

THE LOBBYISTS

Interest Groups and the Shaping of
Public Policy

KERNAGHAN WEBB

A lawyer and public servant defends publicly funded interest groups.

Interest groups do a number of different things in society. They provide services and they oftentimes advocate certain positions to government, to society, urging that society or government adopt a particular policy or a new law or a new program. When interest groups provide services, they're not directly, necessarily, touching on government. When they want to change a policy or a law or program, that's when it's something which directly affects how government operates.

The problem is if one were to just say, "Let all flowers bloom, let all interest groups come forward as they may," some interest groups would naturally be able to get together and have a strong resource base and be heard. Whereas other groups, which are not necessarily groups advocating a position any less valid, would be lost in the shuffle due to certain problems that are now well understood in the economic literature. They are at a disadvantage in terms of how they're organized and how they're structured. So they would have a tendency to be lost.

I think initially you could say that governments everywhere became interested in the question of how do we get an equal voice, with all of the various interest groups out there who are all trying to say something which could be useful to us, which we need to know. In Canada one of the approaches adopted was to provide some funding in a variety of different ways, through the tax system and through direct grants and contributions, which are just fancy names for money coming out in one form or another.

That approach essentially went without criticism until the 1980s, when suddenly somebody noticed there was another meter running — the accounting finance meter. And although the total of the expenses provided to interest groups by the federal government is relatively small, it's still quite significant when looked at outside of government. The question of why one interest group got this funding and why another group did not receive money also grew to become quite a contentious issue in a number of different contexts.

It led to a lot of different soul-searching reviews within individual departments and government-wide, as the case might be, and not just here at the federal level in Canada, but also at the provincial level and in other jurisdictions. We came in trying to provide some way of sorting out the different types of interest groups that are out there. Trying to come up with a system which would allow us to distinguish between a vast cacophony of voices all vying for the attention of government and the media, and society generally.

The approach that we adopted essentially focused on one key problem and that is that everybody always frames their particular position in terms of it being in the public interest — no matter whether you're a manufacturer of a specific product or you are a victim of something somewhere with no commercial interest whatsoever. It's standard practice to say that whatever position you're advocating will be in the best interest of society generally. So essentially what this led to on our part was this conclusion: that the term "public interest" as it is right now has been inflated by so many people using it in so many different contexts that it is essentially meaningless.

We need to come up with a more precise set of vocabulary to distinguish between groups, and the idea that we came up with is to distinguish between three different types of groups. They are public-interest groups, special-interest groups, also known as private-interest groups, and charter-interest groups, which is a particular animal known in the Canadian context which doesn't necessarily relate to other jurisdictions because other jurisdictions don't have a charter the way we do. Public-interest groups, so called, are groups which advocate a policy that does not benefit the members of the group any more than anyone else in society. To distinguish that from a private-interest group, let me give you a quick example. Say there are two environmental groups. One environmental group consists of average citizens in Canada all concerned with deteriorating air quality. The second group consists of property owners downstream from a pulp mill and they're also concerned with air quality. But they're particularly concerned with air quality affecting their property and their property values. We would say that the one group, the group that consists of average citizens of the country who are all concerned with air quality, would be a public-interest group because even if they're successful in getting a change in policy, a new law, they're not going to benefit the individual members of that group. They are not going to benefit materially or physically any more than any other member of society. Whereas the property owners downstream from a pulp mill, if they're successful in restraining or somehow or other restricting the odours and emissions from a pulp mill, their property values will go up, so they would be a private-interest group.

That's a key characteristic of private-interest groups and a point of distinction between public-interest groups and private-interest groups. It's about the benefits and who gets them. This also, however, highlights the key problem with public-interest groups because everybody benefits equally whether or not you're a member of the group. What is the value for you as an individual in joining? As a consumer, if I can benefit from the Consumers' Association of Canada's work without joining, then why should I bother joining? So there's this problem that public-interest groups have because their members are not benefiting any more than anyone else is. They have a tendency to have difficulty attracting members.

Whereas private-interest groups, where the members are going to receive some benefit that other people in society will not have, have less difficulty attracting members. They still might have some difficulty but not to the same point. So this led to the conclusion by our study team that it's the public-interest groups that might not be heard otherwise, were it not for some type of additional support of one sort or another from government or perhaps from some other agency, as the case might be. So those are the two main groups. The public-interest groups on the one hand and the private-interest groups on the other.

The reason behind funding these various interest groups was to create an equal playing field. But it is not correct to say only the public-interest groups have been funded thus far by the government. Up until now, essentially, the classification system that we're suggesting has not been in existence. It hasn't been applied or understood as being the basis for understanding and distinguishing between which groups might need funding and which groups might not.

The other thing is that there's nothing necessarily wrong with government funding a private-interest group in the right set of circumstances. Say, for example, a group of people have all suffered from the same problem. So they're all victims of the same symptoms or disease or malfunctioning product. It may very well be that the federal government or a provincial government might want to fund this group in order to better understand the problems that this particular group is having, even though that's clearly a private-interest group. Frankly, I don't see anything wrong with that. If you know that this group is the only group out there that's capable of supplying you with that information and that information is useful to you, it would make sense to me that that group should receive some funding.

You have to look at the individual circumstances of what the business group is and the context of what issue they would be funded for. What we're suggesting as an approach is that if the federal government wants to fund groups for specific issues, where certain groups have that expertise and others don't, then they should engage in essentially a competitive tender process like for any other contract. And may the most qualified and lowest bid win the day.

At another level the problem is, which groups out there are going to survive or not survive depending upon whether or not they receive funding? That's what we call sustaining funding. On the issue of sustaining funding, the types of groups which should receive government funding, in our view, are public-interest groups because they are the ones who suffer from that free-rider problem. That is to say, they have difficulty in attracting members because all individuals can receive all of the benefits even though they're not members of the group.

I don't know whether we all could be part of the many groups out there. The distinction I make is between a collectivity and an interest group. A collectivity is, say, for example, women. Women represent a collectivity in our society. They all have a certain characteristic that distinguishes them from other people in society. But NAC or Real Women or thousands of other groups out there represent groups who draw on some members of that collectivity.

The interesting question is when those groups stand up, do they say, "We represent all women in Canada"? I suggest you might want to check and look at that. Often times you'll hear someone stand up and say women in Canada are not going to stand for this or that and the logical question that comes to mind is, how do we know all women are standing behind this particular spokesperson for the cause? I think that's a major problem. We have a suggested approach for funding public-interest groups which to our minds is more open and fair and legitimate — transparent is another word that's used — and which in some ways would assist groups in their ability to stand up and say we represent X or Y.

My research into the area suggests that there was a change that occurred at about the time of World War II in terms of the attitude of government as to what it could accomplish in society. In turn that led to — at or about the same time, it's difficult to say which happened first, the chicken or the egg — but in turn that led to a proliferation of interest groups. My understanding is that, essentially, with the ability of the Canadian government and other Allied governments in World War II to bring together society and put out more munitions, armed forces, etc., the needs of the war effort persuaded the government, people and members of society generally that government can do a lot more than what it had been doing prior to that time. Prior to that time it was involved in only the most basic of services: policing, lighthouses, military, roads and that kind of thing.

So what happened after World War II was a gradual expansion in the role of government. It started establishing more and more socially oriented programs, assisting various disadvantaged groups and trying to address more and more problems than it had addressed prior to that time. In the process of so doing, examples being environmental or worker health and safety or what have you, they set up regulatory regimes instead of it just being a general law which said you cannot do this, you cannot do that; instead they had these elaborate administrative structures underneath the laws.

And so there was an awareness within the general community at the same time as this bureaucracy was being created that key decisions regarding the welfare of individuals were being made by this bureaucratic structure. So there came to be, I wouldn't want to call it a shadow government, but a parallel group of concerned individuals clustering around each individual regulatory regime, consisting of beneficiaries or regulated parties or what have you. They all had their own particular perspective on how the law was being applied or how the law could be changed.

Parallel with the growth of government is the belief that government could do more than it had before and that government could solve many of society's problems. This growth of interest groups went alongside that belief, a good example being the environmental area. Where 30 years ago there might have been two or three conservation groups, the Audubon Society and things like that, alongside of the development of major environmental laws there is this huge proliferation of environmental groups representing a spectrum of positions.

That's essentially the situation that we have up until the 1980s, when somebody noticed, wait a minute, all these regulatory programs and some of the funding programs that are associated with them for interest groups are costing us a lot of money. Indeed, we're receiving a lot of flack for some of them as well because it's not perceived as legitimate. People asked, "Why did this group get this amount of funding and not that group?" It comes down to the question of the way it is up until now that government has funded interest groups.

Ultimately it comes down to an individual bureaucrat operating with the full knowledge and authority of his or her minister, pointing fingers and saying, "You're a winner, you're a loser," in the sense of "We're going to give you some money, we're not going to give you some money." This produced a lot of controversy in the interest-group community itself because it created a certain amount of legitimacy. In other words, legitimacy was essentially bestowed by government in giving funding to one group and not to another.

It also, arguably, distorted or at least altered the patterns of behaviour of those interest groups because they realized, depending upon what I say or how I organize, I might be more eligible for funding than I would be otherwise. So they became essentially outward-looking rather than looking to their members or society as a whole. There is a danger there when there is potential for that type of abuse.

I'm not saying that decision making in our government has become very politicized through the proliferation of interest groups. There's an expression that's used in law: "Justice must not only be done, it must appear to be done," and it applies here equally. Regardless of whether or not there was any political role in the decision making, there's a perception to an outsider that if an individual bureaucrat is making a decision at the behest of his or her minister, that because this group happens to be flying a red flag rather than a blue flag, that's why it got more funding than another group. This happens, rightly or wrongly.

So there's a perception problem and a legitimacy problem that flows from that and is potentially leading to a non-democratic way for interest groups to behave. They start to realize, rather than looking at my own members, if I just look to the particular spigots within government where funding is coming out and address all of my attention to that, that's how I will continue to exist and flourish. So it's kind of a change in perception which could lead to a change in actual positions on particular issues, which could be a problem for government and for society generally.

We suggest that a better approach would be to avoid having individual bureaucrats be put into that difficult position of choosing one group over another, even if they had the most legitimate reasons for choosing those groups. Instead, the approach we suggest is one based on membership. In other words, the quantity of money coming to a particular group would not depend upon what that particular group is saying; it would depend upon the number of members in society as audited by a third party. So a group with 200,000 members would get 200,000 times a particular ratio to be decided, whereas a group with only 10,000 members would only get a much smaller proportion of money. No one can say at that point that the reason why this group is getting more money is because of some individual bureaucrat's particular proclivities or biases or what have you. Instead it's clear. It's because more people came to that group. What we feel is that this approach will lead to a more democratic way of behaving in the groups themselves because they realize, if my sustaining funding depends upon how many members I have, then the most important thing I can do is try to get more members. So they will become pretty much focused on members rather than on the spigots that are coming from government.

I think the rapid growth and expansion of public-interest groups showed the promise of government. It was very easy for any individual, whether they're in government or not, to believe, if government has this expanded role to assist us in levelling out booms and busts in the economic cycle, perhaps it has a similar larger role to play to address other societal problems. And in the prosperity of post–World War II, revenues were coming in from all sources. Everybody wanted to buy. There was a pent-up demand for products, etc., so all the conditions supported that type of interpretation that the sky was the limit in terms of what government could do, that there would always be more money. So nobody thought to look at the gas gauge and see whether or not we were running on empty. Later on when the economy did in fact go down, then suddenly that became more of a concern. Not of course just for Canadian governments, but indeed around the world.

There is indeed a symbiotic relationship between government departments and interest groups. Groups definitely feed off government and government departments feed off interest groups. They work together and sometimes they work at odds in ways that are ultimately also in the best interests of the people involved. One thing is for sure — any news is good news if you can get your name in the paper. That means that that particular issue which a particular department is concerned about is achieving some degree of profile, and that's going to assist the minister the next time he or she goes into Cabinet and suggests that we have to move on this. It is the clamour from the public, so it's very definitely a symbiotic relationship.

The welfare state in a general way is a state that is concerned with the individual well-being of its citizenry and attempts to provide services or protect its citizens in a more wholesome way than other approaches, for example, the strict laissez-faire or free enterprise approach, which would say leave all individuals to fend for themselves. I don't know whether or not you can say conclusively if government has created a dependency environment or not, but surely one can put forward that this is a real potential. And that's really all you need to know. If there is this potential for abuse and if there is a potential for that dependency and it can be avoided through another technique, then maybe it's time to explore that other technique.

We suggest the process be designed so that there would be envelopes or pockets of money for each particular issue that you're talking about

— say environmental or health or consumer issues. That money would be finite. There would be limits on it. So if there are more groups all vying for the same money, it will mean that there will be less money to go around to those groups. So you may find that the groups will reorganize themselves into one larger group, if they feel that would be more effective in getting their message across. Or they may disband, as the case might be.

Indeed, the financial limit is not infinite. As it stands now, a particular grant and contribution program within a particular department will only have a set amount to use. That may expand from year to year, but there are limits there. But I will add one important caveat: the tax system. There are no ceilings on tax deduction. So that's one area where there are no limits. The sky is the limit there. For example, if you're in a business, you can claim certain lobbying-related expenses as business fees and they are deductible under the tax system, and there's no ceiling. The federal government does not say, "Up until a certain amount and then after that we will not allow any more tax deductions to go to any more businesses." In reality the financial limit expands with the number of businesses which claim the deduction.

It's the same thing with charitable status. Once you become a charitable group you become a filter through which more and more money flows, and there's no limit on the amount of money and donations that you can receive. It's a form of indirect grant or government expenditure that comes to those interest groups because it would be money that would otherwise be coming to government revenue.

From my experience in government, we do have individuals going forward and saying we should cut back. Indeed, there has been an important cutting back over the last few years, so that's not an unheard of proposition. One of my basic slogans, as a civil servant working for essentially Canadian society, is that it's our role to speak truth to power. We must go to our superiors and say, "I'm seeing something and I don't think it's for the better, Mr. Minister or Ms. Minister or Assistant Deputy Minister," whatever the case might be. "It's my position that we should be doing less rather than more. I see a harmful relationship developing."

That does happen. It's possible for departments to work with groups without there being funding. There are other forms of currency out there, such as when a particular policy being advocated by a particular group is adopted. Then that's a currency to that group. That group has achieved success and they can then go to their own members and to society at large and say, "We stood up to government and said we ought to have this, that and the other, and now they're doing it." And that might lead to more funding coming to them. It's a Nader type of approach.[1] The Nader situation is somewhat different because he's a very charismatic individual, but there's nothing stopping that from happening in a particular interest-group setting here.

Interest groups provide a useful source of information that might not otherwise come out, so we don't want to squelch that. The trick is to develop techniques that improve the democratic processes of Parliament or legislatures rather than detract from them. I think that the idea of a membership-based funding system is a good example of a more democratic, participatory type of approach. Indeed, it becomes a situation of, where individuals decide to put their membership, that group will have a more legitimate voice in society. They'll be able to stand up and say, "Pardon me. In comparison with these other groups that are also appearing before you Mr. Minister or Ms. Minister, we happen to represent the vast majority of members, therefore listen more carefully to what we're saying than to others."

It's the nature of the democratic process that you have only one vote but there are other techniques and there are other ways of participating in the democratic process. Indeed, we're seeing governments everywhere using these other techniques. We're talking about environmental-impact assessment processes where there are hearings held in the affected communities, or prior to a law being passed there will be consultations in every affected community and an attempt to contact all possible stakeholders. This is the new way of governing. One could call this a form of administrative democracy, which supplements the parliamentary democracy that already exists.

We're not all interest groups. We're all potential members of interest groups. The difference is that an interest group is something that has been organized with the specific objective of trying to get a change of law or a change of policy. In that sense, with some rare exceptions, you will see people forming an interest group and they will be the only member of it. Or they and a handful of neighbours will be. Then they will write a letter to the editor and it will seem to have more credibility because it will say the so-and-so association rather than just Bob Triple. And so that will carry more weight.

Indeed, they are immediately susceptible to criticism when they are exposed as just being two or three people afterwards. That is the danger of that type of combining of an interest group and an individual. Essentially what happens is that you get more accountability through this type of membership-oriented process. I should draw another point of distinction. There are other types of groups that have very few members, such as the Canadian Arctic Resources Committee. It has an extremely high reputation in, I think, all circles as being a provider of expert advice on environmental matters in the North and they have demonstrated that in hearings.

These types of groups would not be cut off from funding. Instead they would only be eligible for funding in a direct contract-tendering basis. Given that they have this reputation for providing extremely solid, well-researched papers and studies, they would have a very good opportunity to do a study on antelope crossing in the North and the effect of putting a pipeline down. They would probably be a logical group to receive that type of funding, contract funding. However, they might very well have to compete with some other groups who say they could do something at a lower cost and who have different sets of expertise. Frankly, that's a wonderful situation when you have that competition for the dollars and an effort being made by each interest group to come up with the resources and expertise that they know will fulfill the bill, and they will get the funding in the process.

When you have everyone essentially acclimatized to this idea that they must head off to Rome, that the answers are in Rome, one way or the other it's easy to think that that's the way things will continue to be. But if enough people go to all the trouble of walking to Rome and they discover that there's nothing there, that there's no more money to be had or you have to meet certain criteria that these groups just simply don't meet, then I think there'll also be a lot of weary travellers coming all the way back from Rome, saying, "My God, we wasted an awful lot of time there. Maybe what we should do is see if we can generate our own source of independence from government. That way we will not be so susceptible to the whims and wings of Ottawa or the provinces."

This is something that is applauded by government in addition to individuals in society, if we can get away from that type of approach. It may mean that we have to go through the Klein/Alberta experience where things are radically cut back and then there is a realization that this means the citizenry is going to have to pick up the slack themselves. Or it may mean the rest of the country can learn from the Alberta lesson without having to go through it to the extent or in exactly the same way as it's going on in Alberta. I don't know. People are slow to change. Governments are slow to change.

But the approach that we're suggesting is much more rigorous than a weaning process. It requires much more of an outward-turning behaviour on the part of interest groups, which will in turn lessen their dependency on government. It should also lead to better policy information coming to government because the information will not be in any way tainted or susceptible to challenges that it is tainted by the fact that this group or that group received funding from a particular department.

This policy of government-guaranteed loans to small businesses that become interest groups, essentially forcing people to go to Rome, frankly that is an area outside of my expertise. My immediate reaction is that it actually forces the companies to go to banks as a first step rather than to Rome. In other words the decision maker is not going to be the Roman, at least not the Roman located within Rome.

At the first level I see that as an improvement, but ultimately the approach that's being suggested by our minister is one which is recognizing the fact that for one reason or another certain commercial outlets are not providing the loans, the commercial loans to that sector. And in the interest of Canada it's been decided that these particular sectors or what have you are particularly economically useful, desirable, so therefore that type of government-guaranteed loan program has been put in place.

It has to do with picking winners, in one way. The process also doesn't have a downside for people who put money into it because they go to the banks but the banks are giving them a favoured kind of loan that banks love — government-guaranteed loans. People are being turned toward something. I'm certainly not going to speak for the minister but I don't think that the minister is doing this enthusiastically. He's doing it reluctantly and he's doing it as a step down from what was in place before.

Let's get back to my point about the Alberta experience or the New Zealand experience. Can we learn from these existing examples and come up with an approach which is humane and tones things down over time rather than leaves us suddenly in a lurch and scrambling? If we can do an approach where the one comes up as the other goes down, ultimately that will be the most acceptable approach to everyone in society, the one with the least amount of upheaval. And surely that's what we all want.

There has been a change in the way we have come to identify ourselves in society. The perception prior to World War II, perhaps wrong, was that we were two founding cultures: the Franco and the Anglo cultures. Essentially we were a homogenous group of former Europeans, immigrants. I say that's wrong because clearly that's missing the Aboriginal peoples who were here before us and they're obviously the most genuine Canadian citizens there are. But rightly or wrongly, that perception, I think, has gone through a severe readjustment and analysis.

As we've come to recognize that in fact we are a society of immigrants from around the world — if you scratch the surface of any one of us, we've come from someplace else, and not necessarily with a European, Judeo-Christian set of values and mores and ideas — what that means is that as a society, it's no longer easy to say what our values are toward any particular issue. We represent so many different people coming from so many different groups. Therefore the old approach of thinking that there can just be reliance on the community to solve problems amongst themselves lost a certain amount of credibility in the eyes of many people in the 1960s and 1970s and 1980s and up to the present.

That helped to lead to this idea that we have to go to government to get answers because our interest is sufficiently precise and narrow in comparison with others in society, so they might not necessarily help us if we tried to do this on our own. Government, on the other hand, is out there to represent all of us, and through the terms of the Charter is specifically mandated to do certain things in that type of context. There's a belief that government has all the answers. Perhaps a knee-jerk reaction on the part not just of interest groups but individuals. Whenever a new problem arises or a twist on an old problem, they'll immediately say there ought to be a law or government ought to do something about this.

I think we're reaching the end in terms of government. I think in society we're finally coming to the realization that there are limitations to what government can do. In fact, there's a powerful amount of energy and positive spirit that exists in communities and individual groups if they can form coalitions and work together. Perhaps they can provide services or work out solutions to problems without having government in the centre of the picture. Whether we're talking about self-regulation, you name the solution to a particular problem as it arises, what we're going to see in the future is an adjustment. This adjustment combines the role of government, citizens and interest groups, with the interest groups doing more amongst themselves and less delivery actually being done by the government itself.

There's a Far Side cartoon which I've seen. I think most people have seen it and it strikes me as being appropriate to describe the situation we're in now. It's the one where there's this auditorium full of dinosaurs and there's a dinosaur up at the front standing behind a lectern and he says, "Gentlemen, the situation is looking increasingly grim. There's an ice age coming. We're cold-blooded and we've got brains the size of peanuts." In some ways I think that's the situation that governments are in.

Governments right now have big bodies and expend a lot of energy trying to keep going. They have to eat a lot of vegetation in order to continue to just carry on their functions. But they have very small brains. The part that's actually doing the thinking is comparatively small. And we need to come up with a different approach where the brain part is large. The policy analysis side is large. The delivery is passed off to other perhaps more grassroots organizations who are out there anyway, and they can provide the services for society more effectively, more inexpensively, and provide a useful side service, in the sense that individual citizens become more involved in the process of living and governing. And it doesn't become an us-them situation of someone in Ottawa or someone in Toronto or someone in Parliament or the legislature somewhere being the only source of the solution to a problem.

I think we are seeing the trend to point fingers at government more and more. I know that my minister, John Manley, just yesterday in a *Globe and Mail* article talked about the fact that consumers have to be more responsible and more resourceful on their own. He's raising a valid point that applies in other areas as well, whether we're talking about health or environment. Something that we know is coming down the tubes, generally, at the provincial and the federal level is this idea about health services. We can't afford anymore to bring in individuals whenever they're harmed in the slightest way and have the problem solved in a hospital.

Perhaps now what we're going to have to do is draw on the families of people who are suffering from some type of ailment to provide either in-home care or to go into the hospitals on the weekends and do some of the logistic legwork themselves to help out. It's not necessarily such a bad thing. It's recognizing that families have got a responsibility to other members of their own group and I think that approach is more universal than just the health area.

NOTES

1. Ralph Nader, a leading U.S. consumer and public policy advocate.

SEAN MOORE

A spokesperson for lobby groups provides an overview of lobbying in a parliamentary political system.

If you want to go right back to the source, lobbying probably started back in the time of kings and princesses, when courtiers to the court were hired by one interest group or another to try and influence a decision of the king. Certainly in more modern times there have been lobbyists, right from the beginning of the Canadian parliamentary system. Some we probably don't want to cite as modern-day examples: some of the scandals we had in this country associated with the building of the railway were instances of perhaps overzealous lobbying. There were railway interests trying to influence the decisions of the government of the day as to where railways were going to go and the terms under which they'd be built.

We've always had lobbyists. They've probably taken on more prominence over the last 10 or 15 years because of more media scrutiny, more examination of the role of people, and because the nature of our decision making has changed. We used to have in this country a system of what was called "elite accommodation," where a lot of those sorts of important decisions were made very quietly and behind closed doors.

It's very difficult to do that these days. In many instances, to a certain extent, we still have sort of elite accommodation but the nature of the elites has changed. The leaders of interest groups have become in some respects part of the elite in Canada. And the decision-making process, for a variety of reasons, is somewhat more transparent than it was before. So this interaction between interest groups and governors is more obvious.

A lobbyist is any individual who tries to influence a decision of government, sometimes on behalf of a client, sometimes on behalf of an employer. There are different sorts of people involved — lawyers, accountants or government relations consultants. They needn't necessarily speak on behalf of their employer or their client to the government. Sometimes the role is as an advisor rather than as a direct representative. A lobbyist is concerned with decisions of government, whether it's to give money or to not tax money, a tax expenditure; sometimes they're there to try and influence the regulations of government or a particular act of Parliament. Governments do a lot of things. There are a number of things that governments can do, which the academics call "governing instruments." And people who are involved in public policy advocacy and lobbying are oftentimes trying to influence any one of a number of those.

Belonging to an interest group is a democratic right but we see lots of duplication and a lot of waste. Governments often hand out money to five different groups who probably do similar sorts of things. There's a lot of frustration with this business of government granting money to organizations. However, one of the roles of government is to provide social control. Part of social control is providing escape valves and providing opportunities for individuals and for groups to, if not participate, at least feel like they're participating in the process.

This sounds incredibly cynical but it's true. Flip it around. Think about it this way. If the policy-making process in government appeared to be only accessible to groups that had the money for the high-price lobbyists that had access to key decision makers, what would we be saying about the legitimacy of our political process and the decisions made by government?

I don't think you have to either hire a lobbyist or be part of an interest group to gain access to government. But it's increasingly difficult for government to make decisions these days without it being able to demonstrate that whatever it's deciding is generally in the public interest. How do you demonstrate that it's in the public interest? One of the ways you can do that is to show that large components or chunks of our society are influenced one way or another by this. And that's in part one of the reasons why we've had this formation of interest groups, as a way of demonstrating the impact of government decisions on chunks of our population. Cumulatively those groups will try to argue for or represent the public interest.

One can argue that part of the problem we have in Canada right now is a lot of Canadians don't understand how governments make decisions. If they think that just walking into their MP's office is the single most important thing they can do, they're probably making a mistake. While talking to your elected representative can be important, we don't really have in this country, despite what some of the textbooks say, parliamentary government. We have Cabinet government. Most of the important decisions in this country are made in Cabinet. Most of the policy options and the spadework that is done in developing public policy in Canada is done at the bureaucratic level.

People who want smart lobbyists or smart public policy advocates have to know that that's where they have to start. They have to start understanding how the bureaucracy's looking at an issue, how they're framing the issue and what the options are because if you don't get involved in that issue, in that level of the policy development process, you're probably lost. Where the lobbyists or government relations consultants come in is, for the most part, they have made a living understanding that process. Understanding, for example, that many government decisions are not made by one person. They're a result of a complex series of intergovernmental, interdepartmental, interagency committees of bureaucrats, Cabinet ministers and the like. It's important to understand what that decision-making process is if you want to have any hope at all of influencing the decision making.

I believe there's no one single explanation for almost anything that happens in society, but among the reasons for the growth of interest groups is the failure of political parties to broker these divergent issues that come as part and parcel of a very pluralist society. The media has a role in this as well because a lot of people find that the best way to give voice to their particular point of view is not through a political party, where there's a certain amount of solidarity, collegiality and discretion that's expected as part of that process, but it's oftentimes a lot easier to get out there and get some media attention for an issue that you feel particularly strongly about. Often interest groups can do that much more effectively by just working as that one group.

It's fairly easy to get media attention. However, a lot of interest groups confuse effectiveness in their public policy advocacy with their effectiveness in getting media attention. It's one thing to be on the evening news and to be quoted in the newspaper. It gives you the sense that you're being effective. You may be effective in terms of raising one dimension of an issue but that's not the same as being effective in influencing the decisions of government. But I believe a lot of interest groups make that mistake. They assume one equates to the other.

Part of the cost to our society with having interest groups is the cost of democracy. If you want to have a democratic system and a policy development process in government that takes into account the legitimate interests of a wide range of groups in society, that's part of what we have to accept. Is there a more cost-effective way of having these interest groups? Governments are reluctant to wade into that because it involves making certain value judgments about who is a legitimate representative of one interest or another.

Democracy is messy. Democracy is noisy. Democracy is expensive. Governments are finding that these days we have this incredible orgy of consultations that are happening on a wide range of issues. You have to sit there and oftentimes listen to a lot of people who really don't know what the hell they're talking about. But they have a right to have that particular point of view. And sometimes government is paying for them to have a point of view.

On a wide range of issues you have what they call "intervenor funding," where government provides money to a particular group so it can research an issue and make representation to the government. Governments have to realize — especially with the battering that the political process has undergone over the last several years, where the credibility and very legitimacy of government has been questioned — that you cannot have a politically acceptable outcome unless the process leading toward it is seen as being legitimate.

The Charlottetown Accord was a pretty good example of that. They're trying very hard to show that there are broad consultations; they're listening broadly and listening openly to a wide range of issues.

That's part of the cost that we are bearing for political outcomes that the government hopes it can then argue are more legitimate and more all-inclusive in terms of considering various points of view that have been offered. Can we afford to finance all these interest groups in the grand scheme of things? It's what some people call budget dust; it's not an awful lot of money, but can it be done more effectively and more economically? It probably can be. But somebody has to be making some decisions about who is a legitimate spokesman for an individual or group in society.

There are some that argue the government shouldn't be giving money directly at all. I think this is something that probably deserves more scrutiny. Should we perhaps be using the tax system so Canadians can speak with their own tax dollars as to who's a legitimate spokesman for a particular point of view? In other words remove that decision making, perhaps, from bureaucrats and politicians and put it in the hands of individual taxpayers. The taxpayers may be able, through a variety of means including some of the deductions that are available right now, to target their money and target those groups they feel are the most legitimate spokespeople for their point of view. There's a problem with that, though. Under the Revenue Canada rules, charitable organizations, ones that can receive money and give tax receipts, are limited in how much public policy advocacy they can do. They can't spend more than 10 or 15 percent of their total resources and total time. So these very groups that you would hope could be more legitimate spokespeople for particular issues, under the current tax system are precluded from doing that.

This actually goes back to a common law tradition of what is a charity. It's a performance of public good or public education. In the last several months we have seen Revenue Canada de-register a number of groups. They've been pro-life groups. Their public education on the issue of abortion, for example, has been seen as being too one-sided, that it's not education, it's advocacy. That's the government's position. So the whole question of whether or not there should be a special provision in our income tax code to channel money to groups that do advocacy in lieu of having government make the decisions is one that really hasn't been receiving much attention. And it probably should, if you want another factor in how that sort of decision making can be made.

When people talk about lobbyists, often they're fairly promiscuous in their use of terms like "influence" and "power." It's like saying there is no water that's not shark infested. Well, no lobbyist is not powerful or not influential. I think that misses the point. The power of lobbyists is in what they know about both the decision-making system, how decisions are made, and the different things you can do to influence that decision. Are they personally powerful in terms of their direct influence on the process? No, I don't think they are. Are they useful in influencing public policy? I believe they are, if you consider the guidance they can offer as to whom to talk to and what different parts of government they should be approaching, what different sorts of arguments should be made and what sort of alternatives government would possibly be amenable to, given its public policy agenda and the political pressures that are on it. That sort of analysis and that sort of advice can be very helpful in influencing public policy. But that's not to say that the individual lobbyists or government relations consultants, or lawyers or accountants are individually powerful themselves in influencing the decisions.

I don't think money is the single most important factor in influencing governmental decision making. I mean, if you have the financial resources to put a full-court press on government, research thoroughly and provide evidence of the potency of whatever you're proposing, that's certainly helpful. What's more important is having a clear understanding of how governments make decisions and how you can influence those decisions. That doesn't necessarily require money.

I think there are three problems encountered by a lot of interest groups, be they general public-interest groups, industrial groups or industry associations. First of all, they equate media exposure with influence on government. Secondly, they often make the mistake of preaching to their own membership rather than actually trying to make a case to government that government will find persuasive. In other words, the internal political situation of whatever that interest group is ends up being the chief determining factors to the nature of the argument that these groups are making to government. Thirdly, as I mentioned earlier, oftentimes an enormous amount of effort is put into getting in to see a minister. They believe that if you can just get your argument across to that minister your day is won, failing to observe that in the Canadian parliamentary system, and this applies at the provincial level as well, what's very important is dealing with the bureaucratic advisors for ministers. They're the ones who usually brief the minister. They're the ones who set out the definition of the problem and the options that the government is facing, the consequences of one thing or another. So if enormous emphasis is not put on the bureaucracy, then a lot of wasted effort is expended.

It might seem like there's a whole group of people making policy decisions, not the elected official, and this is part of the great frustration that Canadians have with government. Their ballot every four years doesn't seem to count for an awful lot, and yet we do delegate a substantial amount of responsibility to these individual legislators. But one of the very important features of the Canadian parliamentary system is fairly rigid party discipline in voting in the House of Commons. Your MP can be very sympathetic to this problem but unless he's able to turn around the entire government caucus on a particular issue, and in particular convince the minister and his bureaucratic advisors of the merit of that argument, it's not going to go very far. It's probably a necessary but insufficient means of influencing the public policy process. Of course all of this is assuming that your MP agrees with you in the first place, which sometimes is not the case.

If Canadians want to influence public policy, they really have to take it upon themselves to learn about how our governmental system operates. Unfortunately our educational system is not very good at teaching that. We're talking about a system that doesn't really exist. What we need to do is have some realpolitik education in Canada that explains how decisions are made and how you can play a real role in that system. And to assume that MPs and Parliament are the real decision-making authorities in Canada on a wide variety of issues is not a very good place to start off.

It's becoming more complex because government is involved in so many parts of our lives. This is not a recent phenomenon. Over the years government has delegated a lot of authority, a lot of decision making, a lot of policy making to regulatory agencies and to other public servants because MPs can't do it all. I mean, MPs, and to a certain extent the Cabinet, make decisions in very broad policy terms. They don't get into the nitty-gritty in terms of how regulations are devised, in terms of how things are implemented. The issues are too complex; the country's too big, time is too short to put all of that on our elected members. Learning and understanding, accepting how to deal with the fact that a lot of important decisions are made by non-elected people, is one thing I think we should stop griping about and perhaps just learn to deal with.

If you feel very passionate about an issue, you can either start an interest group or at least join one that already exists. Part of the problem in our politics today, and in particular with political parties, is that people who feel strongly about issues aren't involved in political parties anymore. They go and join an interest group. I think there's some legitimacy to that observation but I don't know if we should be complaining about it so much. It's another manner of expression. Political parties have to find a way — it's one of the challenges that they face — of accessing and trying to get the involvement of these groups more and more within the political parties.

In the United States, and to a certain extent in Canada, you're seeing some parts of that. Some of the political parties have, for example, women's commissions or Aboriginal commissions. Some of them have individual caucuses within them that represent a particular point of view. This has been very common in the United States. In other words, it's trying to bring the influence of those interest groups within the political process.

One of the problems with that from the participants' point of view is that it doesn't give you a lot of freedom in terms of expressing your point of view in the media, which is a very powerful influence in this country. One of the big advantages of interest groups is they often don't want to have to worry about other competing arguments from the outside influencing what they can say to the media. Otherwise they have a pretty significant influence with the media and, at least, access to the media and the media's diffusion of that message throughout the system.

It bothers people to no end to see that the National Action Committee gets half a million dollars a year or that a number of environmental groups get $2 million or $3 million a year. But focusing on that as a problem, as a symptom of some malaise in our political system, is sort of just nibbling away at the edges. Again, one of the biggest problems in our political system is that the public expectation of how the system is supposed to work isn't anywhere close to the reality of how it works. That's the case even within political parties.

Political parties have these grand policy development processes where you have meetings across the country. In every constituency they come forward with policy proposals and resolutions for conventions. These things get debated for a day and a half, they get voted upon, they get written down and then they're forgotten. Now, what can breed more cynicism than people who are passionately putting all that time into the policy development process and then seeing it disappear into the ether.

It seems there is a lack of recognition of public-interest groups, that we're all somehow involved with a narrow interest that we're trying to promote. The best line is, "They've become us." I like that a lot. We belong to all sorts of groups whether we know it or not. You take out a membership in the Canadian Automobile Association for their tow truck service and all of a sudden you're a member of the Canadian Automobile Association and their lobby against higher gas prices. Society is increasingly being organized on this interest-group basis.

One of the things I believe is frustrating for people is that we have this cacophony of interests in society all of whom are saying, "I'm different, I deserve special treatment." It's what some are calling the politics of difference. And I believe one of the frustrations is that increasingly Canadians are asking themselves, "Don't we have anything in common? Isn't there anything that's speaking for us and the common experiences and common values that we have?" You can't blame people for thinking that that doesn't exist anymore. All this could lead us into a long discussion about communitarianism, a school of thought that says we need to be relying much less on government and try to bring more decisions, provisional services and decision making back to communities. But to do that we need to revitalize some of the concepts of community the government has absorbed over the last 60 years. Underlying all that there needs to be a much greater emphasis on the notion of personal responsibility rather than a sort of a counterweight to this rising crescendo and demand for rights that we've had over the last 25, 30 years.

In part this is a debate over the redefinition of government and what government should be doing. It's about how far government should reach into our lives and who the hell is making decisions on behalf of government. Because it isn't our individual members of Parliament. It's all a matter of delegated authority. I think you also have to ask who exactly is upset about this? Not everyone is upset with everything the government's doing.

Some farmers in Western Canada may be particularly upset at the particular strength of interest groups and government that want to control the use of guns, but they may be wholly in support of the idea of a supply-management group — groups like the Canadian Wheat Board, which provides them with a relatively high base price for their commodity. Arguments over economic issues are a very big part of it. I'm not denying that. Somebody's paying for it and we don't realize who's paying for who.

On the other hand, the things that seem to be setting people off more than anything else are the non-economic things. I'm talking about issues related to values, whether it be human rights commissions or the right of government to debate about whether physician-assisted suicide is appropriate or not. A lot of the values discussion goes back to the economic issues as well. For a country that has had a history of collective decision making and a collective approach to dealing with issues, one of the manifestations of this increasing pluralism we have in society is that people are rejecting these collective approaches to decisions.

I don't think this growth of public-interest groups has resulted in a total politicization of everything. I don't think you need lobbyists or government relations consultants to be effective in public policy advocacy. Especially if you take the time to learn yourself how decisions are being made and what the most important factors are in the minds of decision makers, whether it be the international dimension, the impact on the fiscal environment or public opinion. I find many Canadians generally, and interest groups in particular, don't take the time to understand how these decisions are being made. As a result they get frustrated and they think there's some sort of magic potion that a lobbyist is going to give them. I don't think that's the case at all. I mean, what is a government relations consultant or a lobbyist in Canada? It's not rocket science these guys are involved in; it's tracking the personal politics and the dynamics of decision making in a complex government.

What might be considered a grant to an interest group in one department is considered a special project funding in another. Part of it has to do with the definition of the particular account out of which that money has come and the particular purpose that it's being spent for. That's a problem with a lot of government spending. When you're spending $140 billion a year, how you actually categorize those different types of funding can be important. So the Treasury Board is a good place to look, but don't be surprised if they don't have all the answers.

An article I read talks about the roles of the social sector. So what is the social sector? It is non-governmental organizations. It's community groups. It's those things that aren't private sector free enterprise but they're not public sector government either. It's those sort of nether-world groups that represent interests that are an expression of values and particular approaches to dealing with issues. This in essence is the key model by which our society is going to be able to deal with issues in the future. The governments are incapable of doing it because of both the cost and immensity of the problems. At the same time the private sector is not going to be able to either because of their industrial structure and the economics of it. What is the role of non-governmental organizations in dealing with issues, not only in terms of representing points of view of government, but actually providing goods and services? When we talked about the role of government funding, we talked about the whole matter of core funding. The level of core funding has evaporated, for the most part, in Canada over the last several years, not just at the federal level, but at the provincial and local levels as well. What it's been replaced with is project funding. In other words government providing money to those sorts of non-governmental organizations to provide goods, services, or in some cases the service is providing an expression of opinion on behalf of certain elements of the population. Of all the areas that have not received very much original thinking and require more attention, it's the political institutions and political thinking that should be studied. In Canada we have a parliamentary system that basically is designed for the buggy-whip age. The whole approach to parliamentary discipline is borne of an age that we left behind 125 years ago, when individual Canadians could vote for a member of Parliament who's supposed to represent them. You find yourself being totally tied up in a very rigid parliamentary process. You're building in disappointment, frustration and cynicism from day one.

Do I have the particular prescription for what our political system should look like? No. I'm not suggesting that it necessarily reflects that of the American congressional system, which has a whole set of problems all its own and that is largely driven by money. So I don't have any particular prescriptions for it. But if there was one thing that I would like to see in this country, it's a revisiting of the political process so that the expectations of voters can have some hope of being realized much more fully than they ever will be in our existing system.

When the Charlottetown Accord was being debated, one of the advantages of that whole process is that we actually had some serious discussion about major change to the political system in Canada. But with its death, talking about political change or political reform in Canada is a bit like farting in church; you just don't talk about it in Canada anymore. No one wants to talk about those sorts of changes despite the level of frustration that we have with it. I don't know anybody who's talking about that these days.

JACK SLIBAR

A self-described "Sherpa" among lobbyists talks about the relationship between interest groups and regulators.

Pluralism is the foundation of a democracy and ultimately, when you do away with that, then you start doing away with the underpinning philosophies of the society. There is no question that government can become more efficient in the delivery of programs between departments. However, if we're going to continue — and I think we are — living in a very complex society where we expect to have input into policy making and whatnot, you have to have the machinery on the other end. The bureaucracy and government in general provide that ear to listen to the various issues. They have to be able to filter the various competing demands that are made on the system and come up with something that is credible, workable and ultimately supportable by the people of Canada.

In a pluralistic society everyone has a right to be heard. As a lobbyist I'm simply a hired gun. An organization comes to me and says, "Hey, we want to advocate this particular view and we want to have a method of bringing this forward" to government officials or to members of the bureaucracy or the opposition parties or whatever aspect of government you're looking at. It's my job to be unbiased: to look at a particular policy that you're advocating and find the best way of packaging it and then presenting it.

You have to bear in mind that when the process starts we've probably 101 other associations, interest groups and whatnot on the other side of the fence that'll be told in one form or another of this activity going forward, and they will be making a counterclaim. The bottom line is, it's up to the bureaucracy and members of the government to determine what's best for the interests of Canadians, or, in the province of Ontario, Ontarians.

I view myself as an educator for the association. I educate them as to how the government process works. I act as an impartial observer to analyze how that association functions, how effective that association is or potentially can be. I ask what some of its shortcomings are and I try to instill, at least in the executive of the membership, the kinds of things they may have to do to alter the way they're perceived by government. Many members don't realize the magnitude of different constituencies they have to deal with in government when they start the process. Many of them have a very skewed view as to how to approach government and how to be effective. Consequently, they probably had failures in the past and that's probably the reason they're calling me in to work on a particular policy or, alternatively, provide them with a strategic type of advice as to how they can structure themselves. Many associations even fall short of understanding how to effectively lobby.

One thing I make perfectly clear right from the start is that I don't peddle influence. Because quite frankly that's not the way to develop good, sound public policy. It's not in the public interest. It's not in the association's interest and it's not in government's interest. What I try to do is show them, all right, you have particular objectives, this is how we get from point A to point B, hopefully. And if we don't get there, you're probably in a better position to take on the next issue or to develop a new campaign or develop a new strategy once you've reached point B than you were when you were initially at point A. So after conducting an audit for an association I once again provide a briefing to the executive of the association. I explain to them where they stand with government generally, where their weaknesses are, where their strengths are, what they can do to alter their perceptions and government's perceptions of them or the bureaucratic perception of them. Then we go through a process of deciding what's important to the association and what isn't. We attempt to harmonize that with the issues that government would ideally be receptive to should the association bring them forward.

There are hundreds of associations and there are a lot of meetings and a lot of position papers that are developed. But ultimately an association really needs two core things. One, an expertise in the area that it's attempting to deal with. Two, an expertise on government and how government works, how bureaucracy works. One of the nice things about government is, in many cases they strike a compromise. Remember that government is also there to look out for the public interest. Not to say that associations are working against the public interest, but almost by definition they'll be more concerned with the narrow types of interests of their particular membership.

So government is a great meeting ground. It's a place where everybody comes and deliberates, debates, makes compromises and then finally, at the end of the process, hopefully spits something out that's acceptable to the groups that are involved. The public in general makes good, sound public policy. Yet it's hard to decide what public interest is. This is a good question. I mean, I would challenge you to have anybody give the proper definition of "public interest." What is public interest? Who's the public? That's the whole point. If you're going to go after a particular policy, you go after groups in society that are affected by that policy. You attempt to solicit the views from that community or the public community, and then you attempt to filter that through the bureaucratic machinery and ultimately, if necessary, bring it through the political machinery and the law-making machinery in the legislature and the Commons to have a new policy enacted.

One way for a concerned citizen to get involved in a policy issue is to become a member. You, as an individual citizen, could potentially join an association, let's say a consumer-interest type of association. You may try to work your way through the ranks or get on the board of directors. At that point in time you may think, hey, this is of interest to me, and you might be able to convince that association to pick up that particular banner and run with it. That's one way of doing it. It's a long journey from having a concern to actually having your voice heard on Parliament Hill. And it's one thing to have it heard; it's another thing to have it listened to. I think that's the element that has to be stressed. It's a complex, dynamic process. It's one that clearly needs experts all along the way. It's the type of thing where in the end I think you usually have effective policy usually made. It's not the ideal system but, you know, what are your choices?

I wouldn't look to the government as the primary cause of the bankruptcy this country is facing. Ultimately, if you're looking at costs, there are ways of streamlining any particular system. There are ways of doing away with waste. You may have a leaner, more efficient system which is receptive to individuals and receptive to the needs of groups in society. But in this country, as well as most Western countries, we are regulated from the cradle to the grave. That requires a large degree of input on public policy that decides how those various pieces of regulations or policies are made. It's a very complex process and it's difficult to get a firm handle on it. There is no definitive book that tells you this is exactly how it is done.

Clearly any kind of downsizing with government will ultimately shape interest groups, just as the taxes the interest groups take shape government. My analysis is that it's going to be a more competitive environment. Issues that require funding are going to be scrutinized more heavily. It's become a leaner system — not necessarily meaner but definitely leaner. It's going to be a system whereby there's going to be much more burden-sharing between government agencies and associations. Again, it's probably going to be more competitive from the standpoint of lobbyists because you're going to enter a spiral and the quality spiral is going to go up, basically. My briefs will have to be better and will have to have more succinct arguments. My client will have to have more succinct arguments and will have to be willing to do more with less.

Relationships between lobbyists and government were always there. It just happens that at this particular point in time — a really dynamic type of period in history, with streamlining, government cuts, threats to the social services — that these issues are coming out of the fold and are being debated more in the public environment. As a result, these groups are being heard more. The general public is being exposed to them more and that's the bottom line. It's just greater exposure in the times we live in. They've always been there and had some form of influence.

Their existence is dependent on whether they're going to have support from the government. This is the whole process of government. It has to make decisions, affect decisions, then society will rebel or you'll have protests or whatnot. It's part of the democratic process. Governments are not infallible and if they make a mistake, they hear about it. They hear it in the media. They hear it in letters. They hear it from associations. They may very well reverse the decision. In some ways it almost becomes the process of being a policeman. Associations, interest groups and whatnot police what government does. What's acceptable? What parameters are expanded? Which are contracted? Where's the harmony? That's what they do.

I think political concerns are an element of all policy formulation. Ultimately you have to remember that legislative time is scarce. Committee time is scarce. Government time is scarce. There are always more issues that bureaucracies or interest groups want to bring forward into the various political arenas than there is time for. Part of determining what the agenda is and what goes forward and what doesn't go forward, that's part of the process of deciding in political terms where the priorities of society are. In election times, when a government goes back to the people and has to account for itself, well, the people have a choice. Did that government make the right decisions, generally, as to which issues they brought forward or not? And people make their choice through the ballot.

The fact is, decisions are made differently closer to election day. It's part of the reality because of the terms of government and because of, dare I say, the fickle attitude of the population or the electorate in general. People don't want to accept hardships for long-term gain and governments have to react to that and they have to realize that. Part of government's mandate and motivating factors is to get re-elected and once again form the next government so that it's able to continue on with the policies that it's advanced either in its political platform or throughout the previous term. As a result, that means often giving the voter what they want.

Working in a short-term parameter, some issues get pushed away at the last minute because it's election time or because of changes in government priorities, changes in the economic situation or a crisis that surfaces. Sure it happens, but it's part of the process, it's part of the political environment. Governments are there in part to please societies and it's a large machinery that does that. In part it's the bureaucracy that deals with technical policy and it's also the government in power. By that I mean the party, and specifically the ministers in power, determine what policies are going to be pursued. It's Cabinet deciding what program gets funding, which program doesn't get funding, where cuts are made, where cuts will not be made. It's a very pluralistic society. That's part of living in a democracy.

Yet it can be volatile. It's a constantly changing dynamic. It's an environment, especially with government downsizing, merging of ministries and elimination of departments, that has to evolve. As a lobbyist, it's my responsibility to evolve with that to provide the best possible service I can to the client. I keep up by, well, I don't sleep very often. No, it's basically a lot of hard work and it's a process of networking and keeping up to date with what the agendas are. I wouldn't say networking is more important or less important. In many cases you find lobbyists that are specializing in particular areas. They may be specializing in business associations or policy areas such as health and welfare, or social policies or regulatory types of policies. We have lobbyists that deal exclusively with government procurements and whatnot, so it's in part specializing within that area as well.

There's also the factor of harmonization to be considered. I'll give you an example of harmonizing. One of the issues now in the province of Ontario is an attempt to get tough on crime and cut expenditures. So if you can harmonize your policy (in other words, whatever you're trying to advocate) with those particular objectives of the bureaucracy or the government, then of course you have a better chance of getting what you want or getting close to what you want. Getting close to what you want, however, is an art. Being able to think in creative ways and trying creative approaches to harmonizing the interests of a particular group or association and trying to mesh them with the priorities of government, that's part of the art.

Once you have that covered, ultimately your first step, depending on where the policy process is, but let's assume that it's still at the very beginning, your first step will probably be with the bureaucracy. You're going to go to the ministry which has a legislative mandate in this particular area, which monitors the regulations within this particular area. You're not going to necessarily start with the minister because quite frankly the minister is a good individual to see to finalize and formalize agreements that have been worked out previously. If you want to get into the nitty-gritty of policy and control and regulation and whatnot, you're going to deal with staff members. It's the whole gamut from a junior individual who's being asked by the director to develop a particular issue right through to the director of the branch, for instance, or potentially the deputy minister.

So many people are involved in this process because we live in a democracy, and the way policy is formulated in a very complex type of environment is that a lot of individuals at a lot of different levels have to have input, sign off, consult. Any particular policy issue is probably too broad and too vast for one particular person, or even one particular ministry, to deal with. I mean, could you imagine if you were a government employee and the scenario was to redraft the entire Criminal Code. It would be impossible. Clearly you're going to have a whole team involved on this process. You're going to have other ministries involved on this. So we have intergovernmental consultation or inter-ministry consultation that takes place.

You may have intergovernmental consultation between different levels of government. You may have the federal government negotiating with the provincial government for that province, provincial governments negotiating with municipalities or regional governments. This is a very dynamic, very complex, very open and dispersed type of system. And that works in most groups' advantage because if I come to you and if you're the only decision maker and you say no, well, then that's it. If it's a very pluralistic type of approach, I can say, "You're being obstinate and you're not going to be very helpful, so I'm going to go around you." Or, "I'm going to approach another ministry which has some interest on this and try to have pressure exerted on your ministry and maybe in the end your position doesn't matter because I have enough support elsewhere."

By and large, I would say 60 to 70 percent of government policy work is done in a very amicable, harmonious type of way. Groups come together, they meet, they discuss, they put position papers together and they haggle over particular policy issues. They try to advocate particular views, they see opposition critics, they see ministers and whatnot, and most of it is just the common course, so that by the time it gets to the legislature you basically have a compromise struck. And it goes through that process of making it into a law and that's it. It's only when you have a very highly contentious issue and you're not necessarily as powerful as you may think you are, or you have another very powerful association and group that has an interest that's opposed to your particular interest, that's when you start having to take your case to the court of public opinion.

The way you do that in the modern day and age is through the media. Ultimately being positive in your media outlook, being able to put forward campaigns in the media to advance the interests of associations, is a crucial element of being able to have an effective government relations program. You have to have a lot of media savvy at some points. A large majority of groups do a lot of work with the government and we rarely hear about them. They are so innocuous you would never even think that they do any kind of lobbying work. I mean, you have associations for all sorts of things. I would hazard a guess that if you look around a particular room and you look at the furniture, paintings, art, anything along those lines, you could probably find an association that represents that particular sector. And to a greater or to a lesser extent they're going to have some formal or informal relationship with government.

The way this happened is that we developed society into a very complex element. We're no longer a group of rural Ontarians or Canadians that don't look to government for a lot of assistance. We look to government now for a lot of things, everything from clean air, to safe cars, to seatbelts that work, to chairs that don't fall apart when you sit on them, to fabrics that don't combust the minute you put a cigarette down on them. This is part of government relations and there are regulations that govern, if not that specific thing, at least the general elements. Governments go to great lengths to make sure that everything is in the open. We can usually get access to documents, minutes of meetings and whatnot through freedom of information requests. We can probably just call up a ministry and ask them for transcripts and they'd be more than happy to do that. I think a lot of it works on the fact that it's a complex process.

I would guess most people don't know how their refrigerator works. They just know it works. And the fact that they don't understand how it works doesn't mean it's not working well. It's the same thing with government. Government works. It filters through the various interests. I think the other thing we have to realize here is that absolutely everybody is a lobbyist to one degree or another. If you're a student, you have interests in what particular associations are advocating. If you're a housewife, it's the same thing. If you're a consumer of a particular product, if you're an exporter, an importer, it doesn't matter what you do, there is probably, unbeknownst to you, an organization that is representing to a greater or lesser degree your particular views.

If you go by the idea that everyone is a lobbyist, the interesting question is, do we even need to get out of this? If there is an organization that represents your views, you may not have the time to learn how the mechanism of government works and you might rather write a cheque for a donation or pay a membership fee. You may be very satisfied with doing that. As a private citizen you could find out what you need to know; it's just going to take you a long time of training, of research, of drive and energy. To take that time, the question is, do you have a year or two of your lifetime to study how government works, to study how the various patterns in society relate to policy making? Do you have that time?

Chances are the answer is no. So if the answer is no, then you may be better off in saying, "Hey, I'm going to hire somebody like a lawyer or an accountant, and in this case a lobbyist, who has that expertise and who I'm naturally going to pay. It's a lot cheaper than my taking a year or two of my life and concentrating on this particular area of study." So in a sense I'm your Sherpa.

Let's talk about the funding of interest groups by government. The argument for funding specific interest groups is twofold. On the one hand you have to look at what type of funding it is. Is it funding to make sure that an organization will exist in order to represent the views of a segment of society that might not otherwise have the ability to participate in the policy process? Let's look at the issue of the economically disadvantaged. Is it likely that the poor will be able to pay $15, $20, $50, whatever it takes to pay an organization to represent their views? Well, the answer to that is, probably not.

In that case you have social policies being discussed. On the other side of the table you have large interest groups that have either corporate or other membership that can fund that particular association and allow it to present effective types of briefs and representation to government. You have to level out that playing field. The way you do that is through core funding for particular groups so that you have the ability to represent views. It's the government's way of trying to make sure that everyone has a fair shake, even those elements of society which would normally not get involved in this type of process.

You'd be surprised, but in many cases the organizations that hire lobbyists are often the small groups because they don't have the funds to hire someone full time or to have someone on staff constantly to monitor issues. In that case they look to the lobbyist as an individual who is paid a fee for a service to provide them with that expertise, where they don't have to pay the benefit packages and everything else. In many ways lobbyists are actually levelling that playing field as opposed to causing the imbalance.

From the standpoint of a lobbyist my purpose is to help associations or other groups that approach me to provide an advocacy role to government. That can be on any level of government: municipal, provincial or federal. What I attempt to do is package the association's wants and desires in such a way that it's understandable from the standpoint of government, that it's packaged in a correct way. In other words, that it conforms with the objectives of the department they're trying to lobby. It's not always about money, though, and I think that's one of the big problems. Most people think that lobbyists, in some shape or fashion, go to government, have a secret lunch in the backroom of a hotel or a private club and a big bag of money changes hands. And then suddenly someone gets a contract. It really doesn't work that way and while I don't doubt at some point in time that that might have happened, lobbying is a very sophisticated kind of business.

In terms of corruption, when you provide money to a politician to vote a particular way, that's illegal. And that's not lobbying. However, government policy is made in a very multifaceted kind of way. The analogy I like to draw is, you wouldn't go to a Revenue Canada audit if you didn't have a tax specialist or, at the very least, your accountant with you. Likewise, you wouldn't expect to go into a courtroom and defend yourself in a criminal matter or launch a civil action suit unless you had a lawyer present. So why would you expect that associations or groups would approach government without someone who has a special knowledge of how government functions?

It's not possible for the normal citizen to come up and knock on government's door. It's not possible from the standpoint of being effective. There isn't a university, to my knowledge, that offers a graduate program in lobbying studies. That just hasn't shaped yet, though it very well might. What most potential lobbyists will go through is some sort of political science, economics or law degree. And they might polish that off with a master's degree or graduate school training in the area of public policy or public administration. In other cases you can actually have long-time serving civil servants who say they've had enough of the civil service and now want to go out into the private sector and use the knowledge gained on the inside for the objectives of clients. So from that standpoint there isn't really a training program. A lot of it is experience. A lot of it is a question of feeling your way around the system. It's an art. It's not a science.

Lobbyists do many things. Definitely there is some aspect with respect to government procurement contracts. That's where you're trying to get a government contract to perform a particular service or supply a particular good. Then there are also avenues whereby groups try to gain benefits from government for their specific membership. In other words, a manufacturing association might want to have a particular tax break, a favourable hydroelectricity rate, say. It depends. You also have the other aspects of very broad types of public policy, where you attempt to influence social policy, medical policy and all those various things. The broader you go, the harder it is to have impact. From the standpoint of associations, though, they're usually very narrow in their approach with respect to their particular sector and government regulations and rules that they have to work in. They have to consider how that affects their membership from a policy standpoint.

From the standpoint of business, lobbyists are really more concerned with a regulatory environment. In other words, what specific, detailed type of rules, which are the results of enacting or enabling legislation in the form of laws, they have to work within. You can be dealing with things like packaging. In the United States you don't have to do that. So that's an added cost. Also, for example, the entire system for the Canadian manufacturer is set up for French and English and that may or may not give you a competitive advantage when you're trying to export that same product, for example, to the States or Europe, on the other end of the extreme. So you're dealing with cost efficiencies. For example, a manufacturer might have to retool to possibly only have an English label as opposed to a French/English label because it might not be acceptable in the market that he's trying to target on an export basis. So it gets very, very complicated and into the nitty-gritty of things. Also, there are a lot of other regulations that people don't even think of. Regulations that affect the business and profitability of groups, even in the non-profit sector.

I think what has to be understood is that policy isn't neutral. Every policy will bestow benefits on particular groups and costs on other groups. That includes groups that are going to bear the cost and not necessarily get the benefit out of it. They're going to want to mitigate that in some shape or fashion, but those groups that can potentially get a benefit from a particular policy will want to advocate that. Then you come to the machinery of government, which tries to find some sort of way to mesh these two particular interests. Lobbyists are usually hired to help the association approach government, develop briefs, provide issues on monitoring types of services. You give an understanding as to how government works, the tone of government parties, their agendas and their priorities. All those kinds of things start to mesh into the entire process of government relations.

There's no question government would be able to form a policy on its own. It doesn't have to consult. However, would those policies then become effective? That's the question you have to ask. Clearly government wants to consult. They want to consult with groups that have a potential of being affected by specific regulations or policies or administrative decisions from any particular department or agency. Likewise, associations or interest groups serve a communication function. They help communicate to government what the priorities of a particular segment of society are. They also help communicate the priorities of government to their general membership. So it's a two-way street and it's one that quite frankly is needed. Think of it from the standpoint of just single consultation. How effective would it be for a legislative committee or a government bureaucracy or a ministry to consult with every Canadian that wanted to be consulted on a particular issue? It becomes very complex and would get very expensive. Much better to have the ability of an association or an interest group which purports to represent a particular constituency and advocate the views of that constituency or, one would hope, at the very least to communicate with them.

Likewise, one group isn't the only one that's at the table. For any particular policy issue you can have hundreds, sometimes thousands, of potential associations or groups that are interested in that topic. As a result, from the standpoint of government you have to have a mechanism to be able to listen to what these various opinions are. And you have to have a mechanism of harmonizing the various policies that are being advocated. So you could have many different groups all making contributions to the policy- and decision-making process. You can have hundreds of groups.

Where a lobbyist comes in is in an effort to provide the service to the specific client that has hired them. They try to create the best package that communicates their message to the effective elements within the bureaucracy, the legislature, the Commons, the Senate, wherever it happens to be. They do it in such a way that that group's view is going to be favoured over another group's view. That's really what it comes down to.

Associations are permanent, to a certain degree. They don't just simply crop up one day and disappear the next. And that's very important from the government's point of view. Ultimately, if government was dependent on organizations that were here today and gone tomorrow, there wouldn't be that kind of continuity that's needed for continuing policy consultation and refinement. Government is interested in organizations that have some form of permanence to them. The bottom line is, if you consulted with somebody a year ago and the policy isn't going to be implemented for another five years or 10 years or potentially maybe just as short as two years, and if they're no longer around, well, you've basically lost.

With any given issue there are generally more interest groups that want to be consulted than there's room for at the table. And I don't want you to think that there's just one table here. There are a number of meetings. But a more interesting question that couples with that is, which interest group does government ultimately listen to? While you're often listened to, the government doesn't necessarily take the advice of that particular group. It depends on the power that association or interest group is able to exert on the various mechanisms of government.

In other words, if you have a very powerful and well-established association that is advocating a particular policy, government at its peril offends that group. It is not going to want to bring forward policies that are contrary to that group's interests or will significantly affect that particular constituency. First of all, there's a political element. If the group happens to represent a broad voter base then you have to be concerned about potential voting at the next election. If it's an economic element, for example, say it's an industry association, one has to be concerned about whether that group picks up and leaves the province or country, in which case jobs are lost and tax revenue is lost. What are the spinoff industries that are potentially lost? So all these things start to factor into the question of how much that particular group is listened to.

The second factor that government looks at is how representative the association is, in terms of the views of the membership it's purporting to represent. In other words, say the association is advocating environmental policies, which is a very broad type of approach, government's going to want to know who they represent, what the membership is. And to what degree does the membership support the views put forward? How have they arrived at the positions they're advocating? In other words, if they're advocating "no dump" within a particular area, well, how have they come to that conclusion? Did they consult with the members? Do they have an alternative approach available? All those things are taken into account by government bodies, but not necessarily elected officials; we're really dealing with the bureaucracy here. I would say 70 percent of lobbying in Canada is done at the bureaucratic or administrative level. It's only the remaining 25 or 30 percent that's done in the legislative arena.

Members of the legislature clearly have the ability to push forward the particular policies they so choose. But I think a good way of looking at this is to divide the function. The bureaucracy in general develops policy, whereas the legislature or the Commons or Parliament enacts laws. I think that's the important element to understand. In any particular legislature the issues that are brought before that legislature to be considered — whether it's atomic energy regulation or agricultural subsidies or a new project that requires government funding or just general social policy — it's likely to be very detailed and technical. Most members in the chamber probably don't have a thorough understanding of that area. Likewise, they don't have the time to be able to research that particular area and try to get a general and technical understanding.

A good way of looking at this is, would you want somebody who is a member of the legislature or the Commons, who maybe has a business background, would you want that individual making very hard and firm decisions without any kind of expert advice on atomic energy? It's not that they can't make proper decisions. They're not fools. They're intelligent individuals. However, they may not possess the expertise to make an informed decision on a particular issue. That's why in most large governments, unless you're dealing with a very small-village type of government level, most governments depend on experts within the bureaucracy to formulate, to develop policies, and then to bring those forward in the form of legislation or regulations for consideration.

If you were a small association, generally ineffective and ignorant about how government and the bureaucracy functions, you'd have a very difficult time advocating a particular policy because you wouldn't know where to advocate the particular views. What you need is a Sherpa. You need someone who is going to take you by the hand and guide you through the process. And this is primarily what I do as a lobbyist. But all I can ensure is that their voice is heard, that the message they're bringing across is packaged in the best possible way for the particular government department or agency that they're approaching.

One of the things I would do is ask the association, "Who is it that you represent? How is it that you're structured? How do you come to decisions? What kind of representation do you have from the sector that you purport to represent?" For example, if you have 100 percent membership, well then, great. You clearly speak for the industry. If you only have 30 percent membership or if you have other competing associations that also purport to represent that same community, then you're going to have a difficult time because you're not seen as being the credible or legitimate representative or the sole legitimate representative of a particular sector.

I ask if the association is structured in a way that has broad geographic representation. Do they also have broad industry representation and formulate their policies in such a way that consults their membership? They need to at least attempt to develop compromises on the various issues their members may not necessarily agree on. Also, I ask, "To what degree can they enforce and maintain the compliance of decisions of members?" In other words, let's say you're involved in a particular consultation with government and then a compromise is struck between the various groups around the table or in the process. Can the association go back to their membership and say, "All right, this is what we managed to get for you. We now expect your compliance." Or are you going to have a massive revolt on your hands.

These are some of the elements that are looked at with respect to how effective we become from the standpoint of lobbying. I go in and I try to show the executive or the board of the association that often the way you're structured depends on how effective you become in the lobbying element. So part of it's internal, and then we start focusing on the external.

There aren't hundreds of millions of dollars being funnelled into the pockets of professional lobbyists. What I think that figure refers to is the kind of money that's being spent by organizations at all levels, interest groups at all levels and pressure groups at all levels, for taking part in those particular types of activities. You can have an employee of a corporation that's charged with government relations or regulatory affairs who may come along and say, "All right, this is my job. I have to communicate with these various levels of government." That would be said without ambiguity, but I'll guarantee you, if you ask that individual, "Are you a lobbyist?" they'll say, "Well, no, I'm not." Well, in essence he or she is. That's not necessarily that individual's entire role. They could very well be the chief executive officer of a smaller association, and they could be responsible for developing insurance packages for their members, or for doing a media relations kind of campaign or an educational campaign. Advocacy kind of work is potentially a small portion of that.

Media relations show how powerful you are in an association. In other words, if you issue a press conference and you have large attendance, then that probably means that your association is relatively powerful and that probably means that association's going to be listened to in the area of the bureaucracy and the government. We live in a world that is governed by electronic communications, whether that's in print in the form of typesetting, or if you're dealing with radio, television, it doesn't matter. The way we get our news, the way we have our news filtered to us, is through the media.

One of the things that many lobby firms do is provide government relations with an internal audit, which is about setting a standard of business for groups. They actually take the association and its various ministries that it may already be dealing with, or some of the policy areas that it's interested in, and then go to various government officials at all levels — that could include the minister, the deputy minister, branch directors, staffers, opposition critics — and ask them how they perceive that association. In other words, is it fair? Is it effective? Is it a voice of reason? Is it technically competent? They ask what kind of influence they think that association has, and coupled with that is the detailed analysis as to where the policy positions of the association may be viewed. In other words, would it be viewed favourably or unfavourably?

Likewise, they ask where the policy is on the agenda of the government or the bureaucracy, if indeed it even is on the agenda. If the group doesn't have enough influence, or their policy does not fit into the agenda or it isn't packaged in the right way, then I'd go back to the association and tell them to take a long, hard look. One of the things you may have to do is restructure yourself so that you are representative of the community you're purporting to represent. I would also suggest to them that if they have limited funding, they should maybe concentrate on other policy issues that have more direct impact on their membership. In other words, instead of going for the whole cake, go for a slice.

I would try to encourage them to be more effective in the areas where they could have potential impact as opposed to areas where they just have no chance. Failing that, what I might encourage them to do is use the coattail effect, whereby they would try to link up with another association they may share similar types of interests with that may have a better perception in the eyes of government or bureaucracy, thereby influencing that association to carry the standard, so to speak, to government. That sometimes works. Other times you'd be looking at broad-based coalitions. Sometimes it's a question of building media relations campaigns to get the issue on the government agenda.

But one of the things that is very, very difficult is suggesting to a group that they shift their mandate slightly to be more appealing to government. Most associations have to answer to some sort of membership, whether it's individual or corporate members. It becomes difficult for them to go back to their members and say, "Hey, what you want us to do, we can't do." However, the savvy association will try to find a way around that. They'll try to strike the best balance, so to speak, between convincing their members that it's in their interest to maybe shoot a little lower or to repackage some of their issues than to have no effect whatsoever. Because the bottom line you have to ask yourself is, do you want to waste your time or do you want to be effective? Better to be effective on something you can have an impact on as opposed to aiming for the stars and not even coming close.

QUEBEC AND THE FEDERAL GOVERNMENT

Maîtres Chez Nous

LOUIS BALTHAZAR

A prominent academic attacks federal intervention in areas of provincial jurisdiction.

The original idea of Confederation came from Macdonald's dream, which was to form a unitary country. Yet, given the fact that Britain had given home rule to its colonies, that the Maritimes and Quebec had reasons to form a federation, we had a federation that was quite decentralized. When the Judicial Committee of the Privy Council in London made judgments about the way power was distributed it tended to favour the provinces. So provinces were more autonomous then than they are right now.

First of all, what happened in 1931 with the Statute of Westminster was Canada became fully sovereign in its foreign policy as well as its internal policy. That created, I imagine, a feeling among the elites of this country that at long last this country ought to be governed from its centre, like most modern countries in the world. Then there was the economic crisis, which was very severe. Lots of unemployment and populist — even socialist — parties, like the CCF, were founded. The CCF if I'm not mistaken, was founded around 1933 with a very radical program.

There was the feeling that Canada ought to do what the United States was doing, having its own New Deal, its own rethinking — one that makes people believe that the central government should play a more important role than it did before in dealing with problems like unemployment, with social and family allowances, pension plans and things like this. With some constitutional reviews like the Rowell-Sirois Commission, which became a report in 1940, the feeling among most Canadian elites changed. They thought the Canadian government should take some jurisdiction over from the provinces in order to become a welfare state and redistribute income to create more social justice throughout the country.

Then you had World War II, which made it inevitable that the central government would take over from the provinces. At the beginning of the war the central government asked the provinces to give up their tax structure so that all income taxes would be concentrated for the war effort in the hands of the central government. All these developments that gave more power to the central government tended to make Canada more of a unitary country and less of a federation. When World War II was over the provinces thought they might regain some power. Certainly Quebec did, as it is different, being French-speaking, having its own culture, its own special tradition. Quebec thought it was important to regain the power it had before the war.

The response of Quebec during the war was that it was all right for government to take over taxes. The Liberal government accepted this during the war. Yet after World War II there was another euphoria; Canada was reconstructing. Canada was becoming a middle power. We had Canadian citizenship in 1947, so there was a feeling that a modern Canada was to be built. Most provinces accepted that the federal government would continue to play an important role, though Quebec was still reluctant, but in a passive way.

Then came Duplessis in 1944 and then came the end of the war. Maurice Duplessis, a very conservative person, said, "When the war is over we want to control our taxes again." Around the 1950s Duplessis had a little war of nerves with St. Laurent and Duplessis won. By winning he recuperated a certain number of points of income tax, and that was the beginning of this provincial autonomy movement. But Duplessis didn't go very far because although he recouped some income tax power, he had no programs. He was against all federal programs that were modern programs: welfare, programs that cared for the arts like the National Film Board, the Canada Council and things like that. He thought education could be served well by the religious communities. He didn't have any social or welfare programs. He thought the traditional institutions of Quebec could care for that. This is why you have to wait until the Quiet Revolution, until 1960, to see this full effect of Quebec not accepting the new distribution of power.

I'm old enough to remember the 1950s in Quebec when, for us, everything that was progressive, good and modern came from Ottawa and the provincial government had nothing to offer to us. This was a time when most progressive or left-wing Quebecers were very, very federalist. They favoured the federal government much more than the provincial government. Yet then came the unexpected, the Quiet Revolution. The Quiet Revolution produced a modern government in Quebec City, one that decided to take over some of the good things that Canada was doing. This was a big break in Canada's evolution. You had this smooth progress toward a Canadian welfare state, toward a central government taking over the role of redistributing income, of governing for the welfare of all Canadians. All of a sudden you had Quebec in the 1960s realizing it's a French-speaking province and that it is different and that it too ought to become a welfare state. So Quebec decided it would offer all the modern and progressive goodies coming from Ottawa to its own people.

There were a good number of French-speaking Ottawa civil servants, people who came from Ottawa to serve in Quebec to create the welfare state. That was a big clash all of a sudden. Not that Quebec wanted to become sovereign or independent or anything like that, but Quebec wanted to enjoy its autonomy as much as the original BNA Act made it possible. That's when the Lesage government, the Johnson government and all the Quebec governments after were clinging for more power, trying to recoup all the powers of Quebec and express some dissatisfaction as to those federal-provincial joint programs.

Quebec wanted to enjoy its autonomy fully. That's what created the problem because most English-speaking Canadians had made it on the long road to achieving a modern nation. It was very difficult for honest, well-meaning English-speaking Canadians to give up this idea that Canada would be a whole nation. All of a sudden Quebec was calling for an asymmetrical nation; but we didn't use the word at the time, that is, to say that Quebec would enjoy a "special status" or would call for more autonomy than the other provinces did. Yet most Canadian political parties came a long way to recognizing this. Lester Pearson was a good negotiator and on the Quebec point of view he was a great prime minister because he was a man of compromise who could listen to Quebecers. The Progressive Conservative Party in 1968 adopted a two-nations platform. They accepted the idea that Canada was composed of two nations. There was the commission on biculturalism and bilingualism and even the NDP accepted the idea that Quebec was different.

Then came Pierre Elliot Trudeau. Trudeau thought, when he went into politics, that Quebecers had put too many of their eggs in the Quebec nest and he wanted to create a balance and to have more French-speaking people in Ottawa. Eventually he would go further than that. He would tell Quebecers, "You don't need your Quebec allegiance. You should plunge into Canada. I'll make Canada bilingual. I'll make you comfortable in the beautiful country through and through." He used the expression "Quebecers don't need a crutch." For such federalists the Quebec allegiance is a crutch.

"You go and be Canadians through and through," he would say and because of that he spent most of his life trying to create a Canadian nationalism. He wanted to make Canadians closer to one another and by the same token make his fellow French-speaking Canadians of Quebec closer to other Canadians. For English-speaking Canadians this was a great message to hear. Here's this Quebecer who is popular in Quebec and who tells us that we don't have to bother about granting any status to the province of Quebec. Let's all be Canadians and the price to pay for that is that there's going to be two official languages. Some civil servants and some elites in Canada will have to learn French, and if we pay that price there won't be any Quebec problem anymore. A lot of people were enthused with that message.

Trudeau succeeded, yet ironically he succeeded much better by uniting English-speaking Canadians to each other. Of course, we could have seen back in 1968, 1969, 1970 that this wouldn't work because 1968 was the year when the Parti Québécois was created. In 1970 the election in Quebec showed the PQ gaining 23 percent of the vote. In 1973 they gained more than 30 percent of the vote. So you had this nationalist movement growing and the Bourassa government calling for more power in social affairs, in health and in the field of communication. He created Bill 22, making French the official language of Quebec, so you could see that things were not working well.

The problem of Canada is that this French Canadian from Quebec built a Canadian nation all the way to 1982, after the victory and the referendum in Quebec. He created a Canadian nation and a Constitution in which there is one Canada, one Charter of Rights and Freedoms, one Supreme Court that rules for all Canadians. The Constitution was very unifying for Canada. It granted Canadian citizenship a meaning it didn't have before. No wonder Quebec refused to endorse the Constitution — not only the PQ government of the time but also the Opposition of the time. The Liberal Opposition refused to endorse the Constitution. The leader of the Opposition, Claude Ryan, didn't go to the ceremony of the proclamation of the Constitution in Quebec on April 17, 1982, because he was opposed to it.

Trudeau's biggest sin is that back in 1980 when he won the referendum, he won it with a 60 percent majority; comfortable enough, yet 40 percent of the people in Quebec didn't agree with his vision of Canada. Among the 60 percent who said no, a good number of these people said no while hoping there would be a renewal of federalism and that the province of Quebec would still play an important role. You see, Claude Ryan had a vision of the Constitution very contrary to Trudeau's. Yet Trudeau did everything between 1980 and 1982 without, it appears, even consulting Ryan.

In a nutshell the drama of Canada is that in 1979 you had the report of a task force on national unity, the Pepin-Robarts task force. Jean Luc Pepin was a former minister in the Trudeau Cabinet in Industry and Commerce, and John Robarts was a former premier of Ontario. They are two loyal Canadians. In fact, the task force was composed of very loyal Canadians throughout the country. The Pepin-Robarts report says this: Quebec is distinctive, and within a viable Canada it should have all the powers necessary to maintain and develop its distinctive character. Any other solution short of this would lead to the rupture of Canada. The Pepin-Robarts report said that in 1979. Three years later you have a Constitution that pays absolutely no regard to that statement. To me, this is the drama of Canada.

Later on came Brian Mulroney and he tried to redress things — without any success because of many reasons that I don't have time to elaborate here. Quebecers would have been very happy with Meech

Lake. I'm convinced that a good majority of Quebecers would have been. Of course you have to keep in mind the 20 percent margin of discontented separatists, but not much more than that. Give us another Meech Lake anytime and there won't be any problem. There won't be any significant sovereigntist movement in Quebec.

In terms of Quebec's response to the federal government encroaching on their spending, it's always been the same rationale. Of course with Duplessis it was conservative. With the Quiet Revolution it was more progressive. But the point is, as Duplessis would always say, that we have our own traditions. We've been, always, different. We have the French language, the Catholic religion, our traditional institutions, and that's why we can't be governed completely by Ottawa. Ottawa's all right for a certain number of things, but leave us our special prerogatives.

People thought that until Duplessis was gone and Quebec modernized that Quebec would accept Ottawa. But the opposite occurred. The same rationale was used in a progressive way in the 1960s. Lesage and the others wouldn't say, "We have our traditions and we're traditionalists" and all that, they'd say, on the contrary, "We want to build the future, we want to build the new, modern French-speaking network. We want to join the community of French-speaking nations throughout the world. We want to develop modern institutions and we need the prerogatives to be allowed to do that."

In 1964 Jean Lesage went as far as saying that Quebec was the political expression of French Canada, that it had become the homeland for all people who speak French in North America. That might have been exaggerated. A lot of people speak French in other provinces and don't necessarily consider Quebec their homeland. Yet what he was saying, basically, is that Quebec had become the only place in North America where you could build a real, modern network of French-speaking institutions. Elsewhere you may have minorities with certain rights, special schools, certain institutions, but the only place to communicate in the modern life, where you can live in French, is in the province of Quebec.

As long as people live in small communities, which was the traditional way of life, this is what happens. Let's say I live in a small French-speaking parish in Manitoba. If I live in my parish and I never go out of it and I communicate to the people around me, it may be very easy to continue or at least it may be possible to live in French if everybody's speaking French around me. But all of a sudden, if I modernize, I can't

stay in my little parish in Manitoba. I'd go to Winnipeg and communicate with people but I'd find a basically English-speaking network of
communication. I cannot live in French if I communicate a lot throughout the province of Manitoba. It's not possible because the majority of
people don't allow it. Whereas in Quebec I can go out of my little community and go to Montreal and Quebec City. And that's what happened
during the Quiet Revolution.

You see, Quebecers started to communicate more than ever among
each other. Television helped that, as did the use of automobiles, and it
was possible to be all French speaking and communicate and form this
network. What was conducive to assimilation in other provinces was
conducive to a new national self-assertion in Quebec. People leaving,
say, Chicoutimi, Rimouski or other parts of Quebec, and going to
Montreal, where the network of communications downtown was still
dominated by anglophones in the early 1960s, were made more nation-
alistic because they were numerous enough. They could come to
Montreal and say, "Hey, how come I'm going to Eaton's department
store or The Bay and I can't be served in French? Or I go to this restaurant or this nightclub or I take the train or the plane and the airline
company that serves Canada, Trans-Canada Airlines (which became Air
Canada) doesn't even have a French name?"

You had this protest, this radical feeling throughout the 1960s, in
Montreal especially, and in the whole of Quebec, that becomes socially
mobilized. We thought we had to take over and impose our language. So
it was just the opposite of what naturally happened in other provinces
where before the government minorities didn't have programs such as
CBC stations, and they tended to assimilate more and more in a very
natural way. Quebec wasn't the only province asking for more of their
own spending powers. Quebec always made alliances, and especially by
the 1970s you had the Western provinces, which also had reasons to be
more responsible for their natural resources.

Basically Quebec was the only province to have this rationale of
culture and language. To some extent New Brunswick could say they
were different because one-third of the population is French speaking.
But New Brunswick rarely used that fact to claim more autonomy.
New Brunswick has always been a province ready to yield to Ottawa
and ready to see that Ottawa had programs for bilingualism throughout the country. That seemed to be, not all the time, but by and large,

satisfactory for many, if not the majority, of Acadians in New Brunswick because they were calling for minority rights. Especially by the 1970s with Trudeau's program, the Official Languages Act and all that, the federal government had programs for the minorities. Yet whereas the federal program had programs for minorities, it did not have a program to recognize Quebec's autonomy.

You have this anomaly right now. There is a constitutional amendment that recognizes that in New Brunswick there are two basic communities. That amendment came in the winter of 1993 and was included in Charlottetown. Since Charlottetown didn't pass, the Mulroney government amended the Constitution by the parliamentary vote. And in the summer of 1994 there was a big Acadian congress. People came from all over the world. Even Boutros Boutros-Ghali, the secretary general of the United Nations, recognized the existence of the Acadian people and praised them. It was beautiful. But in the meanwhile nobody would recognize the existence of the Quebec people. Why? Because Quebec is a province, and the recognition of a Quebec people would imply that you had a distinct society. People don't like that because then you couldn't talk about the equality of all provinces, particularly because there's a sovereigntist movement in Quebec and that might be dangerous. Yet, if there is an Acadian people in this country, why shouldn't we recognize a Quebec people?

Money coming from Ottawa just couldn't be refused, especially in the 1950s when Duplessis was so parsimonious about education. For instance, Duplessis didn't like what the Faculté des Sciences Sociales was doing at Laval University. They wouldn't get any money from the government and they'd get money from other sources; but if the federal government gave money to universities, of course Quebec universities would welcome it. That money was frozen for some time because of conflicts in jurisdiction, and eventually it was picked up from the Association of Universities and Colleges of Canada.

The Quiet Revolution changed that because then the provincial government of Quebec was ready to spend. Yet Ottawa would continue to pour money in and the provincial government would tend to say, "Hey, if you have money to spend in matters like education or welfare, give it to us. We're the ones responsible for it and we can do it." Little by little, the Government of Quebec had its own hospital insurance plan. When Ottawa was thinking about a Canadian pension plan,

Quebec came out with its own provincial pension plan. It was the great victory of Quebec. It's probably the biggest victory of Quebec ever in this federal-provincial conflict. Around 1965, 1966, the Quebec Pension Plan was so well organized that Ottawa had to adjust the Canada Pension Plan on the Quebec one. Quebec created its own pension organization and that's how the famous Caisse de Dépôt et Placement du Québec (the Quebec Deposit and Investment Fund) came about, which was so important for the development of French-speaking institutions in Quebec.

Another aspect of the Quiet Revolution is one I'm old enough to remember. In the 1950s I'd walk in the downtown district of Montreal and whenever I'd see something big, a high-rise building of some important institution, it would have to be English speaking. The Montreal Stock Exchange was a place where English-speaking people were. St. James Street, the business street of Montreal, was very English. Most department stores were English. The Sun Life Building was a place where anglophones were. Then in the 1960s came the nationalization of all electric companies and a giant corporation rose in the Montreal skyline — Hydro Québec. All of a sudden you see a big building and as a French-speaking Quebecer, I say, "It's ours." Of course anglophones work for Hydro Québec, but the majority of the people who work there, the executives, the engineers, they're French speaking. So Hydro Québec became a sort of symbol of the re-conquest of Quebec by the French-speaking community. Then you had La Caisse de Dépôt et Placement du Québec, which has assets now of around $45 billion, if I'm not mistaken, so it's a lot of money that could help the enterprise take over other enterprises. The Caisse de Dépôt was very instrumental in having Domtar Canada coming into French-speaking hands, and Provigo, the retail grocery store, and lots of other companies that were taken over. La Caisse helped Bombardier in the beginning and there is SNC Lavalin and all those other companies that form what we call today Québec Inc.

All of that was helped in one way or another by the economic institutions created in the 1960s. I didn't talk about the Société Générale de Financement (the General Investment Society). It was another government organization provided to boost the economy and help especially the French-speaking majority to play a role in the economy, which it had done so little of before. It took time to produce results, but by the

1980s there was Québec Inc., which was a result very much of that, but also in great part the result of government intervening to create a French-speaking business network.

In the 1970s when I came to Laval University, there was a business school there. Most graduates in our business school were going to what we call autonomous corporations, you know, quasi–Crown corporations, such as Hydro Québec. Why? Because as French-speaking graduates they didn't feel very comfortable in the mainly English-speaking business network of Montreal. Not that they didn't learn English, but there was a feeling of a sort of a co-opting among businesspeople. By 1980 most of the graduates of our business school at Laval University were going to the private sector. So you had a big change between 1970 and 1980. Why? In my opinion it's mainly because finally there existed a French-speaking business network.

If you take a plane between Toronto and Montreal, you'll hear a lot of people speak French. It means there are a lot of businessmen — and businesswomen for that matter because the women move very much in that field — doing business in Toronto and coming back and forth from Montreal. All these people speak English yet they treasure speaking French among themselves and forming their little network. To some extent there is a form of nationalism in the business community. It's not this kind of nationalism calling for sovereignty or waving the flag but it's being proud of being from Quebec, being French speaking and wanting to take over their business deals within their homeland in Quebec as much as they can.

The response in Quebec to Ottawa seizing power and spending in the province is negative. In a nutshell Quebecers accept Canada. They accept the Canadian community, the Canadian union, the Canadian government, Canadian foreign policy, the Canadian Armed Forces. Yet they are not comfortable in the Canadian welfare state because for Quebecers the welfare state ought to be in Quebec. They could accept, as European nations do, some norms and some accommodation. People are very happy if they can transfer the health program from Quebec to Ontario or Alberta if they travel, yet most people would like to see the welfare state here in Quebec.

Let's just take a field like education, for instance. This is supposed to be provincial jurisdiction and yet you see federal intervention in so many sectors. There is talk about a national daycare program. Daycare is the beginning of education, so why wouldn't we deal with it in Quebec? Then there's federal intervention in the field of literacy, which is another educational matter. Federal intervention in school dropouts is a concern because there are too many young people leaving high school. Again Quebec is concerned with that and could deal with it. You have federal intervention in manpower training and it seems that Ottawa doesn't want to give up there because it's tied up with unemployment insurance. Quebec's very keen on recouping that.

You have the federal government moving in the field of research, of university training and all that. Even the sacred cow of education is felt as being invaded by the so-called spending power in the federal government. Spending power — big word. Now that the federal government is broke, what's going to happen with the spending power? That is a very good question which may transform Canadian federalism. It may transform it eventually to the satisfaction of Quebecers. So far the smoothing down of the spending power is such a new phenomenon that most Quebecers are skeptical that it's going to produce any results. On the one hand the federal government with the Martin budget tells us that they're going to be less involved. They say there's going to be one Canadian social transfer and provinces will be free to take that money either for education, for health or for social assistance. Yet at the same time the provinces are convened so norms would be established. What are these norms going to be?

So a lot of people here in Quebec say, "Hey, they don't have any money to give, yet they want to impose norms." Of course some norms may be very reasonable and very acceptable. Some others may not be. Who is going to be the referee? Are we going to have the power to say that we don't accept this norm? We don't know so far. This is why, even though there is a perception that there might be an evolution of federalism in the direction of decentralization, we're still very skeptical about the very nature of this.

The concern often expressed is that Ottawa is shovelling its problems, its deficits or its debt, into the provincial backyard. We are told they take over but they take over with a lot of shortcomings and lots of problems. So there is resentment because of this. For instance, there was a bill coming from the Senate around the early 1980s, I think it was. It restricted the Quebec Deposit and Investment Fund, La Caisse, to invest money in some transportation companies because La Caisse wanted to take over a certain number of shares from Canadian Pacific. This became law. Then you had the whole business community of Montreal opposed to it.

That happened then, but lately, I must say, there hasn't been much conflict about that except that the creation of a French-speaking business network made it possible for some people to contemplate sovereignty with a different attitude. Some economists, they're still the minority I guess, but I know of one prominent French-speaking economist in Montreal, born in Northern Ontario, Pierre-Paul Proulx. He claims that sovereignty might be good because even though we live in the world of globalization, of economic interdependence, the small units have an advantage because they can produce more of what he calls "synergy" in French. He says they can put their act together more easily in order to go to the outside world. In other words, Proulx would say there was a Team Canada formed by the federal government, and the provincial government he called Team Quebec could be much more effective because it would be more of a cohesive unit. It would be easier for Quebec to produce some cohesion and to go to the outside world.

Not being an economist myself, I wouldn't dare pass judgment on that, but I say this is one kind of argument that can be used to say, after all, sovereignty would not be so bad because we have our own organization here. That makes us less dependent on the rest of Canada. Yet I must say the federal government has been very aware of Québec Inc. and has been very open to help Quebec companies like Bombardier and others. For that matter, the directors of the largest French-speaking companies of Quebec are usually dead-set against sovereignty and for the continuation of federalism. For example, Laurent Beaudoin, the CEO of Bombardier, and Paul Desmarais of the Power Corporation are certainly very much supporters of Canadian federalism as it is.

By and large, if you talk about welfare, that is to say programs concerning education, manpower and social assistance, the tendency in Quebec is to say that we want all of those — because the understanding of the original Canadian Constitution in Quebec is that all these programs should be run on a provincial level. We understand that other provinces may have reasons not to be responsible for these programs, but we cling to the idea that it's better if we would do so. Unemployment insurance is an old thing, you know. It was transferred to the federal government back in 1941, I believe, so Quebec hasn't always asked for it. But in the long run, to be logical, we should recoup that with the rest. So Quebec would accept some programs that are certainly federal, such as transportation, communication, although communication is another field where, because of language, Quebec wants much more than what it has right now.

But if you talk about welfare as such, Quebec's very ambitious there. With literacy, a practitioner in this field will say we realize a good number of people still don't know how to write. And the federal government says they're going to deal with that. Then there is the problem of school dropouts. It's a big international program and most international figures don't mention provinces but they mention a certain number of illiterates and school dropouts in Canada, so the federal government feels we should do something about school dropouts. Then there is manpower training and university education and research. Again the federal government enters. We're supposed to be autonomous in the field of education but they're everywhere. We're invaded. I mean, is there anything we can do by ourselves if you come to our house and you come in the morning and say, "Can I help?" and you come in the afternoon and say, "Can I help you?"; you come in the evening — "Can I help you?" — and then say, "You know, I am doing something here, you see."

For some provinces it may be relatively easy to balance a budget as long as they are junior governments. The main government, the main provider, is in Ottawa. That is the government that has the problem. But Quebec has this pretension, this claim of being a senior government, of being a national government, of being a welfare state. So, not unlike Canada, it has to deal with the main issues of welfare and this is why it's as difficult for Quebec to balance its budget as it is for Ottawa. This claim, rightly or wrongly, of being a national welfare state even if it's within a broad country called Canada makes it especially difficult for Quebec to deal with its debt, its deficit and all that. This doesn't mean that Quebec is not going to deal with it. I think it should. I think it will, eventually, and I don't see why Quebec wouldn't do what the federal government is trying to do. But in a sense it's as if Quebec and probably Ontario are in the same ballpark as Ottawa, whereas other provinces are in different ballparks.

I read *The Globe and Mail* every day and it's constantly talking about Canadian provinces. It's a national newspaper about all Canadians and every day when I read it I say, "Yes, I'm a Canadian but this 'we are all Canadians' idea doesn't fly here in Quebec." Most commentators, even people that are not very politicized, are going to say, "we are Québécois," I think much more than in any other province because the language is different, you know.

MONIQUE LANDRY

A former federal minister discusses decentralization of programs from federal control in order to achieve effectiveness and economy.

It's a tough time for the younger generation. You have reason to be worried about the future of Canada. It's now or never. I think if the provincial and federal governments don't make the right decisions in terms of the debt crisis, the next generation will pay for it. I do think the debt problem is at the top of the agenda of all governments and there's as much talk of the problem of the debt in Quebec as there is anywhere else in Canada. I mean, everybody's complaining about the federal debt but there's also a lot of concern on provincial debt. This means that the federal level seems to be giving less money to provinces, the provinces are giving less money to the municipal level and so on. It's an issue that people are very much concerned about now.

For years the media has said that Quebec is always complaining, asking for more subsidies. I don't think it's fair. If I go back to my previous responsibility in government, I felt, not only as a Quebecer, but I think all Cabinet people felt that that was very wrong. I think all provinces get their share of potential resources from the federal government, they just might go about it differently, depending of the need of the provinces. I don't think Newfoundland has the same needs as in the provinces of Quebec or Saskatchewan. I think there's a way of trying to make things quite fair for everyone. Unfortunately there's been a lot of bashing of Quebec.

Looking back at my time in government, there was definitely a big concern for the debt and the deficit like there is now. Maybe our problem at the time was that the population was not sensitized enough. I mean, we've done our work and now this government is maybe benefiting from our efforts. There was a big concern and I think we've made some hard decisions on cutting expenses. Though the big difference in the management of our government was the lack of revenue. We've maintained our cap quite a lot on the cuts in the government; the revenue had not been what we were expecting.

During the 1980s it was a new situation. If you recall, in the beginning of the 1980s, when we took over in 1984, it was the beginning of the huge deficit, created under the previous government. So it was the beginning of this new reality. We tried to make our concern known to the population. There was a lot of discussion about it. But I don't think that the population was well enough sensitized to it to accept the fact that the government now comes with huge cuts or acts in the way that Ralph Klein does. I think it's been a built-up sensitization to the people, which makes the facts now easier to accept.

Quebec has raised the issue of decentralization for the last 30 years or so, maybe much louder than any other province, which I think makes sense. Quebec wanted to be able to manage more of the money that would go to their people. I think it makes sense, in a way. The closer you get to the people, the better services you should be able to give. The federal government is a big machine that's quite away from the population's concern. In that way Quebec has been pledging for more power and it makes sense to me.

While I was in government we had the issue of the Meech Lake Accord and Charlottetown, which concerned a lot of Quebecers. It was on the agenda on a regular basis but there were other concerns. It depends on what events were happening at the time, but I think all caucuses must have specific topics to discuss. I did not attend the other provincial caucuses, but when we had the national caucus you could feel that the issues of concern were sometimes different from one caucus to the other. This is because of the different agendas of the various provinces or the local industries. As I said, a province like Newfoundland doesn't have the same kind of basic industry that Quebec or any other province has, so it makes the agenda of provincial caucuses quite different.

I don't think that requests for decentralization and cultural and language concerns should be linked together. Cultural or language issues are well managed by the provincial government and the province has the power to be able to legislate in those fields. Federal and provincial levels are managed by two governments, so that kind of discussion is about getting more power for provinces. I'm not talking only Quebec. I think some provinces also prefer having certain issues regarded at their level, which again makes sense because the smaller the machine is, the better the results you can provide for the people.

Decentralization makes sense in the way that it brings projects and programs closer to the people, where public decisions should be taken. In a way, if you look at the federal government, let's say an area like mortgages which has application in each province, in that case they should be able to consider the local implementation of the program. Decentralization completely makes sense if you transfer the funds to the provinces so they can manage closer to the people. I don't think layering has increased the debt. To me the biggest problem of debt is when parties campaign for different issues and just want to be re-elected; often they don't cut programs — they add programs. That's one of the main problems of our debt.

When you're new in Cabinet the political life doesn't give you time to really look deeply into all government operations. You're a member of Parliament, you're a Cabinet minister, but you have your own department and you've got the House and Question Period and the meetings, so you don't really have time to go deeply into all government programs. You make your judgments based on what other ministers come to Cabinet with. If a Cabinet minister comes up with a new program because he evaluated that they should give more than the previous government, that it's a new program and it makes sense to look at it for this, this and this reason, that's a good thing.

A good example is this problem of dropouts. When Jean Charest was minister of youth, Jean came to Cabinet with a new program for dropout kids. I mean, it made sense. There was a big need in this area. I don't remember the amount of money we put in, but it was a good

311

program. It was administered at the local level and I visited schools when that program was put into place. It really made sense but it meant more money being added to a program. They do this but they don't remove whatever else you do, they add. So that's a very good example of what we've done. It's a very small, single issue yet it gives you the idea that if every administration adds a program, it only builds on the machinery of government. You need to hire more civil servants to administer that program and it's just added to another program.

The federal government should be and is able, in its own way, to offer different types of arrangements with provinces. If a province like Quebec is ready to manage more of a certain jurisdiction, as in manpower or health, I think they should have the possibility of dealing with that. Maybe other provinces don't want the same kind power and that's fair enough. The federal government should be flexible enough to be able to discuss with different provinces where they want better arrangements.

As a matter of fact, it's already been done with some issues. Immigration or manpower in Quebec has made some arrangements between federal and provincial levels and I think that's fair. Provinces may not have all the same needs. They may not want to deal with the same issues, so I think there should be that kind of flexibility between governments. Right now the flexibility is often there in the minds of politicians but it's very hard to exercise it. The machinery of government is very slow, which can make it tough to put this idea of flexibility into practice. The will of the politicians is sometimes difficult to apply on the machinery of government and different levels of approval.

In the government machinery it's part of the job to make some arrangements and deliver programs. Maybe it's the politician that often doesn't like the way things move because they don't move fast enough. The fact that it doesn't move fast enough surely frustrated me when I was in government. I had an automobile testing centre in my riding, which is the only one in Canada. To me it was common sense for our government administration to privatize that centre. I started campaigning for that when I was elected in 1984, to work on that dossier. On a regular basis I pressed my colleagues or the government. In the 1993 campaign I finally got the approval of the minister responsible for that dossier. So it took me nine years to be able to have that fact accepted. They've made studies to show that a minister can approve one thing and then another can come along and we'd have to start all over again. So again the machinery of government makes for a long and very difficult process.

Whether or not you have the patience to drive the issue through for nine years depends on your personality. I was very much involved in my riding but I had not made a specific promise. I said I would try hard because I had a lot of representation from mayors and private sector people who felt that the centre would be better used if it were privatized. As well, I was knowledgeable of the issue. The government hired firms that I met with to discuss the evaluation they were doing. Finally, I made up my mind that it made sense and I would start pressing on the ministers to be able to privatize it. But the machine didn't want that. The department didn't want it at all — that I knew. So I had to fight, not at the political level, but at the civil servant level, the machinery of government, which was completely opposed to it. They would make it difficult for the minister to make a decision and they'd order another study to illustrate another point of view and, as I said, it took me nine years and finally I got it because I went to the prime minister with it.

Decentralization can be done differently. We've tried to constitute a new agenda, a new way of working with the provinces, but it didn't seem to have the accord of all Canada, so I think that maybe we should work it differently. Charest is advocating right now to put in place some bilateral arrangement with provinces to see how it works and in a few years, maybe in 10 years, I don't know when, it will be accepted and well in place. Then we could constitute a new agenda at that time. I think we've got to work things differently. I think there's enough flexibility right now to be able to take spending powers away from the federal government. I say this because a lot of subjects are under split jurisdiction, so I think there's a way of working the arrangement very well, to the satisfaction of provinces. And that can be inserted in the Constitution in some manner later on.

I'm sure that problems at the federal level in Ottawa are the same as at the provincial level. The accountability issue is a complicated one that forces government to operate more slowly. Civil servants hire consultants to make sure that they have proof of whichever decision they recommend to the minister, that they have a good record. Otherwise they would be scared of their own decision. Accountability makes the government very cumbersome in the way of delivering programs. I'm sure it's the same at the provincial level. Being accountable to the people of Canada or a province makes the machinery of government much less flexible than the private sector. The private sector works on the results, but they too have to be responsible, they have to be accountable. The government works very differently.

As much as decentralization has been accepted, I think on certain issues it's a question of the provincial government wanting the same kind of decentralization. Maybe we've tried too much to formalize that before trying it, though we've been experiencing some good results in decentralization. Should we go faster? Maybe. It's a question of will on both sides and I think we were there and governments will continue in that same direction. If we think of rationalization or downsizing, we've been doing it. Maybe it doesn't show that much but we've been doing it. Are we doing it in a good way? Are we doing it because we've got to cut some programs or should the government be evaluating more of the whole issue of area of involvement and restudying some of them? Maybe we should cut certain programs altogether instead of just downsizing on an equal basis, which might make things more difficult.

I would not say that the centralization of money and federal taxing has made the debt much bigger. I think our system, our democracy, perhaps makes the political party in power want to maintain power. In doing that, they get into the habit of promising or delivering more programs to the people. And one government that comes to power does not just cancel what the other has put in place. They add to it. So year after year we've been adding programs to try to keep the electorate happy and make sure they re-elect us and I think that's a problem. But that's our democracy. Is there an answer to that problem? I don't know. At all levels, municipal, provincial and federal, parties just want to change things. They want to be elected. They want to make a difference by offering other services to the population. But that forces government to spend more money. I guess their different point of view on how to do things in the recession is one of the reasons for the debt.

The government or a party that wants to be elected has to have the support of the population. It's very difficult to balance the need for government to make the right decisions versus the support by the population. If you compare that to a private sector company, whenever they decide to rationalize their operation, they take the decision and here they go. They cut some expenses and they lay off some 100, 200, 300

people. They don't have to be re-elected. They just make the decision
and that's it. The fact about democracy is that government makes hard
choices and applies them, but they've had to take into consideration the
fact that they want to be re-elected. They need to try to balance this in
a way that is well perceived and accepted by the population.

I do see a possibility for a change. Just look at what Ralph Klein is
doing in Alberta. I think governments have been a bit scared of going
that far in cutting programs but I think now people are very much
aware of the problem of the debt, and they don't want the government
to keep on spending. They really want the government to rationalize. So
I think Ralph Klein is a good example of how you can manage government spending and maybe still be popular. Government now knows
they have to cut spending on a very large level, and I think we might see
the light at the end of the tunnel.

The last federal budget wanted to transfer more money to the
provinces, which I think serves the request of Quebec wanting more
services at their level. I think we're moving toward that direction. The
government, being so big, now realizes that they've got to be less inter-
ventionist and give more money and more programs to the provinces. I
think we're moving toward that. And I don't think governments at the
provincial level would necessarily overspend. They would probably
know in advance about what money they would get back from the federal government. So in a way you're saving money because if each
province would have their taxation system, it would mean more civil
servants for the taxation process.

That's an issue of collecting the money because you've got just one
central government collecting the money then redistributing it. To me,
that's not a big issue. When provinces look to the federal government to
fund specific programs, that's just the way our system works. Federalism
means redistribution of riches. It's been the base of our system. If you
remove that, you'd have individual provinces managing their own
money. Probably a province like Newfoundland, being less prosperous,
could not afford the same type of spending toward the population. So I
think that's the base of our federalism — redistributing wealth around
the provinces.

I don't think Quebec's desire for decentralization can be equated to
this idea of redistribution of wealth. It's not an issue. It's much more a
question of power. Quebec just feels that they should maintain the

French language and manage their own services to the population, which I think makes sense in a lot of fields they were requesting. Other provinces also want that. If you think of Meech Lake, approval was given all over Canada except in one province. We were almost there. I think there was an understanding of some decentralization of powers to the provinces that wanted it. Even if the provinces didn't want that kind of decentralization, I think there should be that flexibility of saying yes to the provinces that want it and no to the others.

I don't think it's possible for a Cabinet minister to really limit spending. The government itself makes the decision. The minister of finance first sets up the amount of money to spend the next year. Then eventually the government makes a decision of where they should cut or where they should add programs. If some sectors of activity in Canada are more needed at that time, then we increase them. Eventually each Cabinet minister has to deal with the cuts the minister of finance makes. That's mostly how it works. Even with the objective of limiting spending we've made some progress. If we go back to our management, I think there were some cuts in the budget. I think the big difference was the lack of revenue. That was the big surprise, for many years, which made the difference in gaining a bigger deficit every year.

On a general basis I doubt if one Cabinet minister would come up with the nice idea of giving back some money. You've got your own clientele that you're serving; for example, I was in the Department of External Affairs and I had a whole group of different organizations coming to me wanting more money. If you think of certain communities in Canada who want money for the Third World, then the business community will want more funds for the project, the multilateral banks will want more. So everybody wants more money. A Cabinet minister that really wants to defend his own portfolio would not go nicely to the minister of finance and say, "Here's some money back." I think you want to get as much as you can because you want to best serve your clientele. The decision is very difficult to make. You need to have a minister of finance who makes the decision after Cabinet has settled the agenda of the government.

It's really up to the minister of finance to make the cutbacks and the hard decisions when it comes to the debt. Cabinet sets up the priorities and decides which direction the government wants to go. The general agenda is fixed by a Cabinet decision, but then the minister of finance would apply the decisions. Then he would call you individually and say, "Here's the objective with your department this year and this is it." Then you have to try to fight for the decision, when the decision is made, try to apply the cuts in your own department the way you think it best serves the interests of the country.

PAULE GAUTHIER

A prominent lawyer and corporate director argues that Quebec's demands for more autonomy within the federal structure are conducive to sound economic principles and effective government management, and that recent experience in other provinces supports this view.

The federal government has had much difficulty giving powers to Quebec. It's just like a family when you have many children and the children think that one is more spoiled than the other is. So the role of the federal government is to remain neutral and fair to everybody and treat everybody the same way, with some exceptions when needed.

In some areas Quebec needs to be treated exceptionally just as in Newfoundland they must be treated differently for other reasons. The same concept applies to each province. Putting language and culture aside, I think Quebec is asking to be treated on an exceptional basis in the economic sphere, but just as much as in any other province. We have economic needs here. We have our natural resources, such as the forest industry, depending on the sectors of activities of industries. We have special needs but that's true for each province. Quebec has always argued for more economic and financial power over its own affairs because it's always felt, being in such a big ensemble in North America with nine other provinces, that it had to have more powers to protect its culture. Also, Quebec wants to develop and expand all its resources, and over the last 30 years it's been able to gain the power that it needs to do that. If you go back to 1954 when Mr. Duplessis was in power, right away he decided that Quebec would take care of collecting its income tax for the province. Step by step the province was able to get more and more power but he never thought it had enough — that's why he was always demanding more and more.

If you look at cultural issues, it's always the one we like to use as an example of Quebec's conflicts with the federal government over economic jurisdiction. There are cases where, for example, Quebecers would ask their government for assistance in building a museum. If the province felt it was not the right time to build it or did not have enough money to build it, then the people would go to the federal government and ask for this money. In some cases they would obtain the money and then the province would have to take care of the new building and operate it. So sometimes this was very costly for the province of Quebec because the federal government imposed this increased spending.

To elaborate, there are many areas of duplication of powers and responsibilities that have been very costly for both levels of government. Quebecers have realized this for a long time and that's why they ask for a division of power in cultural issues, environmental issues, in manpower training, etc. In terms of manpower, many Canadians and Quebecers have lost their jobs because of this present recession. They have to be retrained in a new position in new kinds of work. Well, Quebec feels that it is closer to its people and knows exactly what the needs of its workers are. They'd like to give them the right training and not be part of training for all of Canada.

I think there is a link between this layering of government and duplication of services and the debt. History will probably prove that Quebecers were right in many of their demands. Since Canada is going through difficult economic times, we see that the federal government will not have the choice and will have to give back some power to the provinces, power that was taken away by the federal government. In that sense I think that Quebec is right in its demands.

Many Quebecers understand that the deficit comes from the fact that there are too many levels of government and that there are duplications of services. They feel it's costly and they want that to disappear. For some the best way to settle the difficulty is to separate; that way you're sure to have only one level of government. For some that sounds reasonable. We know that for the majority that doesn't sound reasonable. Quite frankly, on a practical side, I'm sure the people that feel that are very honest. But they don't believe in federalism anymore. They don't believe it's important to be together and to share and to help where it's needed, and they want to do it on their own.

It's easy to say that Quebecers get tired of making all these demands. But I think if you're a real Quebecer and you want the best for your province and the best for your country, you'll continue to try to explain what you want to the rest of Canada and the people involved in the federal activities. There are ways to explain it and the best way is through negotiation. Negotiation is key. Quebec wants to be part of Canada and we're not part at the moment — since 1982. We want to be recognized for what we are. We want to obtain some guarantee that what it has and what it was will always continue.

Often the rest of Canada points to numbers saying Quebec gets more out of Confederation than it puts in. It's always a fight over numbers and Quebecers know that you can have numbers that say whatever you want, and they lost confidence in fighting over numbers so they're not really impressed. They would probably be ready to accept it if they felt the numbers reflected the truth, but they're not certain about that. What is easier for them to understand is that there are two levels of government and it's costly. This is much more practical and easy for them to realize and to accept than just numbers. And it would certainly be more visible to them if there was just one level as opposed to two.

I'm not an expert in the field of what specific powers Quebec would like to grab hold of, so I might be completely wrong, but certainly the cultural field is very important. Education and manpower training is also very important. The social programs I think are of much importance to the province but the national rules, the national criteria, Quebec abides by these criteria and it's not really a difficulty. But culture and education I think would be the two most important fields.

Other provinces might not agree with the reasons why Quebec often asks for more power. But the present recession and a huge deficit show that Quebec's demands are well founded. Other provinces have come to the same conclusions and are trying to cut expenses as much as possible. We know that other provinces are requesting the same demands as Quebec. I know the reaction of Canadians outside of Quebec is not always very positive. Other provinces are tired of hearing about the demands of Quebec, but with time and more information, and also maybe with some pain for everybody, people will understand that maybe Quebec's various demands might apply to them. As well, our example may be of some help to the other provinces.

The response from Ottawa has created a very long and ongoing debate between Quebec and the rest of Canada. I think it's also now part of our tradition in Quebec to fight against the federal government and to gain a little bit here and lose a little bit there and continue on. You have to take into consideration that all Quebecers are very nationalist. We know that the majority is not separatist but nationalism is going to continue. Someone can be a federalist and a nationalist at the same time, and the reputation of federalism on the international scene is very important for Quebecers. But in their hearts they are nationalist and it goes very well together; there's no difficulty.

Of course, Quebec has a bad reputation in some parts of English Canada. It's a bad reputation just as the rest of Canada has a bad reputation in Quebec. But when people are serious and want to really understand the objectives of the requests and want to work together and co-operate, I think all this could disappear very fast.

MARCEL CÔTÉ

An economist and former advisor to Prime Minister Mulroney surveys federal-provincial history in respect to tax collection and shared programs.

There is a tug of war between the Quebec government and the federal government over control of economic affairs. Systematically the Quebecer tends to side with the Quebec government. It started in the late 1940s, early 1950s when the federal government kept the taxes it took during the war years and decided to spend the money on social measures. Even in the late 1940s and early 1950s the Quebec government opposed government spending for higher education and there was a fairly famous clash between the two levels. Indeed, back in 1952, 1953, the Quebec government decided to have its own corporate taxes, and this was right in the middle of a clash with the federal government. That's why only in Quebec the government collects corporate taxes. This started in Quebec because of these clashes.

Now, the people in Quebec were quite happy with federal government spending. The way spending occurred in Canada is that it grew bit by bit, every year a little more, and I guess people just looked at the good side of it. They looked at the spending side of it and didn't realize that the tax increase they had a few years after was due to the goodies they received. But the Quebec government always stood up. Starting in 1960, instead of just standing up to the federal government, they started negotiating with them.

That's where they had the shared programs and that's why the opting out was developed. Then we started to have parallel programs and that's why, in a sense, the social safety net is much more decentralized in Quebec than elsewhere in Canada. We have, for example, the Quebec pension funds and our tax system, which is very different from the tax system in the rest of Canada. We have the Quebec family allowance and the federal family allowance as well.

The federal government took taxing powers away from the provinces during the Second World War because they were fighting the war. They started increasing taxes, they took the income and consumption tax, they had a manufacturers' tax, which is now GST, plus the individual income tax. Most of the money collected by income tax went to the federal government and over the years that has eroded. First provinces got the responsibility for managing the health system in Canada. This was a big chunk of money. They also got the responsibility for managing the social welfare services and that was also a big chunk of money. What evolved over the years was a situation where the federal government collected taxes in the area that really belonged to the province. They sent big cheques to the provinces and the provinces spent the money. That's what we have now. The federal government collects and the provinces spend.

After the war the taxing power wasn't given back to the provinces because they found a new use for the money. See, they discovered unemployment insurance. They discovered free hospitalization. They discovered all kinds of things, including free university education. They discovered needs to be serviced, and they decided to service those needs on a national basis. They even built the Trans-Canada Highway in the 1950s. This was one of the biggest pork-barrel programs we ever had in Canada and it was built by the federal government and the provinces, but under the leadership of the federal government. We built the highway in the name of national unity and the voters bought it because they didn't realize that they were paying taxes for it.

The Quebec government resisted the most. Actually, Ontario went along with the project and the Western provinces went along too, but Quebec was the bad sheep the whole time. It was important to Quebec to maintain those powers. I guess all premiers would have opposed Ottawa if they knew that their own people, their own electorate in the province, would have backed them. Only in Quebec did the electorate back the Quebec government. In the rest of Canada people more or less sided with the federal government and then the premier decided to listen to the people that went along with the wave. That's the reason basically.

As I said, the federal government was collecting taxes but the provincial governments were spending that tax money. There is a problem with that because the one who spends should be the one who taxes. That way they would spend a little bit less. There are two reasons why the system evolved in this way. The first reason is that managing health care, for example, had to be done by the province. The federal level was not equipped by the Constitution of Canada; it was not in the business to do so. So the federal government had to get into an agreement with the provinces to run their health-care system on the principle that has evolved over time, that all hospitals in Canada are publicly owned. We have a publicly owned health-care system. Why, I don't know, but this is just religion in Ottawa. In a sense they more or less agreed with the provinces. If the provinces would respect these constraints, the federal government would give them the money to manage.

The other reason was to redistribute to make sure that the have-not provinces received the same level of service as the have provinces. What happened is that the system really got lost into bigness. In a sense the federal government is collecting $100 billion of tax and basically, among the provinces, it redistributes less than $20 billion, about one-fifth of it. And the rest is just money taken from one province, going to Ottawa and then back into the province. That's most of the federal budget. It's very inefficient.

The more you can put in closer to people, and the more you can put the responsibility of the decision to tax close to those who spend the money, the better it is because then it disciplines the politicians. Politicians love to do things for the people as long as the people don't realize that they're paying for it. This is what we call the "political market." It's trying to give goodies to some people and making sure that you pass the bill to somebody who doesn't realize it. That's the way politicians get re-elected. We get re-elected by spending other people's money without the other people realizing it.

If a province delivers programs it can't afford, it just adjusts the program. For example, Toronto is a high-cost city. Rents are high. Wages are high. Why should we have the same spending per capita for the health system there as in a low-cost city such as Timmins? Or in a small town in Quebec where wages are much lower? I'm talking about the same level of service, but the wages aren't the same so we should have a lot of variation across the land. This is not the case when there's a central financier, and this is what we have now. So if we put the taxing decision close to the spending decision, a lot of local politicians would decide, "Maybe in our town we will spend a little bit less or we'll do things differently." There's nothing bad about doing things differently. We all dress differently. We all have different tastes. So why shouldn't we have difference, variety and diversity in our social systems?

We all want flexibility and that is not the way things have been; but we're slowly going back. The pendulum, I think, is swinging back now. I hope it takes less time to swing back and correct itself than it took to build it up. It took 40 years to create this mess. Part of it was messy and part of it in fact was very inefficient. But part of it also was good, and I guess Canadians are not ready to trade away their health-care system and their social service system and even their unemployment insurance. But we should get rid of all the inefficiency. There's a lot of it there.

There is no need for centralization except that people, politicians, like power. They like to grab power and no politician likes to tax people. So in a sense the federal government, which has probably the biggest taxing powers, really stuck with it because it cannot spend very efficiently, it has to deal with the provinces. But if it spends, it says, "I'm paying for it. I call the shots and I make the rules." And that's what the federal government is trying to do — make the rules and make them uniform across the land. I'm sure when you went to Alberta you probably heard people complaining about the federal government determining what's good for Alberta. Alberta should be able to do it. Quebec has been saying that also for 40, 50 years.

Historically Quebec has suffered a bad rap for being more vocal than other provinces in this regard. The reason why Quebec is more vocal is because it has the support of the people, and this has nothing to do with political science, it has to do with language. But now the Ralph Klein government in Alberta has the support of the Albertan to do it the Albertan way, and now they're also making their presence known. In a sense, if they keep on doing that for 20, 30 years, they'll get a bad rap, which is most unfortunate. It's most unfortunate because there's no reason why we should not have diversity across the land in the way our system operates.

Right now there's a perception in Canada that revenue sharing is the glue that keeps Canada together. If that's the case then we use a lot of deadwood along with the glue. The provinces with surpluses, Alberta, B.C. and Ontario, contribute to the system more than they receive, about $19 billion. The other provinces receive that $19 billion. So there's $19 billion there. Government, altogether, is spending something like $300 billion in Canada. So they are really taxing to redistribute $20 billion. If that redistribution would be the glue that keeps this country together, well, we need a lot of taxes for so little redistribution.

There's redistribution within each province. For example, tax is collected in Toronto and used in Sault Ste. Marie and vice versa. But between the major areas there's much less than people think. There's a lot more trade between these areas than there are taxes coming from one pocket to the other one. The region that receives the most money per capita is Atlantic Canada, by far. That's only eight percent of the population of the country. And nobody wants to abandon Atlantic Canada. If we would solve Atlantic Canada's problem — and there's a huge dependency problem that we've created there — we would solve at least nearly half of the revenue-sharing problem of Canada. We created the problem when we went to vote and elected one government after the other one, and the politicians are really just responding to the wish of the electorate. Now, the electorate doesn't really think all these things through, but the politician will say, "We were supported." And indeed they were supported.

Redistribution has both a positive and negative force. We redistribute $20 billion but we tax $300 billion. There's quite a difference there. There's a 15:1 difference and that's huge. We seem to be taxing a lot for the little redistribution we're doing. Redistribution can sometimes create a culture of dependency. We've seen it now in Atlantic Canada. We are more or less keeping people in the areas where they shouldn't be, where they don't have any opportunities, where they don't really have the level of service. We should encourage these people to move out or do something different and yet the system is not doing that. The system is just patting them on the back and saying, "Don't worry, wait till next year and we'll see." That's what the system is doing.

There are three provinces that are higher than the average on the national income, per capita. There are seven provinces and the two territories that are below. Quebec is slightly below. So Quebecers receive about $400 per capita from the system. People in Atlantic Canada receive $4,500 per capita, and in Manitoba and Saskatchewan, somewhere in between. In a sense those who are receiving more than they're paying can say, "Hey, this is a good thing." But this is really a short-term view. If we took a long-term view we would say, "Why can't we create a condition that will spur economic growth? One that will allow us to create more wealth and to get out of the rut that we are in — in great parts of Quebec, in great parts of Ontario, throughout Atlantic Canada, in great parts of the Prairies?" These are places where we are not really creating wealth; we're just consuming — receiving the cheques at the beginning of the month and spending them.

I have said that it's difficult to create long-term economic growth on a federal level, which implies that provinces can do it better than the federal government. I say this not because provinces are smarter but because they're closer to the level of people, in a sense. We don't necessarily need governments to create wealth. We just want government out of the way. The last things we want are government rules and constraints that prevent people from creating wealth. Or high taxes paid to Ottawa or Queen's Park or Quebec City, money which people would otherwise save and invest. In terms of the federal government, the further away you are from the people, the further away you are from the action. And that hinders the natural dynamism of the entrepreneurs discovering new ways of doing things and really creating wealth.

As a businessman in Quebec, it's not as though I've found it difficult to create wealth. You don't really see it this way. We're just like fish in the water and we don't know where the water is cold or warm, but if the water is warm, you realize there are a lot more fish. If the conditions are better, a lot of people will start their own businesses and will be enthusiastic about developing their business and watching it grow. But if government is taking 40, 50 percent of their profit because they have to finance the whole social infrastructure of this country, suddenly profits are less attractive because instead of having $100 of profits you have only $57 of profit. In that case you tend to be less inclined to invest in making more profits. Government influences these conditions. When you realize that provinces are heavily taxed or regulated, you see there's much less activity and much less growth.

One example is in the Quebec construction sector. There's no sector in Canada that is as regulated as the Quebec construction industry. I don't think you can hit a nail without getting regulated. Suddenly we realize that despite all the encouragement and all the nurturing and all the assistance of the government, the committees, and civil servants looking after it, there's less and less construction in Quebec. In fact, half of the big construction firms are owned by non-Quebecers. When they can move out of Quebec, they move out of Quebec. Look at the fisheries industry. If you look at the number of fishermen or the number of fish we catch, both are decreasing. But the number of civil servants looking after the fish has increased and the two lines crossed quite a few years ago. By applying restrictions and by telling people, "This is the way you should do it," you have less and less innovation. You have less and less flexibility in the system and less economic growth. Economic growth means doing things differently and doing things better. You don't ask a civil servant how to do something better, you ask an entrepreneur. With their innovation, suddenly something works well and the company grows very rapidly. But when you put bureaucrats in the middle of that process, it's just like putting too much sun over a garden — it just dries it.

Governments are headed by politicians and politicians think they have to be busybodies to be re-elected. So they stick their nose in everything, and unfortunately we elect the busybody. That's most unfortunate. I wish there were more people of principle getting into politics, not sticking their noses in everything and keeping the bureaucracies from trying to fix everything. Let the markets and let the people fix things.

Politicians are always virtuous when they talk and very far from being virtuous when they act. Their deeds are very different. Whenever an election comes, they usually spend and then in the first year they try to counteract to reduce spending. But the Quebec government is one of the worst culprits. It's most unfortunate that the governments for the two biggest provinces are the least disciplined. In fact, the three biggest governments in Canada are the three worst governments. The three most irresponsible governments are the federal government, the Quebec government and the Ontario government. It seems the bigger you are, the more irresponsible you can be; and you can count on the politician to take all the leeway to the markets, and that's what has happened in Ontario and in Quebec. The Quebec government right now, May of 1995, is probably the least disciplined of all the governments in Canada.

Politicians go on the circuit to try to get re-elected. They promise they'll reduce the budget and balance their books but they never do it. In Quebec we've had that example since the early 1970s. Politicians have been running in elections and saying, "We'll reduce the deficit. We'll balance our books." It's the same in Ontario and the same at the federal level. It seems at the federal level there's been a change of heart. Who has put the pressure on? The answer is most unfortunate. It's not the Canadian. It's the foreign lenders who have finally got our politicians to listen. Those that lent money to government have said, "If you keep on, this time it'll be for real." Finally, government isn't listening to the electorate but listening to the lenders, and the lenders are curtailing their spending habits. In Ontario and in Quebec this has not happened yet.

Ottawa's basically taking transfers from the provinces and giving it right back to them. It's inefficient but it's an issue of control. They tell them what to do with the taxes and they love that. In Alberta they tried to prevent the federal government from adapting medicare or the management of the health-care system. In a way that seems to be fair for those who elect the Government of Alberta. They cannot do it now because the federal government won't send cheques if you don't do it their way. Politicians love the high level of control over lower-level politicians.

In Germany they've solved that problem. The federal government there does that a little bit but then the provinces, or states in Germany, control the senate. The senate has to approve all the bills. All the laws have to be approved by the senate. So it controls the federal government, although that doesn't stop even the federal government from getting very, very fat. Our excuse is the social welfare system; they use another excuse. Over there they use reunification with East Germany. And they became bloated, so they too have this problem. All governments in this world are obese.

The debt is not a transaction cost; the debt is the sign of the responsibility of government. Government has the taxing power, so those who lend know that government won't go in bankruptcy. They know that they'll always be able to tax people. So what they do is finance the government deficit and the government rationalizes the deficit, saying it's good for the economy. They bring it back to Keynes and old economic theories that say it's good to spend. And there's no doubt it's good to spend, but there's a limit to spending without having the money. They put us into deficit and indebtedness and now we are fairly in debt to foreigners. That means every year interest is going to other countries to pay for that.

I would say the contributing factors to the debt in Quebec are the same in other provinces. I think politicians are the main contributors. The fact that politicians were able to spend and finance their deficit on the market is the prime reason. Politicians will give you all kinds of excuses why they had to go into debt, but we don't have to go into that. In a recession suddenly it can happen: your revenue will drop very suddenly. But two years after you're back to normal, there's no reason then why you shouldn't be able to run a surplus and balance your books. I'm sure if you talked to a Quebec politician they'd say it's because we speak French or because of the cultural integrity or because of this problem or that problem — hogwash. I mean, it's because these politicians get cheered when they spend and get boos when they tax. And they don't tax enough.

Ontario's a very good example. Ontario got into this mess before this recession. It got in this mess in 1989, in the middle of the biggest boom ever known in Ontario, and it started to run these huge deficits. It started to get tangled into a huge spending program. The decision was made in 1988 and 1989 and even 1990. And we have to be fair to Bob Rae; he's not the one who created the mess. Robert Nixon is the one that created the mess. This is fairly well known among economists.

The problem with Ontario Hydro is it's a big monopoly. It used to do everything by itself. Then it just got old and they weren't able to fire anybody. They weren't able to change, but good people left and we were stuck with a lot of deadwood. Suddenly it reached the crisis point. Why did we have to wait until the crisis? Because a monopoly is shielded from the pressure of competition, which would have let Ontario Hydro change continually. They weren't able to change because of their monopoly and they ended up in a crisis. That huge debt has nothing to do with the taxpayer. It has to do with the politicians who decided Ontario Hydro would have a monopoly; that's the main reason.

One example in Quebec is our school system. We know our schools in Quebec are very bad. It's doubly important in Quebec because we have French schools. We're educating and transmitting a fairly unique culture in a very isolated fashion. This is very badly managed. In many ways it's very centralized in Quebec City and the collective agreement doesn't favour innovation. The collective agreement doesn't favour flexibility. We have a system now that is crumbling and we can see it in the dropout rate. We can see it in the results on exams, which are done on a national basis. Indeed, pressure is so strong now that they're trying to change the system, but who's to blame? It's the politicians that created the monopoly in that case.

In Quebec the problems in the business community are a lot more complex than merely the lack of innovation due to government policies. As you know, Montreal is more or less caught between a rock and a hard place in the constitutional tangle because there's a fairly big English community and a French community, and we're always dragging through that constitutional quagmire. So that's one reason why we have some problems. There are also some problems with regulation, which doesn't help in Quebec. I must say that on the whole the entrepreneurial spirit in Quebec rekindled sometime in the late 1970s and early 1980s and it went well. There has been change in the taxation that favours investment and favours entrepreneurial investment. In a sense we have a lot of innovation. But all the gains the entrepreneur made, the government came and confiscated them or the constitutional crisis confiscated them, and that's the most unfortunate thing about Montreal. It's caught in a battle between the Quebec government and the federal government.

In a sense this is one barrier to innovation. Another barrier to innovation is the government interference in the economy, which prevents the economy from developing its own structure. For a while there was a dearth of venture capital in Quebec. This was corrected four or five years ago but the main reason for the dearth of venture capital at the time was because there were too many grants. I'm not sure but I would vouch that because government is showering so many grants on the private sector in Atlantic Canada, it's killing venture capital. Venture capital is much better capital for a firm than grants because a company will get along with venture capital, will get the know-how of the investor, will get the discipline of the investors. I could think of other examples, but again, the dominant factor in Quebec is the constitutional dilemma and the economic uncertainty stemming from it. That has been very bad for business in Quebec.

Does Quebec have politicians that are different from those in the rest of Canada? The answer is no. So Quebec, although they won decentralization from Ottawa to Quebec, doesn't necessarily decentralize from Quebec to the regions. We talk a lot about *les régions* in Quebec. But what do we do? We probably do less than in Ontario. The Ontario system of government is probably more decentralized than the Quebec system of government, although I'm sure we've been talking a lot more about it in Quebec than in Ontario. The Quebec government and the Quebec politicians and the senior bureaucrats in Quebec City are as guilty as the ones in Ottawa when it comes to decentralization. That has to do with the system.

Ultimately it all depends on the values of the people, which get translated to the values of society, and to what extent they trust government for solving problems. There was a time in the 1950s and the 1960s and up to sometime in the 1970s where we really trusted the government to solve the problem. But we've seen the government in action now. There has been a fundamental switch of attitudes where we are mistrusting government and that'll show up gradually in political attitudes and in the type of politicians we get elected, and then it'll show up in their decisions. I think in the future, because we've seen the failure of big governments, we will have a lot more decentralization than we had in the past. And that'll be for the better.

CLOSING THOUGHTS

Parting Words of Wisdom

CATHERINE SWIFT

A representative of Canadian small business presents an insightful critique of the taxation system.

Taxes have changed an awful lot over the last 10 to 15 years, relative to 20 or more years ago. They've increased over the last decade for businesses and individuals alike, from roughly 30 percent of gross domestic product to almost 40 percent. Even though we might be roughly on par now with a few European countries, their taxes have been gradually inching up over time, whereas we really hit the mother lode very quickly. I think this accounts for a lot of the anger we see right now in all Canadians.

In particular it has been interesting how taxes have changed for business. What we've found, representing small firms, is that during the 1980s the burden of taxation shifted from being based on corporate income to being based on things like payroll and property. Corporate income tax is just like individual income tax: when you're not making money as a business, you don't pay it. And if you're making money, you pay it, which is reasonable because the tax is geared to the stage of the business cycle.

The problem with things like payroll taxes, and I include unemployment insurance, the Canada Pension Plan, workers' compensation and many provinces' health-related taxes, like the Employer Health Tax in Ontario (Quebec has its own version, as do other provinces), is that they're stable. They're levied in good times or in bad, whether we're making money or not. Property taxes at the local level are exactly the same.

The change has made our tax system very insensitive to fluctuations in the business cycle. I believe that the reason we had a record number of bankruptcies and very high levels of unemployment in the early 1990s when the recession hit was that the 1980s governments had taken advantage of good growth to really pile on the type of taxes that didn't decrease later. When people weren't making money anymore they were still there. Instead of, say, adjusting the corporate income tax payments, they let businesses go bankrupt. I don't think that was a particularly beneficial move in the structure of our tax system for the whole economy.

Businesses are incensed today. And this change in the tax structure falls way more heavily on small firms than on large firms. For example, small firms are more labour intensive. They're creating all of the new jobs in our economy these days. And large multinational corporations are now moving the labour-intensive parts of their operations to Thailand, or wherever. They don't have them in Canada. So this shift in the tax system has very heavily penalized the job creators, the small firms, but the larger corporations have not taken the same hit.

I think the reason for the level of anger and disgust in the small business sector is that they know they're bearing a disproportionately heavy part of the overall business tax burden. And because of the burden, capital is leaving this country on balance. For a long time we've enjoyed quite a happy inflow of capital in this country, which has been good all around. That was partly because for a long time our resource-based economy was highly desirable. We know that's not worth as much anymore. The economy has been moving more toward manufacturing and information technology in recent years. And because of our fairly high-cost business environment and the heavy regulatory burden we've imposed on businesses relative to a lot of other economies, we've seen capital either leaving or deciding not to come to Canada, deciding to go elsewhere. It's very difficult to measure that.

Revenue Canada is the messenger for the tax system, and one could probably say that our members would like to shoot the messenger in this case. Naturally it doesn't set policy; that's the Department of

Finance, or maybe some other department. But it very much delivers the auditing and all the paperwork that a smaller firm has to deal with. There are very strong rigidities. A little bit of flexibility in difficult times, you would think, would be beneficial in the long run to a government, for example, if somebody missed a deadline once and didn't have a record of doing that, this should be taken into account. If there's one department we lobby the most in terms of relatively small matters on behalf of certain small businesses, it's Revenue Canada — because of all these little, nitpicking, niggling ways that they have.

To be fair, Revenue Canada has improved a bit over the past few years. They've made an effort to pay at least a little more attention to all of their users, businesses as well as individuals. But one thing we still find is that if you phone three different people at Revenue Canada, you get three different opinions on a given tax issue. It's definitely a real bugbear for all small firms to deal with, and for some more than for others.

Now Revenue Canada is going after the underground economy. This whole issue took off like a shot after the GST came in. Historically governments all around the world have had the notion that they could root the dollars out of the underground economy. But goodness knows, all of the facts run contrary. The reality is, if you overtax people and lose their respect for government — because it's not just overtaxation that's necessary to give a boost to underground economic activity; it's also thinking your tax dollars are being wasted — you end up with a situation where government spends $2 to collect $1 in the underground economy. It's simply not efficient. We have examples from European and South American countries, examples all over the world. It's a politically motivated exercise to pretend they're doing something. Some deluded bureaucrats probably think there's a point in doing this, that maybe if they nail one guy on Main Street they'll scare everybody else. But it's also very much blaming the victim because the real causes of the problem are overtaxation, lack of respect for government institutions and the belief on the part of the taxpaying public, right across the board, that the government is misspending their money. For example, a lot of our members tell us, "A consumer comes in here and says, 'What's the price without tax?' If I say, 'I can't give you that,' the consumer says, 'I'm out of here.'"

So the notion of targeting small businesses as the culprits is just totally wrong. And in a realistic sense, concerning this notion that they're actually going to root out enough tax dollars to make their spending worthwhile, again there's absolutely no indication in the history of tax around the world that they'll ever be successful doing that.

I just don't think Revenue Canada's initiative is the solution. I think they'll blow their brains out, in terms of what they're going to spend versus what they're going to collect. They're also going to make themselves even less popular than they already are among the taxpaying public, and that's pretty hard to fathom.

The unfortunate aspect of an underground economy, generally, is that it only ever grows. If you look at other countries that have had underground economies of serious proportions longer than Canada — and Canada really is a latecomer to the underground economy fraternity — you see that because of a new tax or a recession, the underground economy will increase. But you don't see it fall off; you see it plateau. Then another event will hit some time later, so it increases again, and then it plateaus again. It can also increase simply because to stay in business the owner says, "What do I do? Do I go bankrupt or do I cut into my own income or go under the table," or whatever the case may be. Bankruptcy is probably the last alternative that most people would choose. It's also very damaging for the economy if you've got lots of firms going bankrupt because they won't play in the underground economy.

So the widespread impact and the fact that underground economic activity always feeds on itself are parts of the problem. You have to treat the disease and make a dramatic change. We certainly saw that with cigarettes. It was the only instance I can think of in Canadian history where we saw a drastic decrease in underground activity, and there was no doubt of the cause. It's unfortunate that it was for cigarettes, in a way, because the product isn't used very positively, but I think that model should certainly be viewed very seriously by governments.

Our approach has always been, "Treat the disease, don't treat the symptoms." Treat the problems of overtaxation. Bring about policies that will earn government some respect for a change, so people will say, "Yeah, I'm paying a lot in tax, but I think it's being reasonably well spent. So I'm not going to go underground. I'm not going to begrudge this as much."

Business in Canada has lost a lot of its trust in government. But I don't think that's restricted to business. I think Canadians in general have lost their faith in government. They've seen promises broken so many times it's laughable. They've heard them say, "We're going to increase this tax, but it's going to go to the deficit, so it's really OK," and we've said, "OK, we'll suspend our disbelief for a while, and we'll buy that." And then of course we see deficits increasing anyway.

There's no question that there has been a slide in the implicit social contract between our governments and the taxpayers. It's very interesting, when you look at history around the world, that it's not high taxes alone that encourage non-compliance. Switzerland is a good example of a country that has extremely high taxes but also has referenda on major tax changes. People feel that they have input into those decisions. Therefore they say, "OK, I might not love having another X dollars plucked out of my pay every week, but I've at least had a chance to express my views on it, so it's not illegitimate."

You may recall that here the GST was only passed through our legislature by Mulroney stacking the Senate. In my view that wasn't lost on taxpayers. I think people said, "There was an illegitimate process to impose a tax that we all despise." That double-whammy has contributed to people's total lack of faith. The drastic increases in our taxes and the lack of trust in governments and how they're spending our money have definitely contributed to a breakdown in the extent to which people feel they should be honest. Add a serious recession, where in many instances people weren't avoiding tax for philosophical reasons, they were doing it because they wanted to eat every day and give their kids a little bit of food too. That combination dramatically changed the attitudes of Canadians over the last few years toward governments and toward their desire to continue to comply with taxes.

It's becoming increasingly difficult to compete legitimately in today's marketplace. Profit in a small business tends to be the individual's income, and unfortunately it's rarely a princely sum. The honest businesspeople who have ended up reducing their own income and feel that they're being put in a corner by competitors offering illegitimate deals, they're the norm and the majority. I've heard that story from our members: "I'm trying to remain in business and stay in compliance with all of the tax laws that apply to me, but in the end my choices are complying with the law or going bankrupt." Needless to say, that's not a very pretty situation.

I think the reason certain industries may be recognized as having a larger proportion of underground, non-declared activity isn't because we have a bunch of tax evaders in some industries and not in others; it's because of the nature of the industries themselves. In construction, home renovations and those kinds of businesses, for example, a large portion of the cost is not for materials; it's for labour and therefore it's intangible. It's harder to track somebody's labour and time than it is when you've got, say, a big machine that represents 90 percent of the price and the other 10 percent is everything else. So the businesses that you find cutting some corners tend to be businesses in which services are a fair portion of the overall price, such as construction. There are also certain sectors that just happen to be dominated by smaller firms because of their very nature, and construction is one of those as well. But so-called illegal tax avoiding is widespread throughout all sectors. Undeclared activity is not limited to the smaller players; it cuts across the entire industry.

Revenue Canada is even going after waiters and waitresses. This petty nickel-and-diming may not be uncharacteristic of the organization, unfortunately, but the notion of going after some poor waitress who might make $18,000 a year and is getting $1,000 in tips that she's not declaring is just unfathomable. I can't figure out what they're thinking. Not only is this not productive in terms of a revenue-finding exercise, it's politically stupid. All they're going to get is a lot of bad press, and they deserve it. I just can't understand their rationale for wanting to try that. This is the ultimate case of blaming the victim. The real problem for people that aren't making much money and are trying to make ends meet is the fact that they're getting so much taxed away from them, not the fact that they may be trying to put a bit aside without paying tax on it.

We never advocate breaking the law, nor do we feel that anyone should sneak out of paying their so-called fair share. However, we believe that we really should deal with the underlying problem here and not just dance around the edges and try to treat the symptoms of the disease. The disease is overtaxation by a government that wastes our money.

The misunderstanding of the way businesses and individual Canadians feel about what Revenue Canada and our government are doing, the thought that chasing down a few so-called offenders is going to be great publicity or instill a feeling of tax compliance across the country, it all just shows how badly they've misunderstood the problem and how mired they are in a way of thinking that's decades out of date. I can understand bureaucrats thinking that way because they can beef up their own numbers and justify their existence by pretending that they're the tax police on a mission from goodness knows where. But all it really acknowledges is that they badly misunderstand how small firms and average Canadians feel about what the government's doing, and that they really should get at the real problem here.

Another government issue is subsidization. We survey our members all the time on all kinds of issues, and we have consistently found very high opposition to any kind of government subsidy for business. There are a lot of reasons for this. In general the belief of our members is that if you have a properly competitive tax and regulatory system, you don't need to offer any subsidies. Subsidies tend to be motivated by a politician wanting to hand over a cheque and shake somebody's hand in front of the media. They tend to be motivated by pork barrelling so that the person gets re-elected next time around. They are very rarely, if ever, motivated by good, sound economic reasons. The companies collecting the vast majority of business subsidies tend to be large multinational corporations. Small businesses don't get their share of subsidies, mostly because a lot of them don't want them, but also, the subsidies simply don't go to small businesses for all kinds of different reasons. Very often we hear a company say, "I was going to locate there anyway, but if the government's going to hand me $7 million ..." We've always said that if you put out a sign saying "Free Candy," there will be people there to eat it. There are program junkies in business just as there are program junkies anywhere. Once you become dependent you need your fix every now and again, and business subsidies are no exception.

One problem with a climate and a culture that promotes subsidies to businesses is that you create "grantrepreneurs." They're not particularly good at running a business, but they're accomplished at getting grants. Subsidization doesn't benefit our economy overall, and as we see our debt numbers climb into the stratosphere, we know that change has to come. But businesses continue to go after it; if somebody is going to hand out money, there will always be people to take it.

Goodness knows, we can count the megaprojects in Canadian history: the steel industry has been the recipient of massive amounts of government aid for years, certain auto sector examples, and the resource sector is full of them. There have been numerous instances where we have literally thrown billions and billions and billions of dollars into sinkholes that ultimately died. These companies didn't even survive; they weren't viable. Much of this money is offered without strings attached, without it really being a problem. As long as you happen to be in the right minister's riding, or in the industry that's the flavour of the month for the government, you can get potentially millions and millions of dollars.

One of the key problems with subsidies is that you end up making one player better off at the expense of the person who isn't taking subsidies. That's why you'd really have to eliminate the whole process of subsidies to business if you wanted to rectify this situation. If you're in a market and you see your principal competitor get handed what will probably amount to their profit margin for that year, and you're not getting that, then it's pretty clear what's going to happen in the marketplace: you're a lot worse off. And like the underground economy type of activity, you may feel that if you don't engage in subsidies, you're dead in the water from a business perspective.

For all of these reasons, well over 80 percent of our members, even in parts of the country like Atlantic Canada where you'd think businesses may be more dependent on subsidy, say, "Get rid of all of the subsidies and make the system fair." If you took those billions of dollars and put them into reducing the GST or another tax, then you would be making an equitable system where everyone could at least share a little bit, and you wouldn't be benefiting one firm to the detriment of its competitors.

There's a massive will among small firms to get rid of the subsidies, and that's whom we represent. I certainly can't speak for large business, but the evidence has not been all that positive on that front. Some of the worst corporate welfare bums are big multinational corporations, and they will continue to put their hands out. We saw big auto companies in Ontario a few months ago moaning and groaning about government debt and then taking millions and millions of dollars in grants and loan forgiveness arrangements. That's disgraceful. Business subsidization is a luxury that was never sound economic policy. It's one we just can't afford anymore, if we ever could.

We also ask in our regular surveys of members, "What is your most important problem?" Number one is the overall burden of taxes; no surprise there. Number two, a very close second, is regulation and what we call "paper burden," the overall load of paper that government dumps on businesses. A large firm will have somebody devoted to filling out and sending in the UI, CPP and taxes every month. At a small firm the owner does that. But the owner's very valuable time should be spent growing the business, hiring more people and trying to make the business more successful and more profitable. In our research we've found that about 40 percent of our members spend the equivalent of one whole day a week pushing paper for government. This is very unproductive time. It isn't spent producing goods and services; it's about simply being bureaucrats. And they don't want to do it anymore. One of the recommendations that we've made to governments at federal, provincial and municipal levels has been that if they could substantially reduce the load of paper they dump on small businesses, it would have the equivalent beneficial impact on the economy as a tax cut. If you take this unproductive time and make it productive, it doesn't take rocket science to figure out what kind of positive results you're going to get out of that.

There was a very interesting example in Newfoundland about three years ago that we've been using as a model of how something can be done to other levels of government. What they did was eliminate a whole pile of little fees and licences, nickel-and-dime things. The government had previously imposed $50 here for a hunting licence, or $100 here for some other kind of little fee, and so on. What the government found was that they did have to forego about $2 million in revenue because this obviously had brought in some, but they actually saved $3 million in administration costs. So they ended up $1 million to the good.

In these days of broke governments who don't have the money to spend but want to give the economy a boost, the smartest and most cost-effective way of doing that — because they can't lower taxes; they're all in debt up to their eyeballs — is to cut that regulatory burden. We believe that will give the economy a really nice push, create some more jobs and reduce government's own costs at the same time. So it's a win all around.

CHARLES McMILLAN

An economist and former advisor to Prime Minister Mulroney attacks many facets of the Canadian political and economic culture.

As a senior policy advisor for Prime Minister Brian Mulroney I had three basic roles: organizing the Cabinet agenda with the PCO; organizing the PM's speech writing and policy within those speeches with the team; and working with the Cabinet committees, who fed policy into the planning priorities of the inner Cabinet on a weekly basis.

I had an advantage when I started to work in Ottawa in that I was an outsider. I went in, perhaps through loyalty to the government, the party and the prime minister. I was only going to stay for two years. And I did retire after two years, but it took me another nine months to get out of there. It was the longest form of pregnancy I'd ever experienced.

I was living proof of what Bismarck said: "There are two things that you should never learn how they're made: sausages and government policy." I worked 71 months at Canada Packers and then four years in Ottawa. Canada Packers was better.

Ottawa is in the throes of a generational transition, much as it was after the Second World War. The state had a significant role in the war effort, building up industry, productive capacity and the military. In the

1980s this all changed. And now there's a global trend of change, from China to the former Soviet Union to all the Western countries. And there are three aspects of why there's change and why Ottawa's missing it. The first is that governments can no longer deliver the way they used to. They still spend money from taxes, but they waste a lot of it. Second, the wealth-creation process is no longer in the public sector. It's tied to technology, small business and the innovative process, and governments are totally ignorant about that whole exercise. Third, governments have not really been accountable. And by this I refer to the bureaucracy and its ways of spending. We've tried the auditor general route and we've tried all kinds of mechanisms.

That's also been true in the United States, England and France. And now there's a taxpayer revolt. It's sometimes direct, as you see in the United States, and sometimes it's indirect. But the public is fed up and so the politicians, who in my view are not the masters but the servants of the bureaucracy, are trying to cope with those changes. Sometimes things work and sometimes they don't. The confusion and the ineffi-ciencies are reflective of a much bigger process where governments can no longer do the things that they thought they could a generation ago.

For Canada the relationship between the government and the pri-vate sector is a central issue. The real form of wealth creation for per-haps a century has been in our raw materials. We dig the minerals out of the ground, we sell the forest, we sell the fish, we flog it all to the United States and around the world. Well, as we saw in the fisheries, that wealth is no longer there. We've overfished. We haven't managed our forestry. We haven't managed our mining. But look at Japan and, in the United States, Hollywood and Silicon Valley; there are new forms of wealth and they're tied to innovation. Chips, computers and software are the new forms of wealth creation. And that's why the Americans, the Japanese and a lot of the Asian countries are getting very wealthy. They don't need our raw materials the way they did a century ago.

What some people are trying to do is turn back the clock and use government as a protective device, as a prop to create wealth. Companies and industries are dependent on the tax system and the gov-ernment. But in fact they're extremely fragile, as a lot of our industries are showing. We're not building enough new industries to replace the old. I don't think many public policy makers, our banking system or even our universities understand the new forms of wealth creation.

We've been flogging wheat to China and the countries in the former Soviet Union now for 30 years, but the real price of wheat today, net of inflation, is probably the same rate as it was in the Depression. The real price of oil, net of inflation, is cheaper now than it was in the 1973 OPEC crisis. The Japanese economy has grown four times since 1973 and today uses 58 percent less energy. If we're dependent on those forms of wealth creation, some people in the oil and gas industry will do extremely well. But as a country we're not getting what the economists call "the rents," the taxes that generate the wealth to pay for other things. Look at our forest products industry. A couple of years ago, 23 of our 67 pulp and paper plants, including the one in Brian Mulroney's home-town of Baie-Comeau, were more than 50 years old. So you're just not going to get the wealth in terms of jobs or taxes that create the money to pay for the huge overheads.

A lot of people don't understand the nature of the innovative process. For example, the tax regime in Ontario is more favourable to real estate than it is to science and technology. There has been study after study, commission after commission, pointing out these kinds of issues. Brian Mulroney gave speeches on this in 1983. Paul Martin has given speeches on this very issue, including those in the *Red Book*.

The barriers for raising equity for small business on these issues have been around for 10 years, but the bureaucracy and the apparatus are not in tune with these kinds of issues. And these are the fundamen-tal issues directing the future of Canada. Huge portions of the private sector are using public policy for their own aims, and not necessarily to promote innovation. The banks, for example, have almost a monopoly culture in Canada. They've taken over the trust companies, the securi-ties companies and huge portions of the insurance industry. Also, by controlling the trust companies and the mortgages, they own huge por-tions of the real estate industry, especially in housing. And yet the Department of Finance has given them a virtual monopoly. By govern-ment legislation they control the pension funds, while foreign banks are restricted to 16 percent of the Canadian market. So they've got 84 per-cent of the market to themselves, by government edict. It's part and par-cel of our monopoly culture, our close business-government relations in certain sectors. We don't have an open economy.

Compare it to the American economy, the Japanese economy or parts of the British economy. The market system isn't allowed to work here. It's selective in its application. Certain private sector companies love our system because they know how to use it. It's subsidized and regulated. Take the beer companies, for example. Historically they've loved our form of regulation. They don't have to make decisions on anything other than packaging because they've got a monopoly distribution system, which they own. The consumer is fleeced with very high prices because he or she doesn't have a choice. So the governments work with private companies, and the private companies love it. Beer companies are one example in a series of industries, including the marketing boards for milk, cheese, whatever, simply because they know they can fleece the customer with high prices.

The Export Development Corporation is pouring money into Bombardier. Now, aerospace is one of the worldwide industries where governments have always been involved. Bombardier would argue, perhaps rightly, that it's what the French government does and it's what the German government does with Airbus. The Americans have a shrewd way of doing it; they just hide it through their military. The Japanese, the Taiwanese, I wouldn't generalize it, but there's no question that the leading aerospace companies know how to tap into the instruments of government for their own advantages. What Bombardier is doing now is using the Export Development Corporation to help subsidize the capital costs of planes being sold domestically. It's a curious use of the EDC, but on the other hand the Americans, the Japanese and the French know how to use these games as well.

But if you look at consumer-related products, from banking to beer to retailing, you see where the consumer is paying in two ways: directly with very high prices and indirectly through very high taxes.

My real issue with Ottawa was that I didn't think the bureaucracy and the leading mandarins were putting priority on the right places. Some of the biggest initiatives were fought by the bureaucracy, including free trade, deficit cutting and cutting back the civil service. The civil service fought these issues tooth and nail, though obviously behind the scenes.

And companies were into the government all the time. They'd get to their local MP. The MP gets to the regional Cabinet minister. Then all of that builds up a head of steam, and eventually that gets to the Cabinet, the bureaucrats or the lobbyists, and suddenly you've got this snowball effect and everybody's saying, "Well, how do we address this 'political issue'?" And it goes back to the old definition of politics: who gets what, when, where. And once they knew that this pot of money was there, companies had to get in on it for competitive advantage. One company would feel that it had to get into the government trough because its competitor down the street was getting money. It shows how insidious the process is. And is that the way to build competitive industries on a worldwide basis? Absolutely not.

There's lots of evidence that some companies have said, "To heck with government. It just isn't worth it." They would rather go on the export side with international markets. But that sentiment, that you had to get in on the government trough to stay competitive, is deeply ingrained. I found that an awful lot of people in government, including senior bureaucrats, and private sector people rather liked the system because they knew how to play it. I can remember all kinds of meetings with deputy ministers who are still in Ottawa saying that we've cut back enough of the government, and that privatization has gone about as far as it has to go because we have cut to the bone.

And private sector people here would get a phone call from a deputy minister to have dinner, lunch or a meeting, and their companies had restructured, downsized, re-engineered and all that, and they would say to this bureaucrat, "The hell with you. I don't want to see you. When you go through the pain and grief that we have in the private sector, then we're prepared to talk to you." Ottawa hasn't re-engineered. It hasn't gone through the downsizing and restructuring that is necessary. It's an empire in itself. Let me give you two examples, and I may get in trouble by saying this but I don't really care.

When I was there in 1984 the clerk of the Privy Council was Gordon Osbaldeston. He eventually left and went to the University of Western Ontario. His job was taken over by Paul Tellier, who's now the president of Canadian National. Let me use Tellier as an example first, but I can use Osbaldeston because he wrote a book about reorganizing Ottawa. In October of last year Paul Tellier made a big speech. "I was clerk of the Council, the number-one kazoo in Ottawa for 10 years. I fought downsizing. I fought restructuring and all that," he said. "But now that I'm in the quasi-private sector of Canadian National, which has to compete with the Americans and with Canadian Pacific, we have to re-engineer Ottawa. We have to downsize. We have to reorganize."

In the first budget I'd made a recommendation to cut the civil service by 30,000 in the first term, over four years. And they fought it: the

PCO, the Treasury Board and the civil service commission fought. They cut it back to 15,000. The end result was that there were more civil servants after 10 years of Conservative government than there were in 1984. History would show that perhaps the Conservative government in 1984 wasn't as small "c" conservative as indicated, and therefore 10 years later huge pockets of the small "c" conservative population left the party in droves. Hence the decimation in the 1993 election. Margaret Thatcher mentioned Mulroney in her memoirs, saying that when he first met her, even though he was called a Progressive Conservative, she thought that he put more emphasis on the adjective than on the noun.

But to go back to the basic issue, governments have had generations, certainly since 1940, of spending more and more money, federally and provincially. The Progressive Conservative government in 1984, even though it wasn't a recession and the economy was ticking along quite well by 1986 and 1987, cut back on the operation side but didn't start addressing the deficit issue.

You still had a massive sea change of policy over a seven- to eight-year period. Had governments understood that? Well, some of the provincial governments, leading with Alberta, clearly have understood that. But we're talking about changing behaviour, attitudes and policies that have been in place over two generations, from 1940 to 1986. It's all moving like a big battleship, and you can't turn it on a dime. The fact is, though, that the public in 1995 is now more aware of the deficit and the debt than they were in 1985. Even Ronald Reagan talked a big story in 1980, but as the evidence showed, if action is the true test and not words, even Reagan and the Republicans through the 1980s didn't pass the test.

It is a two-way thing. There's a leadership side, in terms of educating the public and changing attitudes, and there is the behaviour itself. It was not a popular message in 1984 to say that we had to cut. I can remember sitting in the House of Commons on November 5 while Michael Wilson announced that we were going to cut $4.4 billion. My own view is that we should have cut almost double that because it was a new government. One of the senior political advisors turned around to me, and he was shocked that we would actually cut government. That gives you an indication of the mood. Keep in mind that very few governments around the world were really cutting in the 1980s. I think that the reading by the politicians was that deficit cutting and dealing with the debt were bad politics. That was true in the second term of the Brian Mulroney government. And it was definitely true with the Chrétien government that got elected in 1993.

My own view was that the best politics went the other way, that deficits can be interpreted in political terms as taxes. As for the debt, we have 40 percent of it held outside the country. Do you want political sovereignty or the IMF? I think there are better ways of selling it. But as somebody said, people like Chrétien and Mulroney learned their politics in Quebec in the 1950s and their business in the 1970s; and we're dealing with a new phenomenon in the 1990s.

It came down in the 1988 election, when the nature of the politics was that certainly in central Canada there wasn't the desire to go too hard on the deficit. The Progressive Conservative Party paid an enormous price for that wrong judgment. But in the end it's the politicians that rule the roost when it comes to these judgments.

The bureaucracy is not comfortable with privatization; it peels away part of bureaucracy's empire. It isn't comfortable with deficit cutting because if you're a deputy minister, you're judged on the size of your little empire within the bureaucracy. The incentives are clearly not to roll back the state.

And then there's the value system. You've been there for 20 years, your budget goes up five percent or seven percent every year, and you largely decide how the money's being spent. Then somebody comes along and says, "You're not getting seven percent. More to the point, you're going to lose 10 percent. And you know these three Crown corporations you've got? We're getting rid of them. And these five agencies? We're going to get rid of them too." That's a culture change that's very, very difficult.

When private sector companies go through restructuring, often an outsider has to come in. Often they have to bring in a very different culture. The mechanisms for this to happen are not easy. In 1984 when the Mulroney government recognized that they were going to get not only a majority but a huge majority, they should have brought in 300 $1-a-year men to go at these issues in a very tough way, and then let them leave. Re-engineer it over the first two years. Downsize it, getting rid of the duplication. Clean up some of these issues. Maybe Peter Lougheed was right about that.

But traditional politics won, the idea of "spend and buy votes." Look at the books and the economics of democracy; spending is another form of vote-getting. And the paradox is that in the 1988 election, where the Conservatives promised the biggest spending, they actually lost votes. From megaprojects to pump priming in Quebec and Atlantic Canada, they lost big. I think that by 1988 the public was far ahead of the politicians and, to be fair, the politicians were far ahead of the bureaucrats.

The public knows what a lot of this means. Canadians, because of our winters, go to Florida, Mexico, Europe and Asia on holidays. They know that the Canadian dollar buys less and less. And they know that one of the reasons we're getting less and less for our dollar is the size of our bureaucracy, deficit and debt. They also know that a huge portion of our debt is held by foreigners. I don't think that the *Wall Street Journal* article about Canada's public spending alerted Canadians to these issues. It rationalized and ratified exactly what Canadians were already thinking. And it's very interesting that the government and the media criticized *The Wall Street Journal* for having the temerity to say the obvious, but you didn't hear that much criticism from the public at large. I think that the public was saying, "My God, *The Wall Street Journal* is right."

The public often doesn't get the right information. The politicians and bureaucrats would rationalize that point by saying that the public can only understand so much and they have to simplify it. There's not a great desire to expose a lot of things. There are a lot of hidden assumptions and hidden agendas about how governments operate. Look at Ottawa. What do a lot of these government departments actually do? What do our embassies do around the world? I got in trouble in 1984 in main Question Period by saying, "Why do we need 600 people in the High Commission in London, or 550 in Paris, or 450 in Rome, while in our second-biggest trading partner, Japan, there are only 80?" You may need a lot of help in Moscow, Tokyo or India, but how much help do you need in Paris or London?

You can examine all kinds of other departments. Think of our big fish crisis. We have the Department of Fisheries in Ottawa, where there are no fish except maybe in the odd little lake. With two coastal fishery areas, why don't we just get rid of the Department of Fisheries, set up agencies on the East and West coasts and dismantle this massive bureaucracy in Ottawa? Just think of it. How could the Department of Fisheries — 20 years ago, if you planned it — have better mismanaged our fisheries? Now there are no fish. We couldn't have done a better job if we tried. We put the thing under government quotas. We let it be managed from Ottawa. We had the politicians, the Department of Fisheries up front and almost acting like a czar: "You get a quota for fish and somebody else doesn't."

Industry after industry, department after department, they're all in cahoots with this bureaucracy. And yet some of the basic operating assumptions have never been exposed, like what do these things cost? Why are we doing this?

I'm not as familiar with Toronto's subway extension debate, but I think it's the old pork-barrel politics, megaprojects. Governments spend, governments create the jobs, and who gets left holding the bag? What is the real cost of the subsidies over the next 25 years? In some cases the subsidies will never be paid for.

We don't have the kind of scrutiny in our public accounts that we should have. We use the auditor general, but even he, with his massive bureaucracy, perhaps should be investigated in the same way. We don't use the committee structures to go through some of these basic assumptions. There are basic assumptions that never get looked at. Does every province get treated equally for every dollar they contribute in tax money? That is an absolute no-no to be investigated. Why? Because of our regional development issues, Canadians supporting each other's physical regime. For example, in Atlantic Canada, where I come from, 80 percent to 90 percent of the money in each industry department, provincially, comes from Ottawa. And yet the provincial governments make the decisions about which companies are going to be subsidized. The money in reality is Ottawa money, but does anybody in Ottawa ever test that?

There were provincial governments, including the Joe Ghiz government in Prince Edward Island, my home province, that had a political strategy of hiring people through the governments and their various agencies for 10 weeks. Those 10 weeks allowed individuals to get their unemployment stamps. Then they'd lay them off and hire somebody else, including some of their relatives. But the unemployment insurance was federal. So the provincial government could ratchet up the provincial spending and turn it over to the federal government. And we had a formal system of public policy allowing that: the 10/42 rule. It's unethical, and it's dumb, dumb, dumb public policy.

Part of the reason that the agendas are hidden is that we have media and a public broadcasting system that are all part and parcel of the same thing: get the money from the government in Ottawa. We don't have a very sophisticated form of investigative journalism. We don't have the think tanks that other countries have that examine this in a number of ways. Even the Fraser Institute, the hallmark of right-wing government and politics, got a grant in the order of $2 million in 1986, and they took that in perfectly good conscience. All of our universities are paid for, as a monopoly culture, through government money. The small amount of money that isn't paid for is paid through tuition. Go back to our basic structure: everything is regulated, and we're paying a very, very high cost because a lot of the real costs are not exposed.

We are a dole culture. It's a reinforcing cycle, through the politicians, the bureaucracy, a lot of industries and a lot of people who receive the money — whether they're the CBC or the universities. It's a self-fulfilling process. And the question is, can we break out of it? Should we break out of it? Well, we have to because we can't afford it. And the single best measure is the debt, which we can't service on the present projections. It's a dependency culture. You get people on unemployment insurance and they can't get off. In parts of Atlantic Canada, eastern Quebec and Ontario the only person who goes out to school in the morning is the kid. The parents and grandparents don't have to go out for a job; they're getting unemployment insurance. We're building second- and third-generation dependency families, all requiring government assistance through unemployment insurance and other forms of policy.

But my fear, given globalization and the international community and the fact that we have basically an open border just south of us, is that some of our best and brightest, perhaps too many, can go elsewhere. They can be sucked into the better opportunities in the United States. That's true of doctors, lawyers, engineers and professionals, not to mention some of the best people coming out of schools and universities.

The other thing, though, is that huge portions of our population might be jeopardized simply because of the cost of government. Medicare or various other social programs may be jeopardized because the costs are too high. And that's the debate about the real cost of medicare because servicing the debt in Ottawa is the single biggest expenditure. It means that we have not only one hand at our throat but two because it's progressively squeezing the other programs to feed this machine called "servicing the debt." And 40 percent of that debt is going offshore, which then has an impact on the dollar and the outflow of money.

I think the academics still treat the Canadian economy as a closed economy. Too many people still see everything as domestic rather than global. But, for example, with the press of a computer key the Japanese banking community can shut off the Canadian dollar or the flow of funds into our government bonds. And that's true of the Germans, the Americans, whomever. It means, for example, that some of our very sophisticated high-tech companies can put a factory into Buffalo or Illinois just as easily as they can put it into London, Ontario.

Within a block from here the Mining Association of Canada had a big conference, and the mood in the business was "ABC — Anywhere But Canada." Across the street one of the major investment houses raised $840 million in 1994, and $800 million of that went to build mining projects outside Canada simply because of the bureaucracy and the duplication with the federal, provincial and regional governments. The cost of all this is just too high. Too many people clue in to what is happening and leave. It goes back to some of these stated assumptions.

I was a consultant to a company in New Brunswick that said, "The hell with it," and they put $5 million into Chile. You know what the joke is? All of that output they're getting in Chile is being sold in Texas and Japan. And where are the jobs? They're down in Chile or in Texas or in Japan. Everybody's mobile today. Everybody's got a phone and a fax. You can deal with Chile as easily as you can deal with Ohio.

Let me give you another specific example. Two weeks ago there was a program on CBC called *Venture*. Brian Tobin was on, not talking about the turbot war with the Spanish, but pointing out that 40 percent of the fish in Norway, which has long, beautiful fiords or inlets, come from aquaculture, which is high technology. What's happening in Canada? Tobin openly said that his bureaucrats in the Department of Fisheries are against aquaculture. It's a new form of business and a new form of technology, and they prefer the traditional fisheries. These debates and the conflicts between the provincial and federal governments have slowed down that industry. But the real issue with what Tobin was talking about was this overlapping jurisdiction between the feds and the provinces. And the fights even within the provinces are slowing down an industry and growth opportunities, in this case in Atlantic Canada. And there are a dozen examples of that every single day.

Too many Canadians feel like they're stuck in this system. But on the other hand, companies that were once dependent on government are starting to say, "Well, we had a good run at it, but the government's broke," and so they're trying to break out of it. But I don't think the mood among young people is such that 100 percent want to leave. I've taught at a lot of business schools and economics departments across Canada, and I think the mood of young people is that they want to compete in the global economy. They don't want the old system. That's why the biggest and most exciting growth area is in small companies, people who say, "We can compete. We can raise the money, use our brains and trade anywhere in the world."

Canada is the territory that they know and like. There's a positive nationalism. They know that when you travel the world, whether you're on holiday or mountain climbing or doing business, the Canadian flag is still one of the best passports. We're not Germans, we're not Americans, we're not Japanese; and in huge portions of the world that's still the best thing going for us. We're seen as a very sophisticated country with very sophisticated, honest people. Don't forget, by the way, in all of the criticisms I've said, I don't think that we're a country of corruption. We're a country of laws and due process. That's something that is still a very positive factor. When we're looking at provincial or federal governments, there may be the odd problem here and there, but we've got a very clean system of government despite the criticisms. And that's not true in a lot of places we've seen: in Mexico, in parts of South America and in Russia.

The other thing is that if you were a skier, like Steve Podborski, or a ballet dancer, like Karen Kain, you'd know that you have to spend a certain time outside Canada. If you want to be a world-class skier, you have to spend time in France or Austria or Switzerland. But you're going to come back. Well, maybe if you're into certain technologies you may have to go to Silicon Valley or Boston or tough it out in Atlanta or Chicago to get experience. But then you're going to translate that experience and come back and build a business here in Canada. I think it's the competitive spirit in a very positive sense. We're in this transition. The economy is being forced to change by dint of technology, globalization and all of these other things.

Look at the 200 top software companies in Canada; they're listed in a major magazine every year. Look at the growth rates, the amount of money they're making, the opportunities and the exports. Some of these companies are selling 80 percent of their product abroad, while we've also got a whole bunch of companies that don't do any exporting at all, even to the next province. Look at the opportunity side of the equation and then the deadbeat side; more and more people are making the shift. And I think this mood of getting out of regulation, government control, deficits and debt is going to accelerate. Five provinces in 1995 have come through with balanced budgets. Give that another couple of years and the public is going to say, "How dare you go into a deficit? Those are my taxes. That's my grandmother. That's my business."

And the current debt situation is not irreparable. With every problem there are opportunities. I think there are interesting ways to fund some of those requirements. Canada's a huge country of savings. There are ways of privatizing some of those obligations.

For the first time there's a clear understanding of what the problem is. It's the deficit and the debt. Action comes when there's such an assessment. That had not been the case for the last 10 years. I also think that the politics have now shifted to deal with some of these issues. Look at Ralph Klein for an example. And that is a big, big change from the last 10 years.

Political decisions are orchestrated in a number of ways. In Ottawa or in provincial governments there's a four-year cycle, basically, when you have a majority government. The old politics are that in the third year you start figuring out what group you have to appease, what votes you have to buy off and what sector you have to get on side. So you start developing this smorgasbord of policies to buy off votes. That's one part of the exercise that's fed by the local MP. He's got this big factory that he wants to get fixed up in his riding. Or this Cabinet minister has to build this mine at Westray in Nova Scotia to get elected. That's the first thing.

The second thing, and it's more insidious, is that governments, particularly Ottawa, have started using, over a decade, the tax code to build certain industries. We've had flow-through shares in the mining industry, tax write-offs in the film business, tax advantages for the real estate industry and accelerated depreciation allowances for capital-intensive industries. We got away from a system of fundamental neutrality across sectors in the tax code. So we've built huge distortions that take five to 10 years to work their way through the system. For example, in the 1980s (and other countries did this too) we put enormous amounts of money into real estate instead of into certain forms of technology. What we've tried to do with the Mike Wilson budgets is slowly get off these distortions, build a system of neutrality and let the market decide.

The third process in this smorgasbord of grants, loans, regional development processes and the tax system has been the megaproject approach — this big oil and gas project, this big manufacturing plant, these heavy oil projects out West. This is a way to spin off jobs. We've had a 10- to 15-year process of using megaprojects as the job generator.

Yet all the academic and public policy evidence is that the best job creation is in small business. And then look at the obstacles to small business, on the equity side, financing and regulations. We should be helping MBAs, not to go into the Royal Bank, but to set up their own businesses. You may hire three or four people very quickly, but then you need to grow that business over the next five or 10 years. It would change the culture. And this, by the way, has been the miracle of Southeast Asia and Japan. They have the largest and most dynamic small business sector, with the largest overseas exporting. This is part of the sea change that's taking place in Canada. There are young people who want to break out of the system but still live in Canada. Well, the best opportunities are in starting up your own small business.

But as long as you allow the governments and the politicians into the marketplace, they're picking the winners because they're dabbling. They're giving money here and there, and that's distorting the system. But they wouldn't call it picking winners. For example, the EDC and Bombardier deal is a form of picking winners. They're saying, "Help Bombardier sell planes in the early stages while they're in the domestic market, and that will help them sell planes around the world in the export market." They're taking a certain amount of money in the public sector and they're not putting it into something else, and that's a form of picking winners. Every time the government spends money and distorts the marketplace, it's picking winners.

The political climate in Canada also does not support innovation in research and development. The evidence is overwhelming on that. On the input side or on the output side of R&D, we aren't using technology as quickly as our competitors are. Perhaps the one area that we're catching up on is in information technology and things like cadcam in industrial processes. But up against the Japanese in some of these areas we're not even in the ball game. A huge portion of American industry has been very slow. Look at the auto industry: Ford and Chrysler have accelerated their efforts to catch up, but the Japanese have moved on to another stage. My own view on research and development is that governments should get out of that business. The real engines of innovation are the generators of ideas, which are largely the academic communities, and the consumer and user of those ideas, which is the private sector. In Japan, for example, 80 percent of research and development is done in the private sector. We have an anemic record on R&D in our private sector, partly influenced by foreign ownership. Too much of our research and development spending is in subsidized universities and government labs. And when we discover certain things, that's where they stay because the incentives are not built in to take those ideas, whether insulin in 1922 or other products potentially in those labs, into the private sector.

That's why I'd love to see Canada deregulate the graduate schools, so that the scientists — and we have some extremely good scientists, by the way, in such schools across Canada — work better on commercialization with companies, foreign or Canadian. We have some good examples of that. And we should privatize, across the board, our government labs to push the commercialization side — or, when you say R&D, the "D" side — to get those ideas into the marketplace, using all kinds of incentives, from patents to hard cash. Then companies can succeed with those products in export markets.

There are two components here. The research and development ideas are a little complex, but there is a role for government in what is called "pre-competitive research." Everywhere in the world governments fund universities and science. They fund this kind of work because it's a public good. Basic research is tied to education at large. The Americans do it. Everybody does it. There's nothing wrong with being part of that because it doesn't give anybody a particular advantage. The problem comes when they take that pre-competitive research and start favouring individual companies or sectors in the commercialization process. Companies love to get that so-called infant industry protection because it's funding. The question is, when do those companies ever get off the public dole?

The evidence is overwhelming that companies don't want to get off it. So you're just creating another form of dependency. In this case it's like a form of unemployment insurance for companies. And it's an extremely inefficient way because in effect companies don't become competitive because they're not involved in the export market. When you're in the export market it's just like playing sports. You've got a test of performance. Getting companies off this dependency culture lies at the heart of the solution. And on the government side the dependency is fuelling the deficit because that's where some of the money is going.

But if you can follow the flow of government payments — good luck! — you deserve a Nobel Prize. Look at Atlantic Canada. How many bed-and-breakfasts could ACOA (the Atlantic Canada Opportunities Agency) fund?

These agencies were set up with some clear criteria and to help build up a private sector. But they didn't apply two basic criteria. Are they using the very best technology around, even if it has to be imported? And are they building exports? But what most of these subsidized projects, such as WED (Western Economic Diversification) and ACOA, got into were local projects for local jobs and therefore short-term political expediency.

Can you find precisely where those decisions were made? Well, I think they were tied to members of Parliament; provincial governments aiding and abetting this process because there's money put into the region; bureaucrats; and a culture tied to the old system of buying votes and jobs. Are those jobs real? Look at the number of companies that closed. They were about short-term expedience. That's why so many people are against this form of using public policy — and public money — to build companies. It doesn't work.

In the bureaucracy there is no individual accountability. That's why the bureaucracy loves to hide behind ministerial responsibility. It's the minister that takes the hit.

If you look at the mobility within the bureaucracy, let's say in 1984, a blackboard big as half of Toronto couldn't show where all these guys have gone. The turnover, and I don't think it's a good thing, is on a 12-month or 18-month period. Do you realize that sectorial bureaucrats in certain countries like Japan are there for 30 years? Let's say you're the computer expert. You never move out of the computer section, as compared to the steel section, of the ministry, let alone moving from one ministry to another. Here we have examples where one month a guy is deputy minister of the Department of Indian and Northern Affairs, and the next month he's deputy minister of the Department of Industry. We have a guy at CSIS, and then the next month he's deputy minister of the Department of Agriculture and he probably wouldn't know the front end of a cow from the back end of a buffalo. We get this rolling process here where in management terms and in specialized knowledge, which is the hallmark of today's world, these guys are being rotated like yo-yos.

So do you think you're ever going to find who actually made a decision? Forget it. And that's why the politicians and these committee structures quite frankly don't work in terms of checking out the accountability of government spending. It's a maze. You'll never find it.

In today's world innovation and the global economy should drive industrial-policy decision making. Governments still have a role. They can help companies export and find markets. They can use embassies abroad, particularly in countries where there may be language problems. But we don't need 500 people in London. There is no correlation between our foreign trade patterns and the number of people we have in our embassies. Zero.

In reality government subsidies and protection drive those decisions in Canada today. The vast majority of Canadian companies do zero trade and zero exports, even to neighbouring provinces. The Canadian Manufacturers' Association is trying to change that and they've got a great slogan: "We're a trading country; we're not a nation of traders." And they were traditionally against free trade. The Canadian Manufacturers' Association and the Canadian Federation of Independent Business, like a number of industry sectors, have gone through a sea change. And the single biggest change in Canada is free trade because it's a fundamental step in saying that we can no longer rely on the old system. It not only means that Canadians have to export, but that foreigners can import. And a Japanese, French or German company located in the United States can bring product here as easily as an American company can. This is what globalization really means. There are also huge changes in the attitudes of our private sector. Free trade is the blunt instrument of our industrial policy. It means the market's going to decide.

The debt that has been left for the younger generation is a tragedy. It's the first generation where there has been a reverse payoff, in the sense that normally parents pass on assets, education, home life and all of that to their children. In effect what this generation has done is seize the assets from the next generation, and it's called the government debt. You can blame the elite for this debt. You have to blame the people that were the principal architects and beneficiaries: prime ministers, Cabinet ministers, civil servants, provincial governments, heads of Crown corporations, and in some ways the academic community because the universities all feed on the government system. This is part of the political resentment in huge portions of the population. A lot of people feel cheated. It shows that our political, bureaucratic and academic elite have let down this generation. There's a fundamental issue here of ethics and morals. What possessed these people to put this kind of burden on the back of this generation?

My own view is that this generation is going to be able to cope, but I think it's a test that in fact will show the resentment against our elite is very profound. And unfortunately we don't have a system of direct accountability. If you put some of these people on the testing block, some would be lynched.

In a world economy it's open, people can vote. Or they can vote with their feet. And I admit that some people clearly have done so. On the other hand a lot of people want to stay. A lot of people of my generation don't have the choice; we've got to cope with the debt because in fact it's our debt. That's why there is such deep resentment. And that's where the political sea change is taking place.

The Conservative government, from 1984 to 1993, was given this fiduciary duty, and in the end they didn't pass the test. And guess what happened? They got wiped.

Now, I don't think morality is the waking thought in the middle of the night for politicians and bureaucrats. What guides the politicians is the next election. And what guides the bureaucrats is their own individual security. I don't think morality ever enters the equation. In the end the marketplace of ideas also works through the political system. And the sea change is that people who don't wake up to that are going to feel it deeply at the polls. The 1993 vote against the Conservatives was the litmus test that every government is going to be facing over the next five years.

The mood has changed profoundly. What you're seeing in the United States isn't a Newt Gingrich issue; he's a symptom of a much larger, deep resentment that people feel. They feel cheated. They feel that politicians and bureaucrats want to use their tax money, intellectual capital, education system and ideas for their own ends. And people have changed their views.

There are also interest groups and lobbyists involved in the consultation process. The whole damn thing should be dismantled. This is another vote-buying exercise. When my twin brother was minister of the environment there were groups subsidized by Ottawa. Four of them went down to his riding, using that government money, to help defeat him in the 1988 election. Ministry after ministry has been throwing money at people in the name of consultation. In effect it's appeasement. It's to buy off their voices. In Ottawa I had the experience that consultation was the simple form of indecision. Part of the problem with the Mulroney government was that when they should have acted, they consulted because they couldn't make up their minds. The interest group and the lobbyist are other insidious factors that feed various spending patterns. It's a self-reinforcing cycle. And the politicians become dependent on some of these groups for fundraising and for workers in the election. This is exactly what happened with Kim Campbell. Her election team was a bunch of lobbyists, fed by the companies who were dependent on government.

There's a system of these different elements that reinforce each other. More active media and more active thinking on some of these issues are exposing it for what it is: a closed system of people using the public trough for their own ends. The net result is a huge debt burden. And the current Quebec and Ontario governments, for example, are still using the old system, buying votes in all areas. The average citizen feels shut out of the process. A lot of the interest groups say they represent the public, but Marie Antoinette said the same thing in France. And what does the public say? "The hell with you. We don't believe you."

What did the Spicer Commission say? They went directly to the people and they said that there was anger in the land. People will rationalize until the cows come home. Of course they will. Today, with electronic media, the beauty of television is that there are no intermediaries. It's direct. The public knows some of these things.

When people vote for a political party, it's given a four-year mandate. But the loyalty to the existing parties, particularly by young people, is not what it was, and there's a huge mobility of votes switching from one party to the next. I think you're going to see a lot of mechanisms during those four years to allow the public to test whether or not a government is doing its job. If you take a course at Queen's University or McGill or wherever, it's a 15-week course. Basically you have to rely on the professor for the subject matter during those 15 weeks. Well, after 15 weeks, if you didn't like him, you go to another course. Life is a process of putting in your trust for a certain period.

Our political system is not the best, but as Churchill said, "Try something different." On balance we put our faith in government with all of these checks and balances, which I think are going to be more severe over a four-year period. But after that the gloves are off. And that's indicated by the amount of turnover. That was the issue in the United States. There was more turnover in the Kremlin than there was in Congress; 91 percent of the people who got elected were already incumbent. And people are saying now, "The hell with it. We don't like that system."

But even four years is a long time in terms of taxes, debts and boondoggles. That's why people like me want to reduce the powers of the state, and either return the money to individuals and let them make their own mistakes or opportunities, or let the marketplace decide. The market is colourblind. There's accountability and it's immediate. If you buy a product, it works or it doesn't work. If you have a cup of coffee at this store and you don't like it, you never have to go back.

The problem with government is the monopoly culture. There's only one place to get a passport. There's only one place to mail your letter. And then along comes technology. Why mail a letter anymore? Use a fax. You have choice. What we've seen in Western countries is in effect the mood to roll back the power of the state because it's a power of monopoly. But do we have enough politicians and bureaucrats that understand that basic issue? That is the issue of the last decade, and it is the opposite of what happened from 1940: building up the state, first for war purposes, then for reconstruction after the war and then to build a welfare state.

Everybody realizes that it has gone too far. More to the point, there are lots of examples around the world of countries that don't rely on government to the degree that we do and are more successful and richer. The pessimist would say that there's very little change in Ottawa, that they're going through the motions. The optimist would say that five provincial governments have already come in with balanced budgets, that the political mood has shifted dramatically. The test will come. There will be five elections in Canada this year. That will be one of the litmus tests. And if the Liberals blow it in Ottawa, there will be a new group coming in that will be very much consistent with these kinds of changes.

Is it happening fast enough? My own view is that clearly it's not happening fast enough, given the measure of the problems. And that gets into the question of the IMF and the perilous state that we have. The test is the falling Canadian dollar because with a floating exchange rate in the global market we have a marketplace for money. If the international community says, "Canada, I think we're going to pass," that puts pressure on our dollar. And I know people within a block of here that say the Canadian dollar could hit 65¢ U.S. or lower this year, as a measure of the lack of confidence in Canada.

And there are offsetting factors. More and more young people will move. More and more Canadian companies will shift some operations into the United States or elsewhere. They will go where the opportunities are. Those are all measurable. It shows up in other ways: very high unemployment; very high levels of taxation; and screams and comments from all kinds of people who like the old system, who say that this is a right-wing agenda, that this neo-classical group of radicals is dismantling the state and not protecting the glories and the beatification of the CBC and all this stuff.

My basic question is, if the CBC disappeared tomorrow, would that mean the end of Canada, in a 500-channel universe? There are three or four basic institutions in this country. When Air Canada was privatized did that mean the end of Canada? Closing down half of these unused rail lines in Western Canada, was that the end of Canada? Take a big one: getting rid of the CBC. Would that mean the end of Canada? It's a basic assumption. And I don't buy it.

The public has had it. It's putting pressure on the politicians to change. But in my view the last Martin budget was only the start. An awful lot of the real stuff is in the out years, against the political cycle, as they move toward the end of their four-year term. There's a closer semblance of rhetoric. But in 1995 we're a long way from getting there.

APPENDIX

People Interviewed in This Book

LOUIS BALTHAZAR has been a professor in political science at Laval University in Quebec City since 1969. He was the co-editor of the Department of External Affairs publication *International Perspectives* from 1974 to 1981. He has published extensively on U.S.–Canada relations and Quebec nationalism.

MARCEL CÔTÉ is a political strategist and economist, and is currently the CEO of Groupe Secor in Montreal. He was an advisor to former prime minister Brian Mulroney and former Quebec premier Robert Bourassa, and is the co-author, with David Johnston, of *If Quebec Goes ....*

JOHN CROSBIE has been in provincial and federal politics for 27 years. In the 1979 Clark government he was the minister of finance, and was justice minister and then minister of fisheries and oceans in the Mulroney government. It was Mr. Crosbie who announced the cod moratorium in his home province of Newfoundland.

DOUG DAVIS is president of D. A. C. Davis Investment Counsel Inc. in Toronto.

PAUL DICK was an MP for 23 years, including eight years in Cabinet. He was the federal minister of supply and services from 1989 to 1993 and the Progressive Conservative deputy House leader in 1984. Trained as a lawyer, he was the assistant Crown attorney for the county of Carlton from 1969 to 1972.

KENNETH DYE was auditor general of Canada from 1981 to 1991.

LLOYD FRANCIS was first elected to the House of Commons for Ottawa in 1963, where he served on and off for many years. He was named Speaker of the House in 1984 and was the Canadian ambassador to Portugal from 1984 to 1987. He has a Ph.D. in economics.

PAULE GAUTHIER, P.C., O.C., Q.C., is a former president of the Canadian Bar Association. She is an expert on business law and is a director of a number of leading Canadian corporations. In her career she has served as chair of the Security Intelligence Review Committee and as an arbitrator and mediator for national and international commercial organizations. Her home is in Quebec City.

MAXWELL HENDERSON trained as a chartered accountant and served on the Wartime Prices and Trade Board during the Second World War. He then worked for Samuel Bronfman in the private sector, but returned to government service as auditor general of Canada from 1960 to 1973. He died in December 1997.

MONIQUE LANDRY was a Cabinet minister from 1986 to 1993. During that period she held the positions of minister for external relations and international development, secretary of state, minister of communications and minister designate of Canadian heritage.

WILLIAM MACKNESS was employed by Scotia McLeod as a senior vice president and was the chief economist with the Bank of Nova Scotia from 1982 to 1988. He was a senior advisor in the federal Department of Finance between 1966 and 1974, and an advisor to Finance Minister

Michael Wilson in 1984. He was dean of the Faculty of Management at the University of Manitoba between 1988 and 1997. He is now retired.

PAUL MCCROSSAN is an actuary and partner in Eckler Partners Ltd., consulting actuaries in Don Mills, Ontario. He was an MP between 1978 and 1980, and again from 1984 to 1988, and served as parliamentary secretary to the minister of employment and immigration in 1979. McCrossan was involved with the changes to the Canada Pension Plan.

CHARLES MCMILLAN was the senior policy advisor to Prime Minister Brian Mulroney from 1984 to 1987. He is now a professor of international business at York University in Toronto and chairman of Midas Capital Corporation.

PETER MEYBOOM is president of P. Meyboom Consulting Services Inc. A scientist and public policy advisor, he has held senior positions in a number of federal government departments, agencies and task forces.

SEAN MOORE is the former publisher and co-founder of the *Lobby Monitor* and *Inside Ottawa*. He also worked for 11 years, holding positions from consultant to president, at Public Affairs International, which was then Canada's largest government relations and public policy consulting firm. He is now a public policy advisor with Gowlings, Strathy and Henderson, Barristers and Solicitors and Trade Mark Agents. He also serves on the advisory board of both Carleton University's Arthur Kroeger College of Public Affairs and *Media Magazine*, a publication of the Canadian Association of Journalists.

FILIP PALDA is a professor of public administration at L'École Nationale d'Administration Publique in Montreal. He is also a senior fellow at the Fraser Institute.

ROBIN RICHARDSON is president and chief economist of R. M. Richardson and Associates. He is a former member of Parliament and has extensive experience in government, private and academic sectors.

GORDON ROBERTSON joined the Department of External Affairs in 1941 and worked for every prime minister from Mackenzie King to Pierre

Trudeau. He was clerk of the Privy Council and secretary to the Cabinet from 1963 to 1975, and secretary to the Cabinet for federal-provincial relations from 1975 to 1979. He was also principal constitutional advisor to prime ministers Lester Pearson and Pierre Trudeau. When he left the government he became president of the Institute for Research on Public Policy in Ottawa.

ALAN ROSS was the senior assistant deputy minister of supply and services from 1986 to 1993 and the director of financial policy for the comptroller general from 1973 to 1978.

DONALD SAVOIE wrote *The Politics of Public Spending in Canada*, the definitive book on the concept of spending in the Canadian political system. He is a professor of public administration at the University of Moncton in New Brunswick, and from 1974 to 1982 held various positions with the Department of Regional Economic Expansion. He was also an advisor to prime ministers Mulroney and Chrétien. His latest book, *Governing from the Centre: The Concentration of Power in Canadian Politics*, is an assessment of the government of Jean Chrétien. He is currently the senior fellow of the Institute for Research on Public Policy and holds the Clément-Cormier Chair in Economic Development at the University of Moncton.

WALTER SCHROEDER is president and founder of the Dominion Bond Rating Service in Toronto.

DAVID SLATER was the general director of the federal Finance Department from 1973 to 1978. He later ran the Economic Council of Canada.

JACK SLIBAR was a public policy and affairs counsel with the Public Policy Group at the time of his interview. He is now the executive director of the Toronto Humane Society.

CATHERINE SWIFT is president of the Canadian Federation of Independent Business.

KERNAGHAN WEBB is a senior legal policy analyst with Industry Canada. He was a consultant on the study *Federal Government Relations with Interest Groups: A Reconsideration*.

INDEX